The World from Beginning to End and the Era of Peace

Eric Bermingham

2018

TABLE OF CONTENTS

DEDICATION

This book is dedicated to Queen Isabella I of Castile (1451-1504), known by her subjects as "Isabel the Catholic." Her zeal to spread the Catholic Faith was perhaps unmatched by any other monarch. Her financing of the voyage of Christopher Columbus led to the greatest mass conversion in history, through the appearance of Our Lady of Guadalupe. Spain and Catholicism were saved from the Muslims and the Protestants, largely due to her efforts.

Isabella was the first woman to be featured on US postage stamps and the first named woman to appear on a US minted coin, a commemorative quarter, all for the 1893 World's Columbian Exposition held in Chicago, Illinois to celebrate the 400th anniversary of the 1492 voyage of Columbus.

She even inspired changes to the game of chess. A report by Elizabeth Nash, in the *London Independent* (March 2, 2004) quoted Govert Westerveld, a Dutch chess historian and former youth champion: "In its original form, the equivalent of the queen was male, a piece known in Spanish as alferza, from the Persian, meaning something like vizier or adjutant. The figure was weak, and its movements limited. Later, around 1475, when Isabella was crowned queen of Castile, the figure became female but able to move only one square at a time, like the king. Not until 1495, when Isabella was the most powerful woman in Europe, were the present rules of chess established, in which the queen roams freely in all directions on the board."

And from www.queenisabel.org:

In the time of Queen Isabella, a poem became famous which referred to her as: "On earth the first / In Heaven the second." In the opinions of the time, this placed Isabella directly after the Virgin Mary in terms of honor and closeness to God.

The venerable Palafox compares her with St. Teresa of Jesus, saying that if St. Teresa would have been a queen, she would have been an Isabel the Catholic, and that if Queen Isabel would have been a nun – "which she truly was by her virtues" – she would have been a St. Teresa of Jesus.

"Isabel the Catholic was a saint, though by the inscrutable designs of God we cannot venerate her yet on the altars ... This woman superseded the queens that were not saints by the virtues of her sanctity, and among the saints who were queens for the heroic deeds of her government."
– Fr. Fray Zacarias Martinez, Archbishop of Santiago de Compostela

In 1958, the cause for the Canonization of Isabella was started by José García Goldaraz, the Bishop of Valladolid. Isabella was given the title "Servant of God" in March 1974. Unfortunately, her involvement with the expulsion of the Jews and Muslims from Spain, and with the Spanish Inquisition, has delayed her canonization.

One quote attributed to her is: "Those monarchs who do not fear God must fear their subjects." The National Security Agency is proof of that. Queen Isabella, pray for us.

ABOUT THE FRONT COVER

The miraculous icon of Panagia Paramythia:
Holy Monastery of Vatopedi, Mount Athos, Greece
From a blog post dated June 5, 2012 by Fr. George Frangos
See also: orthodoxwiki.org/Panagia_Paramythea

The miraculous icon of Our Lady, Panagia Paramythia "Mother of Consolation," is found on the wall of the right-hand choir in the chapel that bears the icon's name and is dated by tradition to the 14th century. It is evocative of Our Lady's complaint to the children at La Salette: "If my people do not wish to submit themselves, I am forced to let go of the hand of my Son." The icon's appearance and miraculous tradition comes from the following story.

On January 21st sometime in the 14th century, after the Orthros service was completed, the fathers were on their way to their cells to rest prior to beginning the day's tasks. It was at that time that the gates of the monastery would be opened for the day. They were unaware that the monastery was surrounded by pirates waiting for the monastery's doors to open in order for them to plunder its treasures. The abbot of the monastery remained in the church, deep in prayer, as was his usual routine.

He was startled after hearing a voice. He looked to see where the voice was coming from and was drawn to the icon of Our Lady in the exonarthex. He listened closely and heard Our Lady say: "Do not open the monastery's gate today, but go to the walls and get rid of the pirates."

He gazed at the icon and saw that Our Lady's image was alive. The Christ child as depicted in the icon was also alive. Christ raised his right arm to cover Our Lady's mouth and gazed at her with a very strict facial expression. He then heard Christ speak in a sweet child-like voice: "No, Mother, don't tell them. Let them be punished as they deserve because they do not keep their monastic duties." Then Our Lady carefully lifted Christ's hand and moved her face gently to the right, repeating her advice for the second time: "Do not open the gates of the monastery today, go to the walls and rid the monastery of the pirates, and be sure to repent because my Son is angry with you." She repeated the same words a third time and suddenly their images became an icon once again.

The abbot, who was full of amazement, gathered all of the fathers quickly and described the events to them in detail. The fathers went to the icon and were all amazed; the icon had changed! It looked nothing like it did originally. The icon appeared as it can be seen today, with Our Lady's hand restraining Christ's hand from her mouth, her face slightly facing to the right, with a calm and motherly expression. Christ's hand attempts to cover his Mother's mouth and his facial expression is stern and strict.

This icon is not made by human hands because it depicts an image that was not painted by human hands but by the grace of God. The monks to this day, out of gratitude toward Our Lady, burn a perpetual flame before the icon and a supplication service is conducted before the icon daily.

ACKNOWLEDGMENTS

I would first of all like to thank God – Father, Son, and Holy Spirit – for creating everything including me, and for redeeming and sustaining mankind and myself. I secondly thank the Blessed Virgin Mary for her "Yes" to God and for her maternal care, and to St. Joseph for his patronage of husbands, fathers, and workers. I would next like to thank my parents for raising me and staying married. I thank those bishops, priests, and laity who are keeping the traditional Catholic Faith alive, particularly Robert Sungenis for his defense of geocentrism and for writing the Foreword to this book. I thank Hugh Owen especially for his leadership of the Kolbe Center for the Study of Creation and for looking over a manuscript of this book.

I thank the saints whom I invoke the most: St. Christopher for safe travel, St. Michael the Archangel for defense against evil, and St. Anthony of Padua for finding lost objects. Finally, I will thank Queen Isabella the Catholic for sending Columbus to the Americas and for her defense of Christendom. I hope that my efforts to defend the Church will bear fruit as well.

FOREWORD

One might think that writing a book titled, *The World from Beginning to End and the Era of Peace* would need to be an extremely detailed and voluminous work comparable to Arnold Toynbee's 12-volume treatise on the history of the world that contains more than 3 million words and 7,000 pages. But Eric Bermingham, an unassuming but competent intellectual in his own right, has given us an abridged version of world history that, pound for pound, is much more insightful than Toynbee's could ever be. That is because Eric's book has one major line of thought that allowed him to interpret man's history in a very simplified manner. Whereas Toynbee struggled in his massive work to find the common thread that summarized all of human culture so that he could analyze any group of people and show how man either evolved or devolved in each successive culture, Eric's perspective is the simple notion of good versus evil as it appears in its various and sundry forms, and how each man responds to that God-given challenge. As such, his book is much simpler and more focused than Toynbee's. It is more like the Bible, since the Bible does not concern itself with all the details of men's lives, but only those in which each man finds himself confronted with a choice between good and evil. Starting from the mysterious but incisive, 'tree of the knowledge of good and evil' planted in the Garden of Eden to test Adam, each man must choose how he will respond. Never has there been a better measuring stick to analyze mankind and his history than this. It makes understanding life very simple. As Moses and St. Paul once told their audiences, we don't need to climb high mountains and cross deep seas in order to find the truth and live accordingly. It is standing right beside us, if we would only call out for it (*cf.* Deut 30:11-20; Rom 10:5-13).

The motivation for Eric's writing of this wonderful book was probably similar to why George Orwell coined the sentence, "Sometimes the first obligation of intelligent men is to restate the obvious." Even to young children it is obvious that good and evil are such an intrinsic and inextricable part of human life as to constitute its supreme essence. But as they grow up and must struggle with the effects of those before them who chose evil and thus decimated the world in which they now live; and when they see that the good are often trampled upon by the bad who make it very difficult to continue to stay on the right path; they need someone to come along and retell the story to encourage them not to give up. Such is Eric Bermingham's book. He certainly restates the obvious, but if there ever were a time in which a loud and clear restatement is needed, it is in our day, a day in which the effects of evil have accumulated to such a degree that the very institutions we have long depended upon to protect us from evil are themselves being overwhelmed like we have never seen before in human history.

Eric's book, in brief, is nothing short of a clarion call to the human race. But it is not a call in which Eric has a brand new solution to human life that will destine his book to be at the top of the *New York Times* bestseller list because it shows how everything can once again be rosy. No, Eric's book is more like how the prophet Daniel would write the history of the world. That is, we have come to a point in which the history of mankind may be reaching its close and Eric is going to tell you what to expect and how to prepare for it. No, there is no date-predicting of when Christ will return; rather, Eric has given us a fascinating and logical connecting of the prophetic and historical dots from Adam to the Second Coming that shows us how the 'good versus evil' theme of human history will most likely play itself out. These are not his predictions; rather, Eric has gathered an incredible list of outstanding witnesses who, in one form or another, have been given a gift from God to tell us what to expect in the not too distant future and how to live through it.

One of the essential elements of the future is what the latter half of Eric's title contains, namely, 'The Era of Peace.' Whereas most Catholics of our day have either given up on expecting Fatima's 'period of peace,' or have been convinced that it came and went sometime in the recent past (although they can't put their finger on just when), Eric's 'restatement of the obvious' shows that neither position is correct simply because neither God nor Our Lady (the Blessed Virgin Mary) could either be liars or half-truth tellers. They meant what they said and said what they meant. As such, we can expect the consecration of Russia to be performed by a good pope someday. At that time good will triumph over evil for a considerable period of time, and to an extent we never dreamed possible. In short, Eric has a message of hope for all those overwhelmed by the evil they see proliferating in the world today. The coming Era of Peace will assure us that God has not forsaken us. In fact, as Eric sees it, God will be using the Era of Peace to prepare us for our next and final battle with the Devil – the battle that will end in his utter defeat and our supreme triumph, for now and forever. Take a read and settle your soul. Eric Bermingham has done the Catholic Church a wonderful service.

Robert A. Sungenis, Ph.D.
Chairman: Stellar Motion Pictures, LLC
Executive Producer: *The Principle* and
Journey to the Center of the Universe
Director: CAI Publishing, Inc.
August 2018

INTRODUCTION

You, dear child of God, most likely have been taught that your Heavenly Father either does not exist, is irrelevant, or is cruel. In fact, he loves you, gave his only Son for your salvation, and will not let anything come between you and him except by your own free will. The Mother of his Son, the Blessed Virgin Mary – your spiritual mother – greatly desires your salvation as well.

You have also probably been taught that your mother earth is nothing special and is drifting through a far corner of space when in fact it can be shown that you are in a very special place. You almost certainly have been taught that you are a product of evolution and are descended from an ape ancestor, but honestly, you are descended from the first man and first woman who were special creations of God.

You might be wondering why any of this matters, since you have perhaps been told that all religions are equally valid, or equally wrong, and that only our perceptions matter. However, the objective truth can be known because nature itself declares it and God has revealed it.

You may have a sense of foreboding that something apocalyptic is about to occur on earth and you would be correct. It has been foretold by certain holy persons that a marvelous Era of Peace is about to be ushered in, but only after a series of distressing events.

St. Augustine in *The City of God* wrote that peace is the

tranquility of order. In Book 19, Chapter 13 he deals with peace on various levels:

> "The peace of the body then consists in the duly proportioned arrangement of its parts. The peace of the irrational soul is the harmonious repose of the appetites, and that of the rational soul the harmony of knowledge and action. The peace of body and soul is the well-ordered and harmonious life and health of the living creature. Peace between man and God is the well-ordered obedience of faith to eternal law. Peace between man and man is regulated fellowship. The peace of a home is the well-ordered concord between those of the family who rule and those who obey. Civil peace is a similar concord among the citizens. The peace of the celestial city is the perfectly ordered and harmonious enjoyment of God and of one another in God. The peace of all things is the tranquility of order. Order is the distribution which allots things equal and unequal, each to its own place."

The history of the world demonstrates a general lack of peace and order resulting in strife and war. The wars of the 20th century were the most destructive of all time. There is no end in sight for the "War on Terror" going on now. At one time when people were asked for what they wished, the response was often for peace in the world. It seems that now, world peace is not even expected or imagined.

However, the Bible describes a time at the dawn of creation in which there did exist true peace. Various cultures around the world have legends of a Golden Age. Unfortunately, this did not last long and ended through disobedience to God's command as recorded in the book of Genesis, and with a general corruption of morals in cultural legends. Still, there is hope for eternal peace in the next life for those who are obedient to God's eternal laws in this life.

God is a loving Father and wishes nothing but good for his creation. He would like to shower us with good things, but our sins – our offenses against him and his laws – get in the way. If he really gave us all the fame and fortune we desired, we would probably ruin ourselves because of our lack of humility, patience, kindness, and all the other virtues, and our attachment to the things of this passing world.

In spite of the perpetual warfare that exists today, there are prophecies in the Bible concerning an era of peace on earth unlike anything seen since the Garden of Eden. Visionaries have also described this era. Even non-Christian and non-religious people are anticipating a time of being in tune with a universal spirit. This is the Era of Peace promised by the Blessed Virgin Mary at Fatima, Portugal in 1917.

You would expect that in a well-ordered society people would be at peace with God and with each other, as well as with animals and nature. There would be no separation of Church and State, or of Faith and Science. All would be for the greater glory of God and the good of mankind. That situation certainly does not exist today, at least not on a large scale. In fact, disorder seems to be the mark of modern times despite all the talk of a "New World Order."

George Orwell, author of *1984*, is known for saying: "The most effective way to destroy people is to deny and obliterate their own understanding of their history." All revolutions want to start with a blank slate. The history of early humanity is contained in the book of Genesis. The creation of the world in six days is described, followed by the global Flood of Noah, and the confusion of tongues and the dispersion of nations from the Tower of Babel.

You would think, based on the opinions of modern scholars, that the Catholic Church is the most corrupt institution to have ever existed (some members of the Church certainly have been very corrupt) and that the Bible is the least reliable ancient text available. But Jesus Christ founded the Catholic Church, and the Church gave us the Bible and the correct understanding of it.

Unfortunately, the literal understanding of the Biblical history contained in Genesis has been obliterated by the acceptance of modern theories, especially by Evolution. The rejection of the concepts of Original Sin and fallen human nature, together with Biblical morality, has led to the demise of the old monarchical Christian order – which was based on those concepts – in favor of the New Socialist World Order and the rise of anarchy.

So how are we going to get from the current situation in the world to the Era of Peace? If the history of the world is any indication, it will only come about through cataclysmic events. Many people seem to be in anticipation of such events. What is known about the Third Secret of Fatima indicates that there will be a time of persecution for the

Church and great disturbances in the world before the Era of Peace. The triumph of the Immaculate Heart of Mary and the Era of Peace are assured, however. It was revealed to Venerable Mary of Agreda that this reward has certainly been gained for us (*Mystical City of God*, Volume 2, The Incarnation, Book One, Chapter XXVIII):

> "I have been informed of a great mystery, which affords us consolation in this conflict of the holy Church against her wicked enemies. Namely, on account of this triumph of most holy Mary and on account of another, which She gained over the demons after the Ascension of our Lord, the Almighty, in reward of her battles, decreed, that through her intercession and virtue all the heresies and sects of the world against the holy Church were to be destroyed and extinguished. The time appointed for this blessing was not made known to me; probably, the fulfillment of this decree is dependent upon some tacit and unknown condition."

Surely this "unknown condition" is the consecration of Russia, by name, to the Immaculate Heart of Mary.

The current period we are living in today has been described as the Minor Chastisement. The persecution of the Catholic Church has not been this bad since the time of Nero. Christians in the Middle East are being slaughtered and driven from their homes. Scandals at the highest level of the Church are in the media. Many are abandoning the Faith.

All of this has been predicted, however. Christ warned his

apostles that such things would happen, especially near the end of the world. Various prophecies say the same thing. The messages given to the visionaries of Fatima, Portugal and La Salette, France are especially timely. We do well to remember that Jesus said: "But he that shall persevere to the end, he shall be saved." (Matt. 24:13)

According to prophecies, the Minor Chastisement will end with the Three Days of Darkness in which all the enemies of God will be destroyed. Only one-quarter to one-third of mankind will survive this event. Those who do survive will not be attached to the things of this world, in part because there will not be much left, and they will be obedient to the laws of God because it will then be obvious what the rejection of God's laws has brought. They will be able to enjoy the foretold Era of Peace which will occur shortly before the end of the world.

Note: All Bible quotes and Psalm numbers are from the Douay-Rheims Bible (DRB – www.drbo.org) with some adjustments for modern language. Bible verse number references following quoted passages are direct quotes, other verse numbers are just for reference.

Warning: I have tried to be both truthful and charitable in writing this, but many people will find something that offends their sensibilities in these pages. In telling the truth, Jesus was not afraid to offend. Apparently, God does not recognize your right to not be offended.

I ask for the intercession of St. Francis de Sales, patron saint of writers, for this work.

1 GOD, TRUTH, AND RELIGION

1.1 Proof of God

Upon reflection, one fact that should be apparent to anyone living in this world is that there is something beyond nature. Obviously, everything comes from something else and clearly there is an order to things. But how did it all get started, and where is it all going, and what does it all mean? Natural science cannot supply the answers to these questions; the answer lies in the realm of the supernatural. It is up to theology and philosophy to give us the answers.

One of the greatest theologians of all time was St. Thomas Aquinas, the Angelic Doctor. He developed five proofs of God in his magnum opus, *Summa Theologica*. They are briefly described as follows:

i. Argument from Motion:

Some things are in motion. In order for them to be in motion, they must have been put in motion by something else, since nothing can put itself in motion. But there must have been something which first put things in motion which was not put in motion by anything else. This everyone understands to be God.

Eric Bermingham

ii. Argument from Efficient Cause:

Every effect has a cause. But there must have been a first cause which was the cause of itself – the first efficient cause. This everyone gives the name of God.

iii. Argument from Possibility and Necessity:

It is possible for things to be and not to be. It is possible that at one time nothing existed. But if nothing existed at one time, then nothing would exist now, which is obviously not the case. So the existence of something was necessary in order for there to exist anything now. The one thing having its own necessity, all men speak of as God.

iv. Argument from Gradation:

Some things are more perfect and some less perfect. But something must be the most perfect. This we call God.

v. Argument from Intelligent Design:

We see that some things which lack intelligence, such as natural bodies, are ordered to an end. This is obviously by design. These must be directed by an intelligence. Therefore, some intelligent being exists by whom all natural things are directed to their end and this being we call God.

So we have five proofs from theology that there must be a God. However, even natural science shows that something must exist beyond the natural world. This can be demonstrated using the First and Second Laws of Thermodynamics.

1.2 The Laws of Thermodynamics

The Laws of Thermodynamics are some of the most firmly established scientific laws. All observations of natural processes conform to them. The way we observe nature is by our senses – seeing, hearing, smelling, tasting, and touching. Any data that we can gather about the universe is through our senses.

One property of the universe that surprises many scientists is the fact that it is so highly ordered. It is only because of the fact that it is ordered that scientific studies are even possible. Without that order, there would be no science.

Yet there is no evidence that matter pops into existence spontaneously. If it did, our universe would be a very different place and we would never know what to expect. The orderliness of the universe has led many scientists to believe that it has been put in order by a Higher Power.

The First Law of Thermodynamics states that energy cannot be created or destroyed. The total amount of energy in the universe is constant and finite. Matter may be converted into energy, and energy into matter, but the total amount of energy is conserved.

This shows that you cannot get something from nothing on a natural basis. As St. Thomas Aquinas stated, if at one point there was nothing, then there would be nothing now. Things do not spontaneously spring into being from nothing in the natural, material world. This "nothing" means literally "no thing" or absolutely nothing, unlike the nothingness given material properties by modern scientists like Lawrence Krauss, author of *A Universe from Nothing*.

This leaves us with two possibilities: 1.) the material universe is eternal, or 2.) something beyond nature created the material universe. But how do we know which one of these is true? The Second Law of Thermodynamics can help us decide.

The Second Law of Thermodynamics states that in any process, heat cannot be converted completely into work. Some energy is always lost to unusable energy. This is why there are no perpetual motion machines. Given enough time, all motion in the universe would eventually stop. Since there is still motion in the universe, it cannot be infinitely old.

Another way to think about this is that disorder increases. Entropy is a measure of disorder. On a large scale, it is always increasing. In other words, left to themselves, things deteriorate: "… the earth shall be worn away like a garment …" (Isaiah 51:6) Locally, things may become more ordered. This can happen by freezing water in your icemaker, or by picking up your room, or by plants growing using the energy of the sun (photosynthesis).

Although ice cubes have more order than liquid water, you have to put more energy into the process of freezing them than what is taken out of the water. The energy you put into straightening your messy room increases the total unusable energy because there was more energy in the food you ate than what was used just to put things in place. (But go ahead and do it anyway, cleanliness is next to godliness.)

Plants convert the energy of the sun into growing leaves using photosynthesis. This process is not 100 percent efficient, so some energy is still wasted. Even the energy that did go into growing leaves would have been wasted if there were not a mechanism to convert the light energy. So merely adding energy to a system will not increase order automatically; there needs to be a way to convert the energy to useful work. Open systems do not solve the problem of entropy. That is why explosions are not creative, but destructive.

The stars in the sky are another example. They are continually burning and would burn out, given enough time. Once that happened, there would be no natural way to reverse the process. The Second Law of Thermodynamics shows this to be the case. Some have called this the "Heat Death" of the universe.

This also shows that the spontaneous generation of stars is impossible. The usual explanation of the spontaneous generation of stars is that gravity will act to compress diffuse gas into a state that will eventually start a fusion reaction. The problem with this explanation is that the pressure pushing the gas molecules apart, due to their motion, is much stronger than the force of gravity pulling them together. So gravity would pull the gas molecules together only to a point where it balanced the force pushing them apart. This prevents gas from reaching the state where fusion can occur.

This can be observed when you blow up a balloon. The pressure of the gas gives the balloon its shape. If you pop the balloon, the gas dissipates because gas molecules do not like to be close to each other. You can see the same thing by opening the valve on a pressurized aerosol can.

Some scientists have recognized this and attempt to counter it by saying that a shock wave from a nearby exploding star could increase the gas density to a point for fusion to begin. However, this only begs the question of the origin of the first star. Other explanations of spontaneous generation of stars are equally implausible. Those "star nurseries" that scientists talk about are only stars that happen to be in clouds of dust and gas. No star has been seen in the process of being formed. However, star explosions have been detected (supernova) and sometimes a single star can split into more than one star. Note that if the universe were really billions of years old, there would be many more supernova remnants.

Since stars cannot be generated spontaneously, the "Heat Death" of the universe would be irreversible. Once the stars in the universe burned out, there would be no natural way to get them back. Gravity is not strong enough. The cyclical universe is impossible. This again eliminates the possibility of an infinitely old universe because the stars would have already burned out if the universe were infinitely old. This leaves only the possibility that something outside or beyond nature created the stars and the rest of the material universe sometime in the past.

We would call something outside or beyond nature the "supernatural." Typically, this refers to God. So natural science, in the form of the First and Second Laws of Thermodynamics, points to God. The Bible says as much in Paul's letter to the Romans: "For the invisible things of him, from the creation of the world, are clearly seen, being understood by the things that are made; his eternal power also, and divinity: so that they are inexcusable." (Romans 1:20)

Note that Paul says that those who do not understand from the visible creation that there is an invisible God are inexcusable. Clearly, things cannot create themselves. Considering that everything deteriorates, the material universe cannot be infinitely old. Everyone who has reached the age of reason can understand this and must use their God-given free will to make a choice to believe or not.

1.3 Attempts to Deny God

Some people attempt to escape the proof of God by suggesting that our universe is just one of many universes that have come into existence. This is sometimes called the "Multiverse Theory" even though the word "universe" generally means everything that exists. Some talk of parallel universes in the same sense. The thought is that our universe is just the lucky one that happened to get everything right for humans to exist.

There is not the slightest bit of hard evidence for the existence of any universe other than our own. Scientists cannot even come up with a natural way for one universe to come into existence, let alone many universes. This is basically circular reasoning at work in assuming that there is no design or purpose in nature, and then imagining how a universe could have come about that has the appearance of order and meaning.

Another attempt to deny the existence of God is what could be called the "Brains in Jars" or Hologram theory, or the Boltzmann Brain theory. The idea is that we are all just brains in jars in some laboratory and that everything we sense is just being projected onto our nerves like a hologram. The general idea is that life is an illusion.

The Boltzmann Brain theory refers to a brain that pops into existence spontaneously with all experiences built into it, and then pops back into nothingness instantaneously. Ironically, this is far more likely from a purely naturalistic standpoint than the Big Bang theory where an entire universe just pops into existence.

This begs the question of how the brain came into existence in the first place. This is simply a non-solution to the question of creation and existence. If it were true, then any concept of reality is illusory and there would no point to this life at all or even discussing it.

People also attempt to exclude God by making everything relative to their own experience. Descartes was famous for saying "I think, therefore, I am." He essentially put himself in the place of God, who alone can say that his existence is independent of anything else (Exodus 3:14). Descartes, in trying to prove his existence, rejected the senses and revelation as unreliable, and decided that the only way he could prove his existence was by reason alone. He made a god of his thoughts and created a universe in his head where he made his own rules.

The French Revolution replaced God with the goddess of reason, following the lead of Descartes. Our modern, godless society is largely a result of this philosophy. If reason alone is the standard of all things, then whose reasoning decides what is right and wrong? In a democratic society, it is decided by a majority vote. This is nothing but mob rule and a recipe for the disintegration of society due to our natural tendency to pursue pleasure and avoid pain – the result of our fallen human nature.

Sometimes people reject the notion of a God due to a bad experience or a bad example. Often, the death of a child will cause a person to question their fundamental beliefs. A serious injury or illness can have the same effect. Abuse or lack of charity from a religious authority can cause a rejection of everything that the authority represents. This is understandable from a human perspective, but it does not objectively show that God does not exist.

Agnostics do not directly reject the idea of a God, they just claim that it is not possible to know if there is a God or to know anything about God. Part of that seems to come from the rejection of absolutes, such as right and wrong. They claim that are no absolutes, so we are not accountable for anything. But to say absolutely that there are no absolutes is a contradiction.

Finally, there are people who reject the idea of a God not on theological or philosophical grounds, but from the moral consequences of admitting that there is a God. If, after all, there is a God, then we should behave in certain ways and not others. If there is no God, then anything is permissible. Some people do not like being told what to do, so they reject God on this basis. Likewise, Satan rejected God because he was not willing to serve him, preferring himself to God (Isaiah 14:11-15). Rejecting God out of preference will give us a dwelling in hell with Satan.

Everything that we experience tells us that there is something beyond the natural world. All cultures have creation stories which involve one or many gods. This shows that the understanding of a supernatural creation is universal. These perceptions and stories have been collected into various world religions. The Bible says that: "The fool has said in his heart: There is no God." (Psalms 13:1) It is contrary to reason, sense, theology, philosophy, and even natural science to suggest that there is nothing beyond the natural world. So the atheists, agnostics, materialists, and naturalists are all clearly wrong in this regard.

1.4 God – What We Can Know by Observation

Since it can be reasonably shown that there must be a supernatural creator, we may then ask about the nature of God. Is God one or many, benevolent or malicious, limited or unlimited? How would we be able to know for sure?

What we can know of God we can know by observation and by revelation. What we can know by observation comes to us from our senses – sight, hearing, smell, taste, and touch.

While any of our senses can be deceived at a given time, it would be unreasonable to think that all of us were being fooled all of the time. That would put us back into the "Brains in Jars" scenario.

Since we know that nature was created sometime in the past by an agent outside or above nature which we usually call God, the very nature that was created should tell us something about God. If nature did not exist at some point in the past, then it must have been brought into existence from nothing. The Bible affirms this: "I beseech thee, my son, look upon heaven and earth, and all that is in them: and consider that God made them out of nothing [ex nihilo], and mankind also." (2 Machabees 7:28) If we consider the power required to bring the universe into existence from nothing, that will tell us about the power of God.

In order to transform something into something slightly different, it requires a certain amount of power. For example, to transform one breed of dog into another breed would require some effort, but still might be done naturally. In order to transform something into something very different requires more power. For example, to transform a cat into a dog would require some rearrangement of DNA and could not be done naturally.

To make a dog out of a rock, however, would require more power than we can comprehend. To make a dog from nothing would then require infinite power. So this tells us that God, in creating the universe from nothing, is all-powerful.

We also observe that nature is orderly – the sun comes up every day, the cycle of the seasons repeats every year, gravity holds us down, etc. That should tell us that there is order in the Creator.

Another thing we see in nature is purpose or design. In the animal kingdom we see that activity is directed toward maintaining life or bringing about new life. Animals are very good at preserving their existence. The more that we look into the details of life, the more we see the design and purpose built into it. Engineers frequently mimic nature because nature is so well designed.

Some people think that the appearance of design or purpose in nature is merely accidental, but that is not realistic. We know that it takes intelligent programmers to create computer programs. We know that it takes intelligent engineers to design well-ordered mechanisms. The orderliness and purpose in nature reveals that there is intelligence behind it all. To have created the universe from nothing indicates an unlimited intelligence.

Consider also that knowledge of something and how it works allows us to make predictions about the future. This shows that God, with unlimited intelligence, is able to predict the future with certainty. The fact that with our limited intelligence we can remember many things indicates that God also knows everything that has happened in the past. This all tells us that God is all-knowing.

Similarly, our own human nature must also be a reflection of our Creator. The Bible says that we are made in the image and likeness of God (Gen. 1:26). On an intellectual level, we all want to be happy and, if we are of good will, would like others to be happy also. This would lead us to want to do good for others and desire that good be done to us. Most societies have some expression of the Golden Rule: "Do unto others as you would have them do unto you." (Matt. 22:39)

The desire for the good of the other is what may be called charity or love. If humans have the ability to love, then God must want what is good for everyone. This tells us that God is all-loving. The Bible says that "God is love" (1 John 4:8). Since the greatest commandment is charity (Matt. 22:37 and 1 Cor. 13), it follows that the very purpose of life is to love God and others. Jesus said that we will be judged by what we did for others (Matt. 25).

As has been shown, the visible world shows that there must be something beyond mortal nature which we call the supernatural, which is invisible. This is the immortal world of spirits. Human history is full of stories of encounters with spirits, who occasionally take a visible form. The Bible says that "God is a spirit" (John 4:24). Therefore, God is an immortal, spiritual being.

Since spirits are not bound by material nature, they are not limited to a physical location. Some saints are known to have been present in more than one place at the same time. With television and the internet, we can be aware of many things happening all over the world. The Bible says: "If I ascend into heaven, you are there: if I descend into hell, you are present." (Psalms 138:8) This indicates that God is everywhere and is aware of everything that is happening.

The existence of pain, suffering, disease, and death lead some people to think that these things are part of the nature of God. The Bible tells us that death and suffering were the result of sin, the rejection of God. If God is all-powerful and all-loving, then he only allows these things to happen to us for our good.

The Bible says "And we know that to them that love God, all things work together unto good." (Romans 8:28) Some people think that happiness comes from getting what you want, and that may work in the short term. But lasting happiness only comes from wanting what you get, since that is what God has arranged for you to have, and he knows what is best for you.

Our ability to put off lesser goods in order to obtain greater goods indicates that there is a greatest good to be hoped for in the future. Obviously, our existence here on earth is not permanent. The near-death experiences that many people have had, and encounters with the spirits or souls of those who have died, indicate that there is life after death. The possibility of life after death makes life in this world a lesser good than eternal life. God only allows suffering and death to bring us to our ultimate good.

The fact that we can put off lesser goods shows that we have the ability to choose; we have a free will. God's foreknowledge of our choices does not negate our free will, however. That God chose to create man shows his good will toward us. Our choice to do good shows our good will towards God. An ill will is a sign of ingratitude for what we have received. Such an attitude will not bring peace of mind. The angels announcing the birth of Christ said, "Peace to men of good will." (Luke 2:14) All of creation is a sign of God's good will.

Everyone has an innate sense of fairness or justice. We do not like it when something is unfair, especially when it is unfair to us. This is a reflection of the justice of God. This desire for justice can, however, lead to a desire for revenge. The Bible counsels against this: "Revenge not yourselves, my dearly beloved; but give place unto wrath, for it is written: Revenge is mine, I will repay, says the Lord." (Romans 12:19) Besides that, if we expect to be forgiven, we must forgive others: "And forgive us our debts, as we also forgive our debtors." (Matt. 6:12)

We can observe that there is much injustice that goes unpunished in this world, and it is disturbing that this is so. However, this is just a sign that there will be a Final Judgment in which all injustices are rectified. The Bible says: "and they were judged every one according to their works." (Revelation 20:13)

Sometimes when an injustice is committed, it is better not to extract the full measure of justice since intentions cannot be completely known and there may be mitigating circumstances. This is to show mercy. If we can be merciful, then it must be within the nature of God to be perfectly merciful. The Bible says that "The Lord is merciful and just, and our God shows mercy." (Psalms

114:5) How God can be perfectly just and merciful at the same time is one of the wonders of God.

History shows that human nature has always been the same. Our basic needs and desires and the way we react have not changed. The four classic personality types – sanguine, melancholic, choleric, and phlegmatic – are based on the way you react. Although the way you initially react to a situation is fundamental to your personality, you can temper your reactions with practice. Interestingly, married couples tend to be opposite temperaments (sanguine–melancholic and choleric–phlegmatic)

Each generation essentially repeats the mistakes of every other generation because we learn mostly by experience and we tend not to learn from history. It is easy to predict what a large group of people will do, given a certain set of circumstances. The ministers of propaganda understand this very well. This demonstrates the stability of human nature. The Bible says that God does not change (Malachi 3:6). By this we know that God has always been the same and will remain the same.

We know that some things are better than others. It is natural to strive to be the best in a given field. We are always looking for perfection. This indicates that God is perfect. The Bible says "Be you therefore perfect, as also your heavenly Father is perfect." (Matt. 5:48) This verse is mostly speaking about unconditional love wherein we can imitate the perfection of God.

Some people look at the imperfections in life and attribute those to God, but these are just shortcomings from perfection. We only know what is imperfect by understanding perfection. Likewise, evil is just the absence of good, there is no evil in God. The Bible says "… God is light, and in him there is no darkness." (1 John 1:5) We are called to be children of the light: "Whilst you have the light, believe in the light, that you may be the children of light." (John 12:36)

Another universal aspect of humans is the desire for the truth. No one likes to be deceived, unless perhaps for the sake of flattery. If God created us with the desire for truth, then it is reasonable to think that he would not want to deceive us. The Bible says that the devil is a liar and the father of lies (John 8:44) and that God is the God of truth (Psalms 30:6).

If God is unlimited in his abilities and created the entire universe from nothing, then there would be no necessity to have another God. That is the argument from simplicity. Therefore, it is reasonable to think that there is only one, almighty God and no others.

So from all this we can know that there is only one, immortal, spiritual God who is all-powerful, all-knowing, all-present, all-loving, of good will, orderly, just, merciful, unchanging, perfect, and truthful.

1.5 God – What We Can Know by Revelation

Apart from what we can know about God by observation, there are also things that we can only know by revelation. Much of what Christianity considers to be divine revelation is contained in the books of the Bible. The Bible is not really a single book but a collection of books by various authors. The Catholic Old Testament contains 46 books and the New Testament contains 27 books for a total of 73. Protestant Christians do not accept seven of the 46 books in the Catholic Old Testament (Protestant Apocrypha or Catholic Deuterocanonical). All Christians consider the Bible to be the Word of God. So how was the list of Biblical books – the canon of Scripture – determined?

The early Christians had a set of Old Testament scriptures that was written in Greek called the Septuagint. It was written by seventy scholars (septuaginta means 70 in Latin – LXX in Roman numerals) around the year 250 B.C. Jesus gave quotations from these scriptures. Today's Jews use the Hebrew Masoretic text which was compiled in the 10th century A.D.

Parts of all but one (Esther) of the books of the Hebrew Masoretic text were found in the Dead Sea Scrolls. It is worth noting that a comparison of the scrolls, which were written in the first and second centuries B.C., to modern copies of the Bible show that the meaning of the verses has been maintained to a high degree. Parts of several of the deuterocanonical books of the Catholic Old Testament were also found among the scrolls (Tobit, Sirach, and Baruch).

The early Christians also started compiling texts written by St. Paul and the apostles and evangelists. These letters were read in the churches of the Christians, as they became available. None of these writings mention the destruction of Jerusalem in A.D. 70, which would have been extremely significant because it was foretold by Our Lord, so they were all likely finished before that event. Ven. Mary of Agreda said that St. John wrote the last gospel in A.D. 58.

The early Christians were persecuted by the Romans and possession of these writings became a crime. That in part led to the question in the early Church as to which writings were considered to be Holy Scripture. The emperor Constantine ordered a set of 50 sets of the sacred Scriptures to be made, which also would have forced the issue. Finally, in A.D. 397, the Third Council of Carthage came up with a list of Old and New Testament writings which were considered to be the list (canon) of Scripture:

> "The Canonical Scriptures are these: Genesis, Exodus, Leviticus, Numbers, Deuteronomy, Joshua the son of Nun, Judges, Ruth, four books of Kings, two books of Paralipomena, Job, the Psalter, five books of Solomon, the books of the twelve prophets, Isaiah, Jeremiah, Ezekiel, Daniel, Tobit, Judith, Esther, two books of Esdras, two books of the Machabees. Of the New Testament: four books of the Gospels, one book of the Acts of the Apostles, thirteen Epistles of the Apostle Paul, one epistle of the same [writer] to the Hebrews, two Epistles of the Apostle Peter, three of John, one of James, one of Jude, one book of the Apocalypse of John."

Note that the book of Jeremiah contained three separate books: Jeremiah, Lamentations, and Baruch. That gives 46 books in the Old Testament and 27 in the New. This list was made dogmatic (official, unchangeable) by the Council of Trent in 1546. For all of his protestations about upholding the Word of God, Martin Luther tossed seven books of the Old Testament and wanted to toss James as well, probably because of the verse: "So faith also, if it have not works, is dead in itself." (James 2:17) Luther also added the word "alone" to Romans 3:28: "For we account a man to be justified by faith [alone] ..."

All the books of the Bible were translated by St. Jerome into the Latin Vulgate around the year A.D. 400. Even as late as 1943, Pope Pius XII could mention in his encyclical letter *Divino Afflante Spiritu* the "authority of the Vulgate in matters of doctrine." The controversial Nova Vulgata, published in 1979, is not the Vulgate of St. Jerome, but a revision of the text intended to harmonize with modern critical Hebrew and Greek texts. It is hard to imagine anyone improving on St. Jerome, however, due to his familiarity with the Biblical languages and culture.

The Rheims New Testament (1582) and Douay Old Testament (1609) were among the first English translations of scripture, coming out before the King James Bible in 1611. Many people say that the Douay-Rheims is the most accurate English Bible that is available, since it is a strict translation of the words of the old Latin Vulgate, not a rephrasing of their meaning.

These canonical books are those considered by the Church to be inspired by God and to contain no error. Various other books were considered, like the Shepherd of Hermas and the Didache, but only the 73 made the list. The Book of Enoch is quoted by many Biblical authors, especially Jude (1:14-15), but it is not in the Bible. There are even books mentioned in the Bible that are not part of the Bible, like the Book of Jasher (Joshua 10:13) and St. Paul's letter to the Laodiceans (Col. 4:16).

The Bible is the written portion of the public revelation of God which ended with the death of the last apostle, John. Oral traditions, such as things concerning Mary and purgatory, are the unwritten portion of public revelation. Catholics know these as Sacred Scripture and Sacred/Apostolic Tradition, which make up the one inerrant, infallible Deposit of Faith to be faithfully defined, upheld, and passed on by the Magisterium of the Catholic Church. Nothing can be added to or removed from these sources, or their understanding essentially changed, otherwise it is not part of the Catholic Faith. Modernists should take note.

But just because the Catholic Church came up with a list of books, does that necessarily mean that everything in them is true? Life involves a certain amount of trust. American money has the words "In God We Trust" on it. Even the people who claim that they do not trust God are forced to trust someone. There just is not enough time to figure out everything on our own, so we end up trusting that someone else got it right. The people who do not trust anyone end up being paranoid.

When you drive down the road you trust that other people do not want to hit you and are able to avoid doing that. When you take food or drink you trust that it is not poisoned or toxic. When you go to sleep you trust that you will be safe and will wake up in the morning. You trust that other people are basically truthful, unless they have demonstrated that they are not. That is why most people like living among Christians, even if they do not profess faith in Jesus Christ themselves.

Many people tell small lies, or white lies, if they think there is no harm in it. Most people recognize that more important matters require more truthfulness. If lives depend on it, we want to know the truth. There are penalties for lying under oath in a courtroom.

So if matters concerning people's lives are that important, then matters concerning eternity should require greater importance. That is why religious truths are held in high regard by people of various religions. The Vedas are very important in Hinduism. The Quran is memorized by many Muslims. The Hebrew scriptures are recited by the Jews daily. The Bible is considered to be the inerrant Word of God by Christians.

It is a Jewish tradition that Moses wrote the first five books of the Bible – Genesis, Exodus, Leviticus, Numbers, and Deuteronomy – the Torah. Christians accept this as well. Moses lived around 1500 B.C. and led the Israelites out of Egypt into Israel. The story of his life is recorded in the Bible, and there are even extra-Biblical legends about him.

Of course, there are many religious stories that we generally do not take to be literally true. Many of the cultural creation myths are so fantastic that it is hard to imagine that they are literally true. Gods and men just pop up everywhere. The gods of the Greeks, Romans, and Norse might not be quite as fantastical, and were certainly taken seriously by many ancient people, but they seem to be more in the world of fiction or myth.

So how can we separate fact from fiction? We know that American legends like Paul Bunyan, Johnny Appleseed, and John Henry have roots in reality, but that the stories became exaggerated later on. How do we know that the Torah is not an exaggeration of Jewish events that happened long ago, and that the New Testament is not just made-up stories of a good man?

1.6 Basis for Truth

We might well ask how we can know anything is true. Our perception of the material world comes to us through our five senses – sight, smell, taste, hearing, and touch. With our intellect we can process this information into concepts that are understandable. There is even the possibility that our soul can communicate with the world of spirits using extra-sensory perception, but that is not a regular means of gathering information.

As far as knowing religious truth, it is usually a matter of what we have heard or read. So it comes down to figuring out how we can know what we have heard or read is true or trustworthy. We might first look at the source of information. Is it dependable?

Our first teachers are generally our parents. Most parents have the good of their children in mind – they love their children. The bond of trust between parent and child is about as strong as it gets. Our relationships with our parents influence our relationships with everyone else. This is why those who seek to control society attempt to remove children from their parents as much as possible.

After forming a relationship of trust over many years, we come to believe that what our parents tell us is true, or at least that they are not trying to deceive us. They may have incomplete or inaccurate information, but most parents do not lie to their children. So we tend to accept our parents as a reliable source because they have demonstrated a long-term regard for our well-being. This also becomes a test for reliability of other sources.

Relationships with extended family members, such as grandparents, aunts, and uncles, can also provide us with love and trustworthy information. Such relationships help humanity to span the generations. That is why those who seek to control society also promote the warehousing of the young and the old, contraception, abortion, homosexuality, euthanasia, and one-child policies.

Since most children go to school and religious services, school teachers and religious authorities become additional sources of information. Even those who seek to remove religious influences from the lives of children are essentially replacing one source of information with another. Just as with our parental relationships, a demonstrated long-term regard for our well-being becomes a key to trust. Of course, fear and intimidation can also be used to form society, and most people will find a way to survive in such an environment even at the expense of the truth. But ideally, we will be free to choose which sources of information to trust.

When we have information from a trustworthy source, we then have something that can serve as a basis of comparison. If I trust that one thing is true, then I can trust that something similar or non-contradictory is also true. Whatever formed our basis for truth becomes the filter for judging other information.

Of course, this assumes that a person is looking for truth. Some people only care about the truth as long as it serves their interests. In the Bible, Jesus tells Pontius Pilate: "For this was I born, and for this came I into the world; that I should give testimony to the truth. Every one that is of the truth hears my voice." (John 18:37) Pilate then responds: "What is truth?"

Pilate was only interested in the truth so far as it allowed him to maintain his position. He had Jesus crucified – a man he believed to be innocent – in order to avoid a riot. Other people, especially those in positions of power or influence, tend to be equally pragmatic about the truth. They would rather avoid any truths that would harm their careers.

Cherished behaviors can also impede our search for truth. If excessive smoking or drinking gives us pleasure, then we do not like to think about the negative consequences. Hallucinogenic drugs and sexual intercourse are other very strong sources of pleasure that some people are not easily willing to give up. Pornography, video games, and excessive entertainment can also be very hard to give up.

God will often allow us to become addicted to these behaviors in order to bring us to a point where we are willing to accept the truth and live accordingly. A person on a quest for the truth cannot allow himself to be distracted by the pleasures of this world. This is a fact that is acknowledged by many of the world's religions. Even people who are professional athletes must avoid behavior that would damage their health if they are to achieve their goal of winning, at least in the short term.

Another impediment to knowing the truth is dabbling in the occult. Witchcraft has been used to attempt to obtain power over nature and other persons for most of human history. This is essentially another form of seeking the good of self over the good of others. The rejection of God by Satan, and then by Adam and Eve, was the choice of the good of self over the good of the other – selfishness. "Do what thou wilt shall be the whole of the law" is the satanic creed.

Even a desire for a comfortable living – to stay in our comfort zone – can prevent us from pursuing the truth. All this must be overcome, however, in order to get to the absolute truth. If we can get past the disordered desires of the world, the flesh, and the devil, we will have come a long way in our search for the truth. It then becomes a matter of who and what to trust.

1.7 How Can We Know What Is True?

So after we figure out who to trust, then how do we know what is true? If we can verify something for ourselves, then we can believe that it is true. For example, if you put two and two together, you get four. Most things are not that easy to verify, however.

Mathematical truths can be determined with mathematics. However, even mathematics is not complete in and of itself. Gödel's incompleteness theorems show that no computer program can be shown to prove all truths about numbers, and that no mathematical theory can prove its own consistency.

Natural science can be used to determine the truth about things pertaining to nature. But it has nothing to say about things beyond nature, and there is much disagreement among natural scientists even about the natural world. Some scientists will not even write books because by the time they are published, ideas have already changed.

Historical science deals with what has happened in the past, and there are ways of supporting this or that theory. However, there is probably at least as much if not more disagreement among historians as there is among natural scientists.

All discussion of truth assumes that there is a language that people can use with words that have accepted meaning.

There are things which also must be accepted without proof, such as that the world is ordered and rational, and that there is truth which can be known. The ancient Greeks believed this. Their philosophy was adopted by Rome and was incorporated into Christianity. The Scholasticism of Aquinas was the peak of this philosophy.

Western thought accepts the law of non-contradiction; that something cannot be true and not true at the same time. Put another way, a statement and its opposite cannot both be true at the same time. The law of causality – that an effect must have a proportional cause – is another accepted concept. Without these presuppositions, any discussion of the truth becomes meaningless and a waste of time.

So if you accept that there is truth and a way to find it, then where do you go from there? You would probably want to start with an organization or system of thought that claimed to know the truth. Three religions that claim to know the truth – or claim to be the one, true religion – are Christianity, Judaism, and Islam. Of course, there are various branches in each of those religions.

One religion that also makes a claim to be the true religion is Mormonism – The Church of Jesus Christ of Latter-day Saints – which is essentially the religion of Joseph Smith. There are about the same number of Mormons as there are Jews in the world today, approximately 13 million. This religion is basically an amalgamation of the King James Bible and American Indian folklore. After the death of Joseph Smith, Brigham Young became the leader of the Mormons. Any reading of the lives of Smith and Young, and of the teachings and practices of Mormonism, should lead you to question the truth of it all.

Other religions, such as most of the Eastern religions, may proclaim truths but they are more systems of thought, like Confucianism, than religions with dogmas, practices, and rituals. They may have collected the wisdom of the ages – the perennial wisdom – such as do this or don't do that, which shows an appreciation for truth. However, they generally do not make a claim to the absolute truth or even acknowledge that absolutes exist. This perennial wisdom (Sophia) is described beautifully in the Biblical book of Ecclesiasticus (Sirach), Chapter 24, which is a prefigurement of the Blessed Virgin Mary. Her Son is the Divine Logos described in the First Chapter of John.

Pagan and primitive religions only have vague notions of the truth, so you probably would not expect to find much clarity there. The farther you get away from rational, reasonable thought systems, the more you get into superstition and spiritism. Satanism, Wicca, Scientology, Theosophy, Gnosticism, and Occultism are all names given to methods of seeking hidden knowledge. This usually ends up badly, as it did for Adam and Eve in the Garden of Eden. There are evil powers out there seeking to destroy your soul: "For our wrestling is not against flesh and blood; but against principalities and powers, against the rulers of the world of this darkness, against the spirits of wickedness in the high places." (Ephesians 6:12) Evil spirits have been causing harm and confusion since the Fall of Adam. So just being "spiritual" is not necessarily a good thing.

So how would you be able to judge the veracity of a religion? You could examine its teachings to see if they were in line with what is observable. Most religions have a version of the Golden Rule – do unto others what you would have done unto you. The Silver Rule is the flip side of that – do not do unto others what you would not have done unto you. Those are fairly universal truths.

A careful observation of nature also tells you what works and what does not – this is the natural law. Even people who claim no religion at all think you should be nice. When asked how a person should behave, Jesus said: "Thou shalt not kill: Thou shalt not commit adultery: Thou shalt not steal: Thou shalt not bear false witness: Honor thy father and mother." (Luke 18:20) Most people would agree with that.

Most religions have collections of writings. Christianity has the Bible, Judaism has the Torah, Islam has the Quran, and Hinduism has the Vedas. What are some ways of judging the truth about historical writing?

If a story is written during lifetime of person or the lifetime of eye-witnesses to the events, we would have more certainty of its veracity since persons living at the time would be familiar with the events. As more time goes by, the events become less clear. The New Testament was written during the lifetime of the people who lived during the time of Jesus. Traditionally, Moses wrote the Torah. And Mohammed is said to have written the Quran. The original authorship of the Vedas has been lost to history.

Archaeological evidence of events described in such

writings would lend further evidence to their accuracy. There are eye-witness sightings of Noah's Ark, although not all of these can be true since some details are contradictory. There is a considerable amount of evidence to support the story of the Exodus of the Israelites from Egypt into the desert and on to Israel as documented by Robert Cornuke in the book *In Search of the Mountain of God*. Joshua's long day is recorded in various ancient cultures. Dozens of names of rulers in the Old Testament appear in writings of other ancient cultures in the region.

Some of the stones in the Wailing Wall in Jerusalem are supposedly from the original temple complex. Many sites in Israel have churches built over them with traditions going all the way back to early Christianity. The Chapel of the Ascension on Mount Olivet has a footprint in a rock that was supposedly left by Jesus as he ascended into heaven.

Independent accounts of religious stories would testify to their authenticity. The global Flood of Noah is held by nearly all of the world cultures. Ancient Babylonian writings speak of the Israelite civilization. The historian Josephus speaks of events of the time of Christ and was written around that time. Civilizations around the Mediterranean Sea record invasions by the Muslims, although Mohammed's alleged ascension into heaven was not witnessed by anyone else.

Stories and writings that are unchanged over time would also be a mark of legitimacy. Jews, Christians, and Muslims are all very careful about preserving the original versions of events.

Supernatural events have long been used to prove the truthfulness of religious claims. One important reason to understand nature and how it operates is to be able to recognize when something is either unnatural or supernatural. St. Thomas Aquinas in his *Summa Contra Gentiles* said, "For an error about creation is reflected in a false opinion about God."

It is said that if you stop believing in God that you will not believe nothing, but that you will believe anything. Ascribing powers to nature that it does not have is tantamount to superstition. God certainly uses secondary causes, so just because we do not understand something does not mean God performed a miracle to make it happen (God-of-the-gaps theory). However, assigning events to causes such as gnomes, elves, aliens, or unknown forces does not get us closer to the truth.

Moses performed various feats that were beyond the natural. He called down 10 plagues upon Egypt which were not natural either because of the timing – certain events can happen naturally, but not necessarily on command – or because of their character. The priests of Pharaoh were able to imitate Moses when he turned his staff into a snake, but they recognized that some of his miracles were beyond their power. The simultaneous death of all the first-born of Egypt was certainly not natural.

The parting of the Red Sea was an event that some people try to explain on a natural basis, but those who witnessed it understood it to be miraculous. When Moses produced water from a rock in the middle of the desert and foretold of the manna from heaven, those too were miracles. His direct communication with God and his bringing back the Ten Commandments showed that he was a true prophet. The Bible says that he even had to veil his face because no one could look at him directly.

The stories of Moses are used to show that he was a prophet sent by God. Another prophet, Elijah, called down fire from heaven several times and was taken up to heaven in a chariot. His successor Elisha raised a boy from the dead. Jesus worked numerous miracles, rose from the dead, and ascended into heaven, all of which were witnessed by many persons.

The foretelling of future events has also been long used to verify claims to the truth. The Bible is full of such accounts. Jesus fulfilled the prophecies of a messiah from the Old Testament. Jesus also predicted his own death and resurrection, and the destruction of Jerusalem.

Miracles and prophecies can be mimicked by magicians and fortune-tellers. Magic tricks are generally just deception. Black magic can involve the preternatural or paranormal, but demonic agencies are at work. Those involved with black magic usually use it for selfish reasons and end up destroying themselves and others, demonstrating that it is evil. Fortune tellers may be very perceptive, and can make good guesses about the past or future, especially if they only speak in general terms. However, only God can know the future for certain. One sign of a true prophet in communication with God is the ability to foretell future events with accuracy.

The lives of the followers of a particular religion can also reveal the truth of its claims. The prophets of ancient Israel led lives that were exemplary. Many of the early Christians were martyrs for their faith. The lives of the saints of the Catholic Church are full of stories of supernatural events such as bilocation, reading of souls, communication with the deceased, visions of God and angels, levitation, prophecy, healing, resurrection, exorcism, power over nature, miraculous wounds (stigmata), ability to live without food or sleep, incorruptibility, etc. St. Simeon Stylites lived on top of a pillar near Aleppo, Syria for years, and the remains of that pillar exist today. He really knew the meaning of the word mortification.

Other miraculous signs indicating the truth of Christianity are Eucharistic miracles, weeping or bleeding statues and icons, and events associated with apparitions such as Guadalupe, Lourdes, and Fatima. In Guadalupe, Mexico, Mary appeared to a native man and left a miraculous image on his cloak. Many instantaneous, complete healings have taken place at Lourdes, France, where Our Lady appeared to St. Bernadette. The miracle of the sun which took place in Fatima, Portugal was foretold months in advance and was convincing even to many atheists.

You would expect that the truth of a religion would translate into followers. According to internet statistics, Christianity holds about 33% of the world population, Islam about 21%, Hinduism about 14%, Non-religious about 14%, Buddhism about 6%, Chinese folk religion about 6%, and the rest about 6%. Judaism claims less than 1% of the world population. The roots of Christianity lie in Judaism, however.

1.8 Moses, Jesus, and Mohammed

The claims of Judaism to be the true religion rest principally on Moses. All questions about Christianity center on the identity of Jesus Christ. Islam rests entirely on Mohammed. The lives of those three men would then be crucial to determining the truth.

Moses was a prophet to the Israelites in about the year 1500 B.C. The Torah, the first five books of the Old Testament – Genesis, Exodus, Leviticus, Numbers, and Deuteronomy – are ascribed to him. The book of Genesis describes the creation of the world and man by God, the early history of man until the Flood of Noah, the building of the Tower of Babel and the subsequent dispersion of man, the settling of Abraham in the land of Canaan or Palestine, and the stories of Isaac, Jacob, and the 12 sons of Jacob – later named Israel – who became the heads of the 12 tribes of Israelites.

Even if the history of the world before Abraham is hotly debated, most people accept him as an historic person. Jews and Muslims claim him as the father of their faith. Christians understand that he is intimately bound up in their faith also.

The book of Exodus tells the story of Moses being adopted by the daughter of an Egyptian pharaoh after finding him floating down the Nile in a basket, then fleeing Egypt for Arabia after killing an Egyptian, having a vision of God in a burning bush on Mt. Sinai, going back to Egypt to gain the release of the Israelites, and leading them through the Red Sea and the Arabian desert into Palestine, while having revelations and receiving the Ten Commandments.

One mark of a holy man is that he can stop demonic or false miracles. The Bible says: "Moses was beloved of God, and men: whose memory is in benediction. He made him like the saints in glory, and magnified him in the fear of his enemies, and with his words he made prodigies to cease." (Ecclesiasticus 45:1-2) Likewise, St. Paul stopped a demon-possessed woman (Acts 16:16).

Traditional Jewish beliefs and practices come directly from the words of Moses. His writings are understood by them to be revealed by God. They have been meticulously preserved for many generations. They have all the marks of authenticity: corresponding to natural law, written during his lifetime, supported by archaeological evidence and independent writings, constant over time, verified by supernatural signs and prophecies, and witnessed by the lives of the subsequent prophets. If any writing can be believed, it is the writing of Moses.

Unfortunately, the Jewish collection of writings known as the Talmud was not written with the same spirit that inspired Moses. It is extremely xenophobic and defends injustice against non-Jews. Anyone who criticizes it is labeled "anti-Semitic." The Kabbalah is occultic and a danger to the soul. After the ancient Israelites turned against God, Ezekiel says that God: "gave them statutes that were not good, and judgments, in which they shall not live. And I polluted them in their own gifts, when they offered all that opened the womb, for their offences: and they shall know that I am the Lord." (Ezekiel 20:25)

One thing that Moses did write was that there would be a prophet to come after him to whom people should listen: "The Lord thy God will raise up to thee a prophet of thy nation and of thy brethren like unto me: him thou shalt hear." (Deut. 18:15) Christians understand this to be Jesus. At any rate, it shows that Moses did not believe that he would have the last word.

The books of the New Testament also have all the marks of authenticity. They concern the life and teachings of Jesus Christ. Jesus himself did not write any of the New Testament, but eye-witnesses to his life and work did. The writings of St. Luke – his Gospel and the Acts of the Apostles – give many details that are highly accurate, especially with names and geography. His Gospel starts out this way (Luke 1:1-4):

> "For as many have taken in hand to set forth in order a narration of the things that have been accomplished among us; according as they have delivered them unto us, who from the beginning were eyewitnesses and ministers of the word: it seemed good to me also, having diligently attained to all things from the beginning, to write to you in order, most excellent Theophilus, that you may know the truth of those words in which you have been instructed."

Jesus claimed that Moses wrote of him: "For if you did believe Moses, you would perhaps believe me also; for he wrote of me." (John 5:46) Jesus also claimed to fulfill the prophecies of the Old Testament: "Do not think that I am come to destroy the law, or the prophets. I am not come to destroy, but to fulfill." (Matt. 5:17)

He is recorded to have performed many signs and miracles, including raising three people from the dead. These were given to verify his message that he was the Messiah, or Christ, expected by the Jews. He plainly told this to the Samaritan women at the well: "Jesus said to her: I am he, who am speaking with thee." (John 4:26)

Jesus said that those who heard, believed, and lived his words would be free: "If you continue in my word, you shall be my disciples indeed. And you shall know the truth, and the truth shall make you free." (John 8:31-32) Part of this being free is freedom from the effects of sin, which is eternal death, so as to live eternal life. Eternal salvation comes only through belief in Jesus Christ (Acts 4:12).

He called himself the Son of God and the Son of man. The Bible records his birth from a virgin, which was a fulfillment of an Old Testament prophecy (Isaiah 7:14). He even claimed to be God: "Jesus said to them: Amen, amen I say to you, before Abraham was made, I am." (John 8:58) The phrase "I am" is a clear reference to how God identified himself to Moses on Mt. Sinai: "God said to Moses: I am who am." (Exodus 3:14) The first verse of the Gospel of John says that "the Word was God," further showing his divinity and St. Thomas declared "My Lord and my God" without correction from Jesus (John 20:28).

Upon his birth, Jesus was proclaimed by angels to be the Christ (Luke 2:11). When Jesus was presented in the temple as an infant, the holy man Simeon – who was promised that he would see the Christ before his death – called him: "A light to the revelation of the Gentiles, and the glory of thy people Israel." (Luke 2:32) The prophetess Anna spoke about him at that time also.

St. Peter declared that Jesus was the Messiah foretold by both Moses (Acts 3:22-23 and Deut. 18:15) and David (Acts 2:34-35 and Psalms 109:1). Jesus mentioned the prophecy of David, implying that it referred to himself (Matt. 22:41-45). St. Stephen mentioned the prophecy of Moses as well (Acts 7:37). St. Paul used the Old Testament to prove that Jesus was the Christ (Acts 18:28).

St. John said that Jesus performed many miracles that are not recorded in the Bible, but the ones that are recorded are meant to show that Jesus was the Christ, the Son of God (John 20:30-31). He also said: "But there are also many other things which Jesus did; which, if they were written every one, the world itself, I think, would not be able to contain the books that should be written." (John 21:25)

No one else in history, who was taken seriously by more than a small number of people, has claimed to actually be God in the flesh. You would have to believe that Jesus was a lunatic, a charlatan, or a megalomaniac if you thought he was not God. The only other possibility is that his followers got the story wrong. But the Bible is the most reliable piece of ancient literature that we have. Once you accept that the Bible is true and that Jesus is God, then it becomes clear that Christianity is the religion of God.

If Jesus is God come in the flesh, then it shows that God is humble and forgiving. He created the world from nothing, and yet he was willing to be born of a woman, live in near-poverty, and die on a cross. There are many Bible verses that say God favors the humble and resists the proud.

Jesus told Pilate that his mission was to preach the truth: "For this was I born, and for this came I into the world; that I should give testimony to the truth. Every one that is of the truth, hears my voice." (John 18:37) He also claimed to be the truth: "Jesus said to him: I am the way, and the truth, and the life." (John 14:6) Jesus did not claim to be just teaching truths, but that he was the absolute truth.

Jesus also taught that he came so that people could have eternal life: "For God so loved the world, as to give his only begotten Son; that whosoever believeth in him, may not perish, but may have life everlasting." (John 3:16) Jesus gave a precondition for eternal life, however: "He that believes and is baptized, shall be saved: but he that believes not shall be condemned." (Mark 16:16)

Jesus was crucified on Good Friday, which he predicted and which is foretold in the Old Testament (Isaiah 53), and then rose again to life on Easter Sunday. There were witnesses to his death and to the empty tomb. He also appeared to many of his followers after his resurrection, showing the ability to pass through locked doors. After spending a short time on earth after his resurrection, he ascended into heaven in the presence of many witnesses (Acts 1).

Jesus said that he would be buried three days and nights (Matt. 12:40). The Bible says that he was buried on Friday evening and rose from the dead on Sunday morning. That seems to be a contradiction, but the expression "three days and nights" can mean any part of three consecutive days.

The cloak of Jesus is preserved in the Cathedral of Trier, Germany. The crown of thorns is kept in Paris. The Cathedral of Aachen houses several relics including the cloak of Mary, the swaddling clothes of the infant Jesus, the beheading cloth of Saint John the Baptist, and the loincloth worn by Jesus at his crucifixion. A piece of the cross, one of the nails, and the INRI inscription are displayed at the Basilica of the Holy Cross in Jerusalem in Rome. The house where he grew up is in Loreto, Italy. The Shroud of Turin is believed by many to be the burial cloth of Jesus. Blessed Anne Catherine Emmerich indicated that it is actually one of three miraculous copies of the original shroud, upon which the image of Jesus runs at an angle. This would be the case if his body were wrapped in it, as is described in the Bible (Luke 23:53).

The followers of Jesus wrote about him, spread his message, and died rather than denying their belief in him. It would be one thing to make up a story about a man, but quite another thing to die rather than changing the story. The lives of the canonized saints of the Catholic Church are another proof of the truthfulness of the Bible message.

So the Bible has all the marks of authenticity and tells the story of Moses, the great prophet, and of Jesus, a man who claimed to be God in the flesh. So we have every reason to believe that the events recorded in the Bible are true. If that is the case, and Jesus was who he claimed to be, then we can believe that what he said is the absolute truth. It was revealed to St. Teresa of Jesus (1515-1582, author of *The Interior Castle*) by Our Lord Jesus Christ that: "All the harm that comes to the world comes from its not knowing the truths of Scripture in clarity and truth."

Jesus claimed to establish a Church that would have the authority to perpetuate his teachings (Matt. 16:18-19). He also said that he would send the Holy Spirit to teach all truth: "But when he, the Spirit of truth, is come, he will teach you all truth." (John 16:13)

The authority of the Catholic Church to determine the books of the Bible and the authentic interpretation of them comes directly from Jesus Christ. Because of that, the Bible and the teachings of the Catholic Church are the two most reliable sources of truth that we have. Two dogmas of the Church are that the Bible is inerrant, and that dogma is infallible and cannot change. If those two things were not true, then we would not be able to know much truth, outside of what can be scientifically proven.

Since we do not have any of the original copies of the books of the Bible, we are trusting that they were faithfully copied throughout the years. Even at that, the texts used by St. Jerome to produce the Latin Vulgate are no longer in existence – we trust that he was able to convey the meaning of the original Hebrew, Greek, Chaldaic, and Aramaic into Latin. Most of us do not even read Latin, so we trust that whatever language we read the Bible in is a faithful translation of the original meaning.

Pope Leo XIII in his 1893 encyclical letter *Providentissimus Deus* – On the Study of Holy Scripture declared that:

> "For all the books which the Church receives as sacred and canonical are written wholly and entirely, with all their parts, at the dictation of the Holy Spirit; and so far is it from being possible that any error can coexist with inspiration, that inspiration not only is essentially incompatible with error, but excludes and rejects it as absolutely and necessarily as it is impossible that God Himself, the supreme Truth, can utter that which is not true. This is the ancient and unchanging faith of the Church, solemnly defined in the Councils of Florence and Trent, and finally and more expressly formulated by the [First] Council of the Vatican."

The First Vatican Council (1870) declared on infallibility of doctrine/dogma that:

> "For, the doctrine of faith which God revealed has not been handed down as a philosophic invention to the human mind to be perfected, but has been entrusted as a divine deposit to the Spouse of Christ [Catholic Church], to be faithfully guarded and infallibly interpreted. Hence, also, that understanding of its sacred dogmas must be perpetually retained, which Holy Mother Church has once declared; and there must never be recession

from that meaning under the specious name of a deeper understanding." (Denzinger #1800)

Pope Pius X in his 1907 encyclical letter *Pascendi Dominici Gregis – On the Doctrines of the Modernists* said that Modernism is the "synthesis of all heresies" and that evolution, primarily evolution of dogma, was the chief point in their doctrines. He quotes Pope Gregory IX saying: "Some among you, distended like bladders by the spirit of vanity, strive by novelty to cross the boundaries fixed by the Fathers [Prov. 22:28]; twisting the meaning of sacred text."

Infallible Catholic Church dogmas can only be defined by a pope, or by a council with the agreement of a pope. Dogmas are usually defined in the form of anathemas or condemnations of their denial, e.g.: "Whoever says this dogma is not true, let him be anathema." The First Vatican Council codified the teaching of papal infallibility. It is only rarely used. The last time without question was in the definition of the Assumption of the Blessed Virgin Mary into heaven (Pius XII, 1950).

Popes use official letters to define dogma. Pope John Paul II only exercised infallible language once in his 27-year papacy – to declare what was always held: that the Church does not have authority to ordain women to the priesthood (*Ordinatio Sacerdotalis*, 1994). Also, in 1995 he reiterated the infallible teaching of the Church that: "direct abortion, that is, abortion willed as an end or as a means, always constitutes a grave moral disorder" (*Evangelium Vitae*)

Infallibility does not imply impeccability. Not every word out of a pope's mouth is the Word of God. A pope can make errors in many things and lead a scandalous life. He is only guaranteed by the Holy Spirit to not make an error when officially defining a doctrine to be believed by the whole Church.

The *Sources of Catholic Dogma* by Denzinger (I recommend the 1955 edition) is a collection of Catholic Church dogmas/doctrines. *Fundamentals of Catholic Dogma*, by Dr. Ludwig Ott is another good source of dogmas. There is no official list of every Church teaching that must be believed, however, which are the de fide "of the Faith" teachings. Things like the law of non-contradiction (that something cannot be both true and not true at the same time) are presupposed by those teachings. Other teachings which may not have the rank of dogma are: Sententia Fidei Proxima (proximate to the Faith), Sententia Certa (theologically certain), Sententia Communia (common teaching), and Sententia Probabilis (probable teaching).

The Church uses creeds (Apostles' Creed or Nicene Creed) to summarize beliefs. The Catechism summarizes teachings, especially those related to the Creed, the seven sacraments, the Ten Commandments, and the Our Father prayer. The Catechism itself is not necessarily infallible; teachings in it which have not been infallibly defined are subject to change.

Islam claims to complete Judaism and Christianity, and says that Moses and Jesus were prophets, but that Mohammed is the last prophet. The religion of Islam and its founder, Mohammed, have similarities to Mormonism and Joseph

Smith. Both leaders claimed to have had visions of angels who gave them divine messages. They both wrote books – The Quran and the Book of Mormon – which define the religions that they founded, which they claim were the true religions. Their religions are a synthesis of the experiences of their youths. They both had multiple wives. Violence was prevalent in their lives, which was justified as part of their religion. After their deaths, succession was a question. Both are heralded as prophets by their followers, but their intentions are questioned by their critics.

The central tenet of Islam, and the very meaning of that word, is "submission" – submission to the will of God. What is the will of God? The teachings in the Quran. What does the Quran teach? Kill the infidel! Who is the infidel? Apparently, the one who does not believe in your interpretation of the Quran. Unfortunately, that leads to a lot of bad behavior. Even Shias cannot tolerate Sunnis.

Although Muslims share the concept of monotheism with Christians and Jews, their concept of God is very different. It can hardly be said that they worship the same God. The Quran shares some ideas with the Old and New Testaments, but its laws are very different. People should study Sharia Law before they start calling Islam a religion of peace. Honor killing and a sentence of rape would be violations of the Commandments for Christians and Jews.

One central tenet of Judaism is an eye for an eye (Exodus 21:24). Although that was an improvement over wiping out an entire town for one rape (Gen. 34:25), it is still brutal. The conquest of Canaan was made after the Israelites were given the commandment "Thou shalt not kill," so a Jew can easily come to the conclusion that God is brutal and is concerned less for Gentiles than he is for Jews.

The history of Israel involves a lot of violence, both in ancient and in modern times. The King David Hotel bombing in 1946 happened just before Israel became a modern state. Some say the motive was to destroy evidence of Jewish terrorist activity. The 1967 attack on the USS Liberty during the Six-Day War was probably another attempt to suppress evidence. Anyone bringing up those two incidents will likely be labelled anti-Semitic, however.

The concept of a "Christian Zionist" should appear to be self-contradictory. A Zionist is one who supports the interests of the state of Israel. But Israel's treatment of the Palestinians can hardly be described as Christian. Besides, the New Testament makes it clear that the Old Testament has been replaced (Hebrews 8 and Acts 4).

Pope Pius XII stated in his 1943 encyclical *Mystici Corporis Christi* (#29): "And first of all, by the death of our Redeemer, the New Testament took the place of the Old Law which had been abolished; then the Law of Christ together with its mysteries, enactments, institutions, and sacred rites was ratified for the whole world in the blood of Jesus Christ." That was stated during WWII and just before Israel became a modern state.

The central tenet of Christianity is to love God first and love your neighbor second (Matt. 22:36-40). Jesus told his followers to love their enemies (Matt. 5:44), that is, have concern for the eternal soul of the other, even if it costs you your life on earth. This attitude is best for the common good. For this reason, most people like living around Christians even if they do not have the same faith.

So if Jesus Christ is God, and Christianity is the religion of God, then the claims of Islam and Mormonism must necessarily be false, and those of Judaism are incomplete. Christianity claims that public revelation ended with the death of the last Apostle (John). So that was all there was to say, and there was not anything substantially new to be said publicly after that. It is best for society when people follow the teachings and practices of Christianity.

It is said that for the person who believes, no proof is necessary, but for the person who does not believe, no proof is sufficient. A person cannot be forced to believe anything. It is a decision of the will. It still requires a certain amount of faith to believe that Jesus is God. There is no scientific or mathematical proof of that. However, we must accept many things without absolute proof. The Bible says, "But without faith it is impossible to please God." (Heb. 11:6) God has given us enough evidence to believe in him. It is up to us to make the decision.

2 CREATION

2.1 Nature by Design

The Bible says that God can be known by his works
(Romans 1:20). The First and Second Laws of
Thermodynamics prove that nature was created at some
point in the past. Some people look at the world and see
design in everything. Other people only see accidents.
Could dispersed gas and dust accidently become a thinking
human being? That is what evolution says. What does
nature itself have to say about it?

2.2 The Cosmos

The commonly accepted story for the origin of the universe
is the Big Bang theory. The Nebular hypothesis is then used
to explain the origin of the stars and planets. But can those
ideas account for what we observe?

The Big Bang theory is taught to most everyone who goes to
school. As has been shown, nature could not have created
itself and cannot be infinitely old. Most scientists imagine
that a small particle of nearly infinite density was the starting
point for the Big Bang. Never mind how it got there.

Have you ever created anything using an explosion? That is usually reserved for destruction. Why do we think there was an explosion? The usual answer is that we can observe that distant stars are moving away from us. The farther away they are, the faster they are moving away.

Of course, if they are moving away faster, then something is accelerating them. But that requires energy that we cannot detect. That is why it is called Dark Energy. But if we cannot detect it, how do we know it is there? The usual answer is that we just know the stars are accelerating away from us, so the energy must be there even if we cannot detect it just now. But how do we know that the stars are accelerating away from us?

When Edwin Hubble looked out at the stars early in the 20th century it was commonly thought that the Milky Way galaxy was the totality of the universe. However, he was able to observe other galaxies with his 100-inch telescope on Mt. Wilson. He observed that the light from distant galaxies and stars was shifted to the red end of the electromagnetic spectrum. He observed that fainter stars, assumed to be farther away, had more of a red shift. He assumed that the red shift was caused by the velocity of the stars moving away from us, much like the Doppler Effect explains why a train horn increases in pitch when the train is moving toward us and decreases in pitch moving away. The assumption was that more distant stars were moving away faster. This assumption is used to estimate the distance to the far stars. Some close stars have a blue shift, which would by the same logic indicate that they are moving toward us.

We can measure the distance to the closest stars using triangulation, using an angle and a known distance. We know that the distance to the sun is about 93 million miles. Distances within the solar system can be determined by radar astronomy and other methods. Every six months we have a different perspective of the stars due to the relative motions of the earth and the sun and stars. This only works for closers stars because of the limited accuracy of the angle measurements. So we can measure that the nearest star system, Alpha Centauri, is about 4.37 light-years away.

Have you wondered how far a light-year is? Here is a comparison. We can measure the distance to the sun to be about 93 million miles. If you scale the 93 million miles between the earth and the sun to one inch, then one light-year would be about one mile on the same scale. The sun would then be the size of a tiny dot, about 0.01 inches in diameter. So the distance to Alpha Centauri would be 4.37 miles on that scale. Compared to other stars in the universe, Alpha Centauri and our sun are relatively close together. Only in binary stars or star clusters do stars get much closer than that. So as near as we can tell, the universe is really big with great distances between large objects.

However, the universe may not be as big as we think, since the expansion of the universe is based on assumptions like the one that says red shift translates into distance and speed. Has that been proven? Not absolutely. In fact, there is evidence against it.

Halton Arp (d. 2013), an astronomer, observed that light coming from certain objects that are physically near each other can have different red shift values. It can be observed that there is dust or gas linking such objects, which is how we can know that they are close together. He believed that the red shift was related to speed and distance, but that there was also another component to it, such as mass or age.

This is documented in the book *The Electric Sky* by Donald E. Scott. This book also explains how little effect gravity has in the universe compared to electromagnetic forces. Stars are plasma which is subject to these electromagnetic forces. Even the craters that we see on various heavenly bodies may have been formed by electrical discharge.

If redshift does not directly correspond with distance from the earth, this clearly undermines the whole red shift assumption and the Big Bang theory. Mr. Arp was thanked by the astronomical society for his observations by being denied access to all public telescopes. We cannot have anyone questioning our most basic cosmic assumptions! There is just too much – careers and dollars – riding on those assumptions. So much for following the evidence.

How about the Nebular hypothesis? Could the stars and planets have condensed out of diffuse gas and dust left over by the supposed Big Bang? It has already been shown in the previous chapter that stars cannot form spontaneously because the gas pressure pushing molecules away from each other is much stronger that the gravity pulling them together.

Galaxies are another problem for materialistic scientists for a similar reason. Spiraling galaxies are not dense enough for gravity to hold them together. Scientists attempt to counter this by inventing what they call Dark Matter which they ⸱ must be there to hold galaxies together, even if we canno detect it. This is just another example of using imaginary concepts to save theories that are unsupported by the evidence.

Planetary formation has the same issues as star formation and galaxies. Gravity alone is not strong enough to bring dust and rocks together to form planets. If it were, then Saturn and Jupiter should have no rings by now, only extra moons. The asteroid belt should by now have formed another planet. But that is not happening, so the Nebular hypothesis has no basis in observable fact.

There are a number of theories on the formation of our moon. Some say that it was formed out of the earth by another passing planet that hit the earth just hard enough break off material to form the moon, but not too hard to destroy the earth. Others say that the moon was captured by the earth as it was wandering by. Still others say that the earth and the moon were formed together out of the same dust and rocks that were present in the nebulous cloud that started our solar system. All of these theories have problems in that they cannot completely explain the situation as it exists today.

Each of the planets in our solar system has properties that confuse those who hold to the currently accepted theories. Venus is spinning in the opposite direction of the other planets. Uranus is spinning on its side, relative to the other planets. Jupiter is spinning much too fast for current theories to explain.

f Creation Astronomy has created DVD's
'ail how evolutionistic models of the solar
 l galaxies do not explain what we can
. ı he Bible says that in the beginning God created
ιιeaven and earth (Gen. 1:1), and that it was created out of
water (2 Peter 3:5). Genesis says that God created the sun,
moon, and stars on the fourth day of creation. The Bible also
says that God stretched out the heavens and established the
earth (Isaiah 44:24).

Science can explain the development of things, but not their
origins. There are no naturalistic origins theories that
adequately explain what we observe in the cosmos. We can
know from the Bible that God created them in the beginning.
We have no reason to doubt what God has said.

2.3 Are We in a Special Place?

The earth is unique in that it supports life. Contrary to
expectations, we have not found life anywhere else, even if
billions of dollars have been spent looking for it. The earth
is indeed a special place.

The Privileged Planet, by Gonzalez and Richards, describes
just how special the earth really is. It begins by explaining
how unique total solar eclipses are – made possible by the
fact that the ratio of the size of the moon to the size of the
sun is equal to the ratio of the distance to the moon to the
distance to the sun. Some atheists have been converted by
considering that one fact.

The book also describes how special our sun is – that it is

just the right type and size, and that it is stable. The location of our solar system in the Milky Way galaxy is also just right for preventing us from getting too much cosmic radiation, and allows us to see out into the rest of the universe.

The conditions for life on earth are of such a narrow range that some have called it the "fine tuning" of the universe. Many characteristics of the universe must be just right, otherwise there would not be a possibility for life. This demonstrates that the universe was designed for life; it cannot be an accident.

Not only is earth a special place, scientific evidence indicates that it is in a special place in the universe – the very center. This is consistent with what the Bible says and with the revelations given to St. Hildegard von Bingen, Doctor of the Church (d. 1179).

Galileo Was Wrong, by Sungenis and Bennett, describes the scientific, scriptural, logical, and theological arguments for the earth being in the center of the universe and not moving. The revelations given to St. Hildegard are described in detail. Her visions indicate that the earth is at the center of six layers of fire, water, and air.

These are the classic four elements. St. Hildegard says of them: "God has built the world by means of the four elements [earth, air, fire, and water], so that no one of them may be separated from the others, for then the world would go back to nothingness if an element could exist separately from the others." So God created the world in a delicately balanced state.

The firmament or world vault or outer space, in the view of St. Hildegard, rotates around the earth and is driven by the cosmic winds. She writes: "And further I saw the world vault, through powerful drifts of the east and the south winds with their crosswinds, allowing it to circulate over the earth from east to west, and there the west wind and the north wind caught it together with its crosswinds and tossed it underneath the earth back from west to east."

In this vision she saw the earth sitting with the north and south poles horizontal and the firmament rotating from east to west. So looking at the earth from above, north is up, south is down, east is right, and west is left. The firmament then rotates over the earth from east to west, then back under the earth from west to east. In her visions there were 12 cosmic winds, each coming from a different direction.

Hildegard was informed that the winds came immediately from God, which indicates that God sustains the universe directly at the largest scales. It could also very well be that God sustains the universe at the smallest scales. Science has no way to detect what is happening inside of a sub-atomic particle. On a logarithmic scale, the size of a man (two meters) is in the center of the range between the smallest and largest single things that are detectable (neutrino: 10E-24 meters in diameter, Lyman-alpha blob: 10E+24 meters in diameter). Considering that God created the universe with Christ foremost in mind, that seems significant.

St. Hildegard also had revelations concerning a counter-current of winds that slightly impede the sun and planets with respect to the firmament. Since the stars move with the firmament, the sun and planets move slightly slower around the earth than the stars. It takes the sun 24 hours to revolve around the earth, whereas it takes the stars about four minutes less. This is sidereal time.

The cause of the seasons in this geocentric system is not the tilt of the earth and its annual motion around the sun, it is that the sun actually rotates around the earth north of the equator in the summer, and south of the equator in the winter (as seen in the northern hemisphere). The relative motions of the earth and stars are the same in whichever system you choose, the only question is the absolute reference frame.

In Hildegard's visions, the stars interact with the clouds and affect the weather – it is actually now known that cosmic rays can cause cloud formation on earth. She mentions that there are 16 large controlling stars in the universe which help to hold it all together. The planets help to stabilize the motion of the sun.

Some might protest that Galileo proved that the earth orbits the sun and that modern science has shown that the earth is just an insignificant planet revolving around an ordinary sun off in some dark corner of the universe. But does the evidence really prove it?

Copernicus (d. 1543) came before Galileo (d. 1642) and spoke hypothetically of a system where the earth circled the sun, instead of the other way around. He managed to avoid trouble with the Church by keeping his views in the realm of theory, and not positing them as fact. He seems to have personally believed that the earth did, in fact, circle the sun.

Galileo used his telescope to view the moons of Jupiter and the phases of Venus, which suggested to him that the Ptolemaic system was wrong. In noting that the smaller moons of Jupiter orbited the larger planet, he assumed that this must mean smaller bodies orbit larger bodies. It was known at the time that the sun is larger than the earth. In a system of rotating bodies, the rotation is actually about the center of gravity. So if the earth were at or near the center of gravity of the universe, it would not need to move.

Also, in the Ptolemaic system, Venus would always be between the earth and the sun, meaning that you would never see all the phases of Venus like you would see the phases of the moon. Galileo was able to see all the phases of Venus, disproving one accepted facet of the Ptolemaic system, but that by itself did not absolutely prove that the earth was orbiting the sun.

In fact, modern science cannot measure absolute motion in the universe. This is because we cannot observe the universe from the outside. We can measure relative motion, but in order to know absolute motion you need an absolute, motionless reference point. We can measure the force due to acceleration, but a body falling through a gravitational field would not experience a force. Astronauts orbiting the earth are weightless because they are effectively falling through the gravitational field of the earth.

Einstein's theories of Relativity are an admission that modern science does not recognize an absolute, motionless reference point. Unfortunately, the phrase "everything is relative" came to have significance in morals as well as in science. The lack of an absolute reference makes it difficult for science to prove anything unconditionally. A lack of moral absolutes makes it difficult to know right from wrong. One aspect of Einstein's theories shows that they have fundamental problems.

In his theories, a body moving near the speed of light will experience a contraction in length and a slowing of time, not to mention an increase in mass. So the story is told that if one twin is on earth and the other twin travels away from earth near the speed of light, the traveling twin would come back a younger person. However, this leads to the so-called Twin Paradox. If you have no absolute reference frame, you do not know which twin is moving in an absolute sense, so you cannot know which twin should be the younger one. One twin cannot be both younger and older at the same time.

Any thought of traveling at or near the speed of light is unrealistic, however. We can barely get subatomic particles up to nearly the speed of light, much less a vehicle able to carry a man. Knowledge of that fact has led some people to imagine that there are "worm holes" in space or even "hyperspace" that would allow travel from one side of the universe to the other.

Another paradox that calls into question the idea that everything is relative is Faraday's Paradox, which has to do with magnets and electricity. If you move a magnet through a stationary coil of wire, you do not produce the same effects as moving a coil of wire past a stationary magnet. In both cases, you are assuming that your laboratory on earth is not moving. The experiment shows that there is a preferred reference frame for the magnet. That is contrary to the theory of Relativity.

Black holes are a mathematical concept that are a consequence of Einstein's theories. The idea is that a super-dense mass would have so much gravity that light would not be able to escape it. However, even though values in mathematical equations can go to infinity, nature is finite and so nothing can be infinite in physical reality. Black holes have never been directly observed.

This shows that although mathematical equations can be used to describe or model physical realities, they do not govern them. Equations are concepts, reality is fact. The physical universe exists independent of our ability to understand it. We may all have our own perceptions of reality, but we are all living in the one reality created by God in the beginning which will continue until the end of time.

Einstein admitted in a speech titled: *How I Created the Theory of Relativity*, delivered at Kyoto University, Japan, Dec. 14, 1922: "I have come to believe that the motion of the Earth cannot be detected by any optical experiment, though the Earth is revolving around the Sun." He also said in his book *The Evolution of Physics*: "The struggle, so violent in the early days of science, between the views of Ptolemy and Copernicus would then be quite meaningless. Either coordinate system could be used with equal justification. The two sentences: 'The sun is at rest and the Earth moves.' or 'The sun moves and the Earth is at rest.' would simply mean two different conventions concerning two different coordinate systems." So he acknowledged that his theories could not prove that the earth is moving, absolutely.

Ernst Mach and Hans Thirring did theoretical work in analyzing what the effect would be on the earth of a rotating universe. Their analyses suggested, similar to Einstein's, that a rotating universe would have the same effect on a stationary earth that we would expect to see on a rotating earth in a stationary universe. This work was repeated by Dr. Luka Popov in an article in the *European Journal of Physics* in Jan. 2013 entitled: "A Newtonian-Machian Mathematical Analysis of Neo-tychonian Model of Planetary Motions."

Other scientists have been forced to admit that it cannot be proven that the earth is moving. Hendrik Lorentz said in his 1886 paper, *On the Influence of the Earth's Motion on Luminiferous Phenomena*: "Briefly, everything occurs as if the Earth were at rest." Lorentz was speaking about experiments that were designed to measure the speed of the earth through the ether. He is famous for his Lorentz transformation equation which supposedly gives the length of an object moving near the speed of light. However, as Einstein suggested, there is no optical experiment that can verify length contraction, since a measuring device would also be affected by motion. According to the philosopher Karl Popper, falsifiability defines the inherent testability of any scientific hypothesis; if any hypothesis is not falsifiable, is it not scientific. Since there is no way to physically test the idea of length contraction, it can be argued that it is not falsifiable and therefore not scientific.

Einstein's Relativity theories (Special and General) were

really all about making everything relative to the observer in order to avoid any admission that the earth was not moving in an absolute sense. Unfortunately, the theories led to bizarre concepts and contradictions. Relativity has also led to the idea that everything is relative – to me. Surely this has greatly contributed to the "me generation" with its disregard for the other person.

There is nothing unscientific about using the earth as an absolute reference frame. Even though aspects of the Ptolemaic system have been disproven, there are geocentric systems that are scientifically valid. Tycho Brahe (d. 1601) lived during the time that earth's position in the cosmos was being debated, and developed a system with the earth in the center and the sun orbiting the earth, and the planets orbiting the sun. In his model, the stars orbited the earth, but other geocentric systems have them orbiting the sun.

In either of the geocentric or heliocentric or the modern acentric (no center) systems, all relative motions are basically the same. Everyone recognizes that the earth, sun, moon, and stars move relative to each other. The question regards the absolute motions. Since natural science cannot give us an absolute reference frame, scientists cannot say what is moving in an absolute sense.

Some people would argue that the Foucault pendulums hanging in science museums around the world prove that the earth is rotating under them. However, a sphere of stars rotating around the earth could produce the same effect. It is noteworthy that those pendulums rotate according to sidereal time, not solar time. You can argue about whether the stars are fixed or the earth is fixed, but the distant stars definitely have an effect on those pendulums. Newton's Laws of Motion do not include that effect.

This also could account for the Coriolis force that causes hurricanes to rotate. Aerospace engineers account for that force in rocket launches, even if they consider it to be only an effect of the rotation of the earth. From the geocentric, earth-centered perspective, the Coriolis force is real and not apparent.

Another argument used against geocentrism is geostationary satellites, which are satellites that remain over a particular spot above the equator all the time. If the earth were motionless in space, those satellites would also be motionless. The standard explanation for them is that they rotate around the earth at exactly the same angular speed that the earth is rotating. This only happens directly above the equator at a particular altitude of about 22,300 miles. That is where we are told that the force of gravity balances the centrifugal force caused by the velocity of the orbiting satellite – which is also the case for any satellite in a stable orbit at whatever altitude.

Anyone with a background in science understands that the equation $F=ma$ (Force equals mass multiplied by acceleration) works pretty well, even if the effect of the distant stars is ignored. That gravity follows the inverse square law is also generally accepted ($F=GmM/r^2$). The centrifugal force caused by an object moving in a curved path can be measured ($F=mv^2/r$). We can put satellites into space with great accuracy using those equations. What is not well understood is the cause of gravity and the effect of the distant stars on the earth.

You can think about geostationary satellites in a rotating earth reference frame, which involves those equations, or you can think about geostationary satellites in a geocentric reference frame, where the satellite is stationary above a fixed earth but moving through a rotating universe. The motions are the same, but the reasons for the motions are explained differently. The satellite in the heliocentric frame is held at constant altitude by the balance of gravity and the centrifugal force caused by its speed, which matches the angular velocity of the earth. The satellite in the geocentric frame could be held at a constant altitude of 22,300 miles by the balance of earth's gravity and the gravitational pull of the distant stars, similar to the L1 Lagrange point between the earth and the sun which is one million miles from earth. Its movement against the rotating ether, which carries the mass of stars, could be sustained by the station-keeping thrust used to maintain its position.

One might object that satellites could also theoretically be placed above points on the planet Mars, using equations that assume Mars is rotating, and it would probably work. It also might seem too coincidental that the forces caused by a universe rotating around the earth are exactly analogous to the forces caused by a rotating earth in a fixed universe, but the math and physics actually work either way. This only shows that in order to know the absolute motions, the witness of someone outside the system is required, which is where revelation comes in. Theologically, Jesus Christ was born, lived, and died on Earth and not on Mars.

Modern scientists might also object that the moon and the sun have a much larger effect on the earth than the distant stars, as shown by the ocean tides on earth. The effect of the moon on tides is about twice that of the sun, but the effect of the distant stars would seem to be comparatively negligible. It could be that the earth is stationary at the geometric center of the universe, but not in the center of gravity of the universe. Interestingly, St. Hildegard von Bingen said that the moon's orbit is the basis "by which everything else is reckoned."

This is where our ignorance of the fundamental aspects of space, time, light, gravity, electricity, magnetism, matter, etc. is exposed. If you do not understand the fundamentals, it is hard to make correct judgments on the cause of the effects. Although we can measure effects, the exact cause can be mysterious. If you reject the First Cause, then everything becomes mysterious. As Etienne Gilson has beautifully explained: "The universe, as represented by St. Thomas, is not a mass of inert bodies passively moved by a force which passes through them, but a collection of active beings each enjoying an efficacy delegated to it by God along with actual being. At the first beginning of a world like this, we have to place not so much a force being exercised as an infinite goodness communicated. Love is the unfathomable source of all causality." (*The Christian Philosophy of St. Thomas Aquinas*, University of Notre Dame Press, 1994, p. 183)

If all that seems complicated, it is. St. Hildegard said that man would never fully understand the operation of the cosmos. The winds of St. Hildegard probably refer to the motion of what has been called the ether, which is that extremely fine material which fills all space. It could be that ether particles smaller than electrons pack the space between atomic nuclei throughout the universe. The distance between the atomic nucleus and its electrons is much larger than the radius of the nucleus, so many ether particles would fit into an atom. The atomic nuclei, being less dense than the ether particles, would essentially be floating in an ether sea and gravity would be a buoyancy force. A disturbance could also travel very rapidly through the packed ether particles and could explain gravity's ability to act nearly instantaneously over galactic distances.

Many experiments were done to understand the ether back in the late 19th and early 20th centuries. The Michelson-Morley experiment was one of the more famous experiments. At that time (1887) it was thought that the ether filled all space and that the earth moved through the ether in its orbit around the sun. The experiment was designed to measure the speed of the earth through the ether. The results indicated a speed much slower than expected, although not quite zero. George Airy performed another experiment with a water-filled telescope which also indicated that the earth was not moving through the ether.

Many people think Einstein did away with the ether, but what he really did was to assign properties to what he called "space." If space has properties, it cannot be empty. So all Einstein did was to give a new name to an old concept. In antiquity it was known as the firmament.

There is physical evidence of an ether. The Michelson-

Morley experiment demonstrated that light moved faster in one direction that it did in another direction, which indicated that there was a moving medium through which the light was traveling. It is also known that GPS satellite signals travel faster in one direction and slower in the opposite direction. It is typically called the Sagnac effect.

Supposedly "empty" space has been shown to have electrical properties. A photon with energy greater than 1.022 MeV can produce an electron-positron pair in space, which then will annihilate each other almost instantly. Could the ether be the "dark matter" that scientist have been searching for?

It could also be that electrical forces in the universe are much stronger that astronomers will currently admit. Stars are balls of plasma and most celestial bodies have a magnetic field, so electrical forces could be significant. It is known that the solar wind is a sort of electrical current and space is full of ionized particles.

Until we understand more about the fundamental aspects of reality, there will be mysteries about the operation of the natural world. God, who created the universe and who is outside of space and time, knows exactly how things operate and has revealed that it is the sun, moon, and stars that are moving, and not the earth. We know from Genesis that he created the earth first, and the sun, moon, and stars afterwards, with their purpose being to mark signs, seasons, days, and years, and to give light on the earth. We also know from the Bible that the sun, moon and stars will not be needed in eternity because God himself will be the light.

2.4 Galileo

So did Galileo prove that the earth was orbiting around the sun? St. Robert Bellarmine, who prosecuted the Catholic Church's case against Galileo, admitted that if it could be proven that the earth truly orbited the sun, then certain passages of Scripture would need to be reinterpreted. However, he did not believe that Galileo had absolute proof.

It is somewhat ironic that the attention paid to the movements of the stars and planets was an aspect of the Catholic Church's desire to set the date of Easter more precisely. It was Pope Gregory XIII (d. 1585) who gave the world the Gregorian calendar which is still in use worldwide today. The understanding that the universe was orderly and that the laws governing it could be understood gave rise to modern science. Unfortunately, the Galileo case started a split between theology and science which has not yet been healed.

Although Galileo was sentenced to house arrest and later retracted his views in a personal letter to Francesco Rinuccini on March 29, 1641, the idea that the earth revolved around the sun came to be accepted as true. As Bellarmine suggested, this idea seems to contradict the plain meaning of certain Bible passages:

"In the beginning God created heaven, and earth."
(Gen. 1:1) – world geocentric at first

Joshua's long day (Joshua 10:12-14) – sun and moon stand still; earth assumed motionless

"… for he hath founded the world immoveable." (1 Chron. 16:30)

"He stretched out the north over the empty space, and hangs the earth upon nothing." (Job 26:7)

"His [sun] going out is from the end of heaven, and his circuit even to the end thereof." (Psalms 18:7)

"For he has established/corrected the world, which shall not be moved." (Psalms 92:1 and 95:10)

"Who hast founded the earth upon its own bases: it shall not be moved ..." (Psalms 103:5)

"From the rising of the sun unto its going down, the name of the Lord is worthy to be praised." (Psalms 112:3)

"Thus says the Lord: Heaven is my throne, and the earth my footstool." (Isaiah 66:1) – God not moving, so his footstool not moving either

"And the city has no need of the sun, nor of the moon, to shine in it." (Apoc. 21:23) – world geocentric in eternity

In the end, the 1616 trial of Galileo resulted in two declarations from the Holy Office as follows:

Consultant's Report on Copernicanism:

Assessment made at the Holy Office, Rome, Wednesday, 24 February 1616, in the presence of the

Father Theologians signed below.

Proposition to be assessed:

1.) The sun is the center of the world and completely devoid of local motion.

Assessment: All said that this proposition is foolish and absurd in philosophy, and formally heretical since it explicitly contradicts in many places the sense of Holy Scripture, according to the literal meaning of the words and according to the common interpretation and understanding of the Holy Fathers and the doctors of theology.

2.) The earth is not the center of the world, nor motionless, but it moves as a whole and also with diurnal motion.

Assessment: All said that this proposition receives the same judgment in philosophy and that in regard to theological truth it is at least erroneous in faith.

Petrus Lombardus, Archbishop of Armagh, et. al.

The idea that the earth was the center of God's creation was accepted by the Jews and Christians from antiquity until Galileo's time. To say that belief was mistaken would have been quite a shock to Christians living in the 17th century. It certainly would have created doubts about the inerrancy of the Bible and the credibility of the Church.

This period of time was also tumultuous for other reasons.

The Protestant Reformation had occurred about 100 years earlier. The New World had only recently been discovered by Columbus in 1492. The Renaissance was giving way to the Enlightenment. New ideas were being spread. The established rule of Christendom was being challenged.

As an aside, Columbus did not believe the earth was flat, nor has that idea been generally accepted for any significant period of history. The orb – a round ball – has been used since ancient Roman times as a symbol of the world, which is a sphere. Columbus did, however, severely underestimate the size of the earth and the distance from Spain to India. Eratosthenes made an estimate of the circumference of the earth in about 250 B.C. based on his observations in Egypt. The sun shone straight down into a well in Syene at noon on the summer solstice, but on the same day and time of the year, a tower in Alexandria cast a shadow of about 7.2 degrees, or 1/50 of a full circle. Figuring that the earth was a sphere and knowing the distance between Syene and Alexandria was about 5,000 stadia, he was able to get a relatively accurate estimate of the circumference of the earth. Posidonius estimated the circumference of the earth in about 100 B.C. using an observation of the star Canopus on, but never above, the horizon at Rhodes, while at Alexandria he saw it ascend as far as 7.5 degrees above the horizon. Unfortunately, his estimate of the distance from Alexandria to Rhodes and confusion about the length of the stadia created a number that was too small, which was the number that Columbus used. Today, satellites and astronauts can confirm the spherical shape of the earth and give us a very accurate measurement of its size.

The fact that the earth is much smaller than the sun, and that bodies revolve around their center of mass, does not prove that the earth is orbiting the sun. Since gravity acts almost instantly across vast distances, the planets and stars have an influence on the earth. If the earth were at or near the center of mass of the universe, then the universe could indeed revolve around it.

A rotating ether sphere would tend to push collections of atoms towards its center. If the universe is such a sphere, that could also explain how the earth could be motionless at the center of a rotating universe.

There is scientific evidence that the earth is in fact at the center of the universe. Astronomers have observed a spherical distribution of stars, quasars, radio wave sources, gamma bursts, and X-ray bursts, with the earth at the center of the spherical distribution. Patterns in the cosmic microwave background radiation (CMB) are aligned with earth's poles and equator, and the ecliptic plane. The binary star systems (two stars) that we observe almost all have axes of rotation that point to the earth. If you were lost in space you could use that fact to find your way back to the earth.

Even the famed Edwin Hubble admitted that science could not disprove that the earth was in the center of the universe, but he rejected the idea out of hand:

> "Such a condition would imply that we occupy a unique position in the universe, analogous, in a sense, to the ancient conception of a central earth ... The hypothesis cannot be disproved, but it is

unwelcome and would be accepted only as a last resort in order to save the phenomena. Therefore, we disregard this possibility and consider the alternative … But the unwelcome supposition of a favoured location must be avoided at all costs ... Such a favoured position, of course, is intolerable ... Therefore, in order to restore homogeneity, and to escape the horror of a unique position, the departures from uniformity, which are introduced by the recession factors, must be compensated by the second term representing effects of spatial curvature. There seems to be no other escape."

The Observational Approach to Cosmology, Oxford, Clarendon Press, 1937

His measurements of the red shift indicated that the earth was in the center of the universe, a unique position. The accepted concept of the universe since the early 20th century is that the universe is uniform – it looks the same from any point of view. For Hubble, to admit that the earth might be in a special place – an "ancient conception" – was an intolerable horror, not from a scientific view, but from a philosophical view. To admit that the Church and Bible are right on this point would force one to consider that Christian moral teachings might also be correct. That is what would really be horribly intolerable.

Hubble would rather curve space ("compensated by the second term representing effects of spatial curvature") than to make such an admission. But can space really be curved? That is a stretch of the imagination.

This brings to mind another quote by a prominent scientist, Richard Lewontin:

> "Our willingness to accept scientific claims that are against common sense is the key to an understanding of the real struggle between science and the supernatural. We take the side of science in spite of the patent absurdity of some of its constructs, in spite of its failure to fulfill many of its extravagant promises of health and life, in spite of the tolerance of the scientific community for unsubstantiated just-so stories, because we have a prior commitment, a commitment to materialism.
>
> It is not that the methods and institutions of science somehow compel us to accept a material explanation of the phenomenal world, but, on the contrary, that we are forced by our a priori adherence to material causes to create an apparatus of investigation and a set of concepts that produce material explanations, no matter how counter-intuitive, no matter how mystifying to the uninitiated. Moreover, that materialism is an absolute, for we cannot allow a Divine Foot in the door."

Billions and Billions of Demons – 1997 Review of *The Demon-Haunted World*, by Carl Sagan

Here Lewontin admits that his rejection of God and the supernatural is not the end result of his scientific studies, it is the underlying philosophy of his absolute materialism. He is willing to accept any absurdity that his materialism forces him to believe rather than considering that there may be a God. St. Paul says of such people: "And will indeed turn away their hearing from the truth, but will be turned unto fables." (2 Tim. 4:4) Those who reject the God who created the universe end up making a god out of evolution or make everything out to be god (pantheism).

Shortly before Copernicus published his beliefs on the rotation of the earth about the sun in 1543, The Blessed Virgin Mary appeared at Guadalupe, Mexico to St. Juan Diego. On December 12, 1531, she appeared to him and gave him a bunch of roses to show to the local bishop as proof of her message. After presenting the roses, an image of the Blessed Virgin appeared on his cloak. This image is preserved in the Basilica of Our Lady of Guadalupe in Mexico City, the most visited Marian shrine in the world.

The image shows Our Lady dressed in royal attire, obviously pregnant, standing on the moon with the rays of the sun behind her. This depicts the first verses of Chapter 12 of the book of Revelation:

> "And a great sign appeared in heaven: A woman clothed with the sun, and the moon under her feet, and on her head a crown of twelve stars: And being with child, she cried travailing in birth, and was in pain to be delivered. And there was seen another sign in heaven: and behold a great red dragon ..."

The image shows the moon, and Our Lady is obviously shown to be pregnant. But what about the crown on her head and the dragon; where are they? To see them you must line up the stars on the cloak in the image with a sky map of the stars at the time of the apparition. If you do that, you will see that the constellation Corona Borealis (Northern Crown) appears on Mary's head. You will also see the constellation Draco with its head immediately opposite Our Lady.

Very shortly after the appearance of Our Lady, the Aztecs converted to the Catholic Faith en masse. Clearly, they were impressed. After worshipping false gods for centuries, including sun and moon gods, the miraculous image convinced the Aztecs that Jesus Christ, contained in the womb of the Blessed Virgin, was superior to the moon and sun. Coincidentally, the pyramids of the sun and moon are located near the site of the apparition.

It is also an interesting fact that Christopher (meaning "Christ-bearer") Columbus sailed with the ships *Pinta*, *Nina* and *Santa Maria* in 1492, shortly before Mary appeared at Guadalupe. The meaning of those names is "Painted, Girl, Holy Mary." The image of Guadalupe looks like a painting of a girl who has been identified as Holy Mary, who is bearing the Christ child.

It is thought by some that in Genesis, God deliberately created the sun and moon on the fourth day, to show that the sun and moon were not beings to be worshipped, but were created by God for a purpose. Perhaps if more people had been paying attention to the apparition of Our Lady of Guadalupe, the split between faith and reason would not have occurred.

The apparition of Our Lady of Guadalupe can be seen as a

warning against the worship of false gods, and ι
much importance to the sun. The timing of th
relative to the publication of the ideas of Co
striking. It seems to have been a divine sig ₋.ᵥ₋ᵤ to
mankind alerting them to the dangers of questioning the
Word of God.

The Bible explicitly says three times that the earth does not
move (Psalms 92:1, 95:10, and 103:5 DRB). Other passages
where it says that the earth does move refer to earthquakes.
It also states three times that the world was created in six
days (Gen. 1, Exodus 20:11 and 31:17). The waters above
the heavens are mentioned three times as well (Gen. 1:7,
Psalms 148:4, and Daniel 3:60). When speaking about the
waters above the heavens, Augustine said: "These words of
Scripture have more authority than the most exalted human
intellect. Hence, whatever these waters are, and whatever
their mode of existence, we cannot for a moment doubt that
they are there." Aquinas agreed with him. This should be
our attitude when dealing with realities that are so explicitly
and repeatedly stated in the Word of God.

2.5 The Origin of Life

If the Galileo case started the split between faith and reason,
then Darwin opened it up into a chasm. What started as the
questioning of one point of Biblical teaching became the
doubting of the first 11 chapters of the book of Genesis and
of some fundamental doctrines of Christianity. Richard
Dawkins is famous for saying "Darwin made it possible to
be an intellectually fulfilled atheist." The general

acceptance of evolutionary theory has had a huge impact on the modern world. But is the theory of evolution based on fact, or is it just an atheistic world-view based on assumptions?

The Bible says that God created the world and all kinds of creatures in six days. This is described in the opening chapters of the Book of Genesis. The words "evening and morning" together with the numbered days affirm that the days are to be understood as literal 24-hour periods. The ancient Israelites understood them in this way, as do modern orthodox Jews. The first miracle of Jesus at Cana (John 2) involved six jars of water being instantly and supernaturally changed into wine, reminiscent of the six days of creation and the creation of the world out of water.

As the wine at Cana appeared fully aged, the creation after six days appeared fully formed. The stars were in place, animals were able to begin reproduction, and Adam and Eve were mature adults. Only after the end of the miraculous six days did natural processes begin to operate. So natural science has nothing to say about the creation of the world, only its development.

It is noteworthy that the Bible describes the earth being created out of water (2 Peter 3:5), Moses being taken out of the water – as indicated by the meaning of his name (Exodus 2:10), and Jesus coming out of the water after his baptism (Mark 1:10). Water is truly an amazing substance which makes life on earth possible. Your body is mostly water. It is a nearly universal solvent. Its molecular structure causes it to expand upon freezing which allows ice to float. If that were not the case, the oceans would freeze solid. It also makes for beautiful and unique snowflakes.

Even though the Catholic Church has not dogmatically defined the six creation days as literal, Pope Leo XIII said in *Arcanum* (1880) that: "We record what is to all known, and cannot be doubted by any, that God, on the sixth day of creation, having made man from the slime of the earth, and having breathed into his face the breath of life, gave him a companion, whom He miraculously took from the side of Adam when he was locked in sleep." Most of the early Church Fathers understood the days to be literal, although Augustine supposed that creation might have been accomplished in one day. Nevertheless, this is an event which is outside the realm of nature; it was a supernatural event not subject to the laws or investigation of natural science. The details can only be known by revelation.

On the other hand, evolutionary theory speculates that the spontaneous generation of life came from a "primordial soup." We know that there now exist living organisms and we imagine that at some time in the past that there were no living beings on the earth, so life must have started somehow. But is there any evidence that life can arise spontaneously from non-living material?

Three famous experiments have been done to show whether or not life could arise spontaneously. The first concerned the apparent spontaneous generation of flies from rotten meat. In 1668 Francesco Redi published a series of experiments that he performed with rotten meat. During his time the appearance of flies on rotten meat was thought to indicate that the meat produced the flies.

In one of his experiments, Redi put meat into an uncovered jar and another one covered by gauze. Maggots appeared on the meat in the uncovered jar, but not on the meat in the jar covered by gauze. This disproved the concept of the spontaneous generation of flies on rotten meat.

The second famous experiment done to test the theory of spontaneous generation of life was done by Louis Pasteur in 1859. It was known that if soup was left in the open that microbes (microscopic life forms) would soon develop in it. Some people thought that the microbes arose spontaneously in the soup.

Pasteur put soup into two flasks with swan necks (S-shaped) and boiled it to kill any existing microbes. He then broke the neck off of one flask, which allowed microbes in the air to fall into it. The swan neck of the other flask was left intact, which prevented anything from falling into it. Microbes developed in the flask with the neck broken off, but not in the flask with the neck intact. This disproved the concept of the spontaneous generation life once again.

The third famous experiment done to test the theory of spontaneous generation of life was done by Stanley Miller in 1953. He created a chemical mixture of what the "primordial soup" was thought to contain and then ran electricity through it to simulate lightning. He was able to produce some chemical compounds, but nothing approaching a living organism.

The saying "three strikes and you're out" should apply to the theory of spontaneous generation of life, but that has not dispelled the myth. We know that the simplest form of life is still very complex. It is absurd to think that such complexity could have arisen by itself from a "primordial soup."

Sir Fred Hoyle in *The Intelligent Universe* (1983) wrote this:

> "A junkyard contains all the bits and pieces of a Boeing 747, dismembered and in disarray. A whirlwind happens to blow through the yard. What is the chance that after its passage a fully assembled 747, ready to fly, will be found standing there? So small as to be negligible, even if a tornado were to blow through enough junkyards to fill the whole Universe."

Some people like to argue against Hoyle's statement by saying that the individual components of life could have arisen over time to finally become life at some point. But that is like saying that if enough tornados go through the same junkyard with all the right pieces, a 747 will eventually emerge.

It took thousands of engineers many years to develop a 747 airliner. It takes many months of skilled labor to put one together. It also takes many intelligent people to keep one operating. The complexity of life reveals that it could only have come about by design. There is simply no plausible way that life could have spontaneously created itself, just as there is no possible way for anything to create itself from nothing.

2.6 Evolution

Just as some scientists like to imagine that life could have formed spontaneously, they also like to think that it could have developed into more complex forms accidentally. We do know that genetic mutations can cause small changes in an organism. But these mutations are almost always harmful, which is why there are mechanisms in the living cell to minimize them.

The Bible says that God creating living things according to their kind and that they reproduce after their kind (Gen. 1:11). We know that some animals can interbreed and some cannot. In the biological classification system of Kingdom, Phylum, Class, Order, Family, Genus, and Species, a "kind" would be at about the Family or Genus level.

Members of the same species are generally able to interbreed. Members of the same genus, but different species, are sometimes able to interbreed, although the offspring can be sterile such as the mule (horse-donkey hybrid). Members of the same family but different genus are rarely able to interbreed. It can happen, however, as in the case of a leopard-puma hybrid called a pumapard. A leopard is of the genus *Panthera* and a puma is of the genus *Puma*.

The theory of evolution says that small genetic changes can accumulate to produce new and more complex organisms. The genetic changes are brought about by mutation, and they are passed down to offspring. A beneficent mutation might give the offspring an advantage over other similar organisms, so that it would have a better chance of survival.

This is the concept of natural selection. If a group of those organisms survived with that particular mutation, it would be said to have evolved.

In this manner it is supposed that single-celled organisms evolved into multi-celled organisms. Multi-celled organisms then evolved into more complex organisms like sponges or jellyfish. Eventually fish were produced which evolved into amphibians, which evolved into reptiles, which evolved into birds. Other reptiles evolved into mammals, which evolved into apes, which evolved into humans. So the story goes. But is there any evidence that anything ever evolved into something else?

We know that bacteria become resistant to antibiotics. It is claimed that this is because of evolution. However, bacteria can become immune by losing the parts on which the antibiotics work. This is a case, not of an increase in complexity, but of a loss of complexity, resulting in an organism that may be resistant to antibiotics, but is less capable in other ways. It has certainly not increased its genetic information so as to be on the way of evolving into something else.

We know that genetic differences limit the ability of different organisms to produce offspring. We also know that genetic mutations are mostly harmful. Many genetic experiments have been performed on fruit flies because they reproduce so rapidly. However, nothing ever came of the fruit flies except more fruit flies, even if they looked a little different.

Experiments on the stickleback fish have shown that certain features can be turned on and off by modifying the genes. However, genetic experiments do not necessarily mimic what can happen in nature. All of the modified fish were still fish, they did not become something else.

In order for a fish to become an amphibian, it would have to develop lungs and limbs. There are some fish that have lungs and fins that allow them to survive outside of the water. However, there would be no evolutionary advantage to developing a half-lung or a half-limb, and the genetic changes necessary to make the jump all at once are not possible on a natural basis. The same is true for the supposed evolution of amphibians into reptiles, and from reptiles into birds and mammals.

The similarities between apes (especially chimps) and men are notable, and they are constantly emphasized by evolutionists in order to convince people that they descended from apes. But the differences are much greater. Although the skeletal and muscular systems are similar, the human posture is much more erect, but the ape is much stronger. The differences in the skull, jaw, and teeth are pronounced. Although apes can communicate, they do not have speech and certainly not a written language, and do not think conceptually or have ethics. Their genetic composition may be similar, but even a one percent difference can mean that millions of DNA base pairs are not the same.

Many scientists have given up thinking that men descended from apes, even if they have not quite given up the idea of a common ancestor. It is really an insult to say that we are just highly evolved apes, however. The Bible says that man is a little less than the angels, and has dominion over all animals (Psalms 8:6-9).

The malaria parasite may have produced more generations than any other organism on earth because of its ability to reproduce, and its prevalence in the world. It is carried by mosquitos which then infect humans. It is one of the largest health problems in the world, in terms of number of people affected. Michael Behe wrote a book, *The Edge of Evolution*, which investigates the ability of that parasite to evolve. He notes that the parasite has developed resistance to a number of medications, but that it has never developed the ability to overcome the sickle cell trait.

The sickle cell trait is caused by a single mutation in the hemoglobin gene. Hemoglobin is the protein in your red blood cells that carries oxygen. You get sickle cell trait when one of your parents passes on the gene. It makes your red blood cells less able to carry oxygen and gives them a "sickle" shape, but also gives you protection against malaria.

Sickle cell trait can give you some health problems such as an increased probability for urinary tract infections. You can get sickle cell disease if both parents have sickle cell trait. Sickle cell disease, however, is a serious health problem and decreases your lifespan.

Since sickle cell trait gives protection against malaria, it is prevalent in areas where malaria is present. This is likely because people who have it survive malaria better than people who do not. Again, having sickle cell trait does not make you healthier, it actually makes you less healthy, but it will protect you against malaria.

Behe makes the analogy of burning down a bridge to protect yourself from an enemy. He goes on to explain how single mutations in malaria have allowed it to become resistant to certain medications like quinine. However, it has never developed the ability to overcome sickle cell trait, demonstrating that there are limits to what genetic mutation or evolution can do.

It is suggested in his book that these limits constrain biological diversity to the order of family (just above genus and species). That could correspond with the Biblical "kind" of organism. The Bible says that God created creatures according to their kind.

Behe had previously written *Darwin's Black Box* which was an attempt to show that irreducibly complex biological mechanisms, such as the bacterial flagellum, could not have been formed in small steps. Charles Darwin, in *On the Origin of Species* had said: "If it could be demonstrated that any complex organ existed, which could not possibly have been formed by numerous, successive, slight modifications, my theory would absolutely break down. But I can find out no such case."

Behe was convinced that he found just such a case in the bacterial flagellum. He uses the phrase "irreducibly complex" to describe a mechanism that cannot be broken down into simpler parts without losing its function. As an example, he analyzes the common mousetrap to show that the key components must all exist together at the same time in order to function at all.

In the theory of evolution, each small genetic step must be beneficent in order for the mutation to be preserved in an organism. However, as Behe shows with the bacterial flagellum, there are biological mechanisms that only work when all of their parts are working together as a whole. The individual parts would provide no benefit to the organism. In that case, Darwin's theory absolutely breaks down.

Another example of an organism that either works as a whole or does not work at all is the butterfly or the moth. It has an egg stage, a larva stage, a pupa or cocoon stage, and a butterfly or moth stage. The butterfly or moth lays the eggs. Some moths do not even have mouth parts; they are designed to mate, lay eggs, and die. The eggs hatch into larva. The larva eats leaves at a prodigious rate and then makes a pupa or cocoon. The pupa or cocoon then undergoes metamorphosis where the entire body structure is rearranged. The butterfly or moth then emerges to start the cycle all over again.

The key to the whole butterfly or moth lifecycle is that it all must work right each time in order for it to survive. It also must have worked right the first time or there would have been no second generation. The metamorphosis phase is so complex that it has only become understood recently with the help of advanced diagnostic machines. It is inconceivable that this could have happened accidently the very first time.

One special trait of Monarch butterflies is that they will only lay their eggs on milkweeds. This is because the larva will only eat milkweeds. They also have a precise navigation system built-in. They spend the winter in a particular grove of trees in Mexico, they then fly north to the US and Canada for the summer. Several generations live and die during the year. The last generation of the year lives longer than the other generations and flies back to the same spot in Mexico, even though none of that generation started there!

This lifecycle, in addition to the egg-larva-pupa-butterfly cycle, has to work right every time, including the very first time, in order for the Monarch butterfly to survive. Additionally, it demonstrates a symbiotic relationship between a plant and an animal. Without milkweeds, there would be no Monarch butterflies.

Many plants and animals are interdependent. Some plants depend on insects for pollination. The clownfish is dependent on the anemone for protection. If evolution is true, then certain plants and animals had to evolve at exactly the same time and same location in order for either one to survive. It takes a stretch of the imagination to think that it could have happened just by accident.

Engineers recognize that the design of certain aspects of nature is so good that they have tried to mimic them. This has been termed "biomimicry." Velcro was designed to mimic the hooks of burrs found on weeds. Shark skin inspired the swimsuits that were worn at the 2008 Summer Olympics. Scientists have been trying to mimic photosynthesis, which is much more efficient than solar cells, but are only just recently having any success.

The fact that so many scientists support the idea of evolution leads many people to believe that it must somehow be true. However, a serious investigation of the literature shows that although the theory has great support, the actual mechanism of changing one organism into another type of organism is full of unknowns. Phrases like "we do not know" or "we do not yet understand" abound. What we do know is that changing a fish into an amphibian into a reptile into a mammal into a man would require hundreds of precise genetic changes which would not only have to happen in a male, but also in a female at the same time in the same place. The odds against that happening are insurmountable.

Besides all of that, the Second Law of Thermodynamics shows that inexorably, things naturally deteriorate; they do not improve on their own. Nature is not self-organizing; that requires intelligence. Some higher animals have enough intelligence to organize things, and some lower animals have enough design built-in so that they can create structures (think of a coral reef). Even minerals have structure and molecular bonds produce snowflakes. However, evolution – biological and cosmological – says that things have continually improved by themselves, contrary to our every observation.

The Catholic Church has never <u>officially</u> endorsed evolution, in fact, just the opposite. The Councils of Lateran IV and Vatican I said dogmatically that God created everything "at once" from nothing, which was compatible with the creation of all things in six 24-hour days or in an instant, but not over a longer period of time. Pope Pius XII allowed for the study by "men experienced in both fields [science and theology]" of the "origin of the human body as coming from pre-existent and living matter" in his 1950 encyclical *Humani Generis* (#36), but added that "the Catholic faith obliges us to hold that souls are immediately created by God." He warned against thinking that the theory was "completely certain and proved by the facts" and that "If such conjectural opinions are directly or indirectly opposed to the doctrine revealed by God, then the demand that they be recognized can in no way be admitted." He also prohibited any idea of polygenism since all men took their "origin through natural generation from him [Adam]."

Since Adam was the son of God (Luke 3:38), we are all then children of God since we all descended from Adam. Perhaps people would behave better if they were taught that, instead of being taught that they descended from beasts.

The warnings of Pius XII were at least in part directed against Fr. Teilhard de Chardin, SJ (1881-1955). Teilhard was an enthusiastic supporter of the theory of evolution. He even had his own version in which everything was evolving to the "Omega Point" and becoming the "Cosmic Christ." He said: "It is Christ, in very truth, who saves – but should we not immediately add that, at the same time, it is Christ who is saved by Evolution?" (*The Heart of the Matter*, 1950) That statement cannot be reconciled with any traditional understanding of Christianity.

In 1962 the Holy Office issued a warning against his ideas: "For this reason, the most eminent and most revered Fathers of the Holy Office exhort all Ordinaries as well as the superiors of Religious institutes, rectors of seminaries and presidents of universities, effectively to protect the minds, particularly of the youth, against the dangers presented by the works of Fr. Teilhard de Chardin and of his followers."

Two fellow travelers of Teilhard, you might say, were Fr. John Zahm (1851-1921) and Fr. Stanley Jaki (1924-2009). Fr. Zahm was Vice President of Notre Dame University for a number of years and was very influential in bringing that institution from a small college with a Classical curriculum to a modern, major university. He wrote *Evolution and Dogma* in 1896 which promoted the idea that God created using evolution – theistic evolution. There is apparently a medallion in the floor of the main hall of the Jordan Hall of Science at Notre Dame which has a quotation from Theodosius Dobzhansky (1900-1975), "Nothing in Biology makes sense except in the light of evolution." Fr. Zahm is probably second only to Teilhard in getting Catholics to reject the Word of God as plainly written in Genesis.

Perhaps third on the list of those most influential in bringing evolutionary thought into the Catholic Church is Fr. Stanley Jaki. He was a professor at Seton Hall University and held doctorates in theology and in physics. It was probably his doctorate in physics that led him to give too much credit to scientific theories. This is apparent when he said in his book *The Savior of Science* (pp. 156-157): "... they [Christians] can only discredit their Christ-inspired sense of purpose if they tie it to a geological timetable measured in thousands of years, or to the specific creation of plants and animals 'according to their kinds,' or to a sequence of creation in which light and dry land come before sun and moon." So much for the plain-sense meaning of Scripture.

In his (non-dogmatic) address to the Pontifical Academy of Sciences (PAS) on October 23, 1996, Pope John Paul II stated that: "… new knowledge has led to the recognition of the theory of evolution as more than a hypothesis." However, he also added that: "A theory's validity depends on whether or not it can be verified; it is constantly tested against the facts; wherever it can no longer explain the latter, it shows its limitations and unsuitability. It must then be rethought." Clearly, the theory of evolution needs to be rethought.

This unfortunate remark by a pope gave many people the mistaken notion that the Catholic Church had changed its position on evolution and the understanding of Genesis. The thought was that if you just add God to a godless theory and call it "theistic evolution," it would be acceptable. This is a use of the Hegelian dialectic of combining opposites – thesis and antithesis – into a synthesis. Modernists are adept at using that dialectic, much to the detriment of the truth.

Pope John Paul II had given an address to the PAS earlier in 1992 on the Galileo case saying: "… the Galileo case was the symbol of the Church's supposed rejection of scientific progress … recent historical studies enable us to state that this sad misunderstanding now belongs to the past." Well, St. Robert Bellarmine did not think it was a misunderstanding. Unfortunately, Pope Pius XII had already capitulated to modernist scientific theories back in 1951 in yet another address to the PAS when he essentially admitted to the Big Bang, evolution, and billions of years. Popes should really stop talking to the PAS.

The real problem comes in assuming that what a majority – even a vast majority – of scientists or theologians think about origins or cosmology is necessarily the truth, especially when it contradicts the Word of God. Most people have been taught that science has proven that the universe is billions of years old, that it started with the Big Bang, that stars and planets were created by gravity alone, that the earth is no special place, that life spontaneously arose from non-life, and that humans are the end result of evolution. But is there positive proof for any of that?

Scientist Stephen Gould admitted that science does not have positive proofs: "Moreover, 'fact' does not mean 'absolute certainty' ... In science, 'fact' can only mean 'confirmed to such a degree that it would be perverse to withhold provisional assent.' I suppose that apples might start to rise tomorrow, but the possibility does not merit equal time in physics classrooms." (*Evolution as Fact and Theory*, 1981) Ironically, scientists like Gould castigate creationists for denying man's descent from the ape by equating it with the denial of gravity (or belief in a flat earth), but the fundamental cause of gravity is not understood by science – we can only measure its effects. Gould was perceptive, however, in realizing that the overturning of belief in geocentrism was the start of the modern scientific revolution when he said: "The most important scientific revolutions all include, as their only common feature, the dethronement of human arrogance from one pedestal after another of previous convictions about our centrality in the cosmos."

Sometimes atheists are more perceptive about the consequences of ideas than churchmen. One of them said this (G. Richard Bozarth, *The Meaning of Evolution*, American Atheist, Feb. 1978, p. 30):

"Christianity has fought, still fights, and will fight science to the desperate end over evolution, because evolution destroys utterly and finally the very reason Jesus' earthly life was supposedly made necessary. Destroy Adam and Eve and the original sin, and in the rubble you will find the sorry remains of the son of god [sic]. Take away the meaning of his death. If Jesus was not the redeemer who dies for our sins, and this is what evolution means, then Christianity is nothing. Christianity, if it is to survive, must have Adam and the original sin and the fall from grace, or it cannot have Jesus the redeemer who restores to those who believe what Adam's disobedience took away. What all this means is that Christianity cannot lose the Genesis account of creation like it could lose the doctrine of geocentricism and get along. The battle must be waged, for Christianity is fighting for its very life."

Some people think that given enough time, nature produces intricately designed structures automatically, just by mutation and selection. But as has been shown, many systems only work if all the parts are present at the same time. There is no way to get there by small steps. Even billions of years would still not be enough time if it were impossible. But is the universe even billions of years old?

2.7 Old or Young?

How do we know if the earth or the universe is young or old? We are told that they are billions of years old but is this only to justify the claims of evolutionary theory? The Bible says that the world was created in six days only thousands of years ago. How do we know who is right?

One argument for an old earth is the layers of rock strata found in places like the Grand Canyon and Glacier National Park. We are told that each layer was deposited on top of the previous layer, over millions of years. The layers make up what is called the Geologic Column, with names being given to the various layers of rock to denote the particular epoch of time. These layers are related to the fossils found in them. It is supposed that the organisms fossilized in the various layers lived during those particular epochs.

The various layers of rock have been observed since antiquity. It was not always thought that they were deposited one at a time over millions of years. Based on a literal reading of Genesis, Bishop James Ussher (1581-1656) calculated that the original creation happened in 4004 B.C. The flood then occurred in 2348 B.C. Before the 19th century, it was commonly thought that the layers of rock were deposited in the Biblical flood. However, several prominent persons were determined to change that.

James Hutton (1726-1797) is known as the father of modern geology. He observed that rocks erode and the sediment is washed into the sea. He also observed rocks being formed from the lava of volcanos. He concluded that this was an endless cycle: "The result, therefore, of this physical enquiry is that we find no vestige of a beginning, no prospect of an end." He obviously failed to realize that there is no such thing as perpetual motion. He also decided that things had been proceeding in the past at about the same rate as they are now. This led to the idea of uniformitarianism – that things have always been about the same way they are now.

Geologist Charles Lyell (1797-1875) published his *Principles of Geology* in 1830. He admitted that he wanted to "free the science [geology] from Moses." He was aware that his views were "anti-Mosaical" (contrary to the writings of Moses). From the biography of Charles Lyell by Edward Bailey we have: "A few days in Paris allowed Lyell to enjoy a lecture by Prévost 'on diluvium and caves, a good logical refutation of the diluvian humbug.'" Diluvian refers to Noah's Flood.

Lyell's thoughts can be summarized by saying "the present is the key to the past." He popularized the notion of uniformitarianism. Lyell's ideas greatly influenced Charles Darwin (1809-1882).

There is a chapter in the Bible that predicted the rise of uniformitarianism long before it happened:

"... in the last days there shall come deceitful scoffers, walking after their own lusts, saying: Where is his promise or his coming? For since the time that the fathers slept, all things continue as they were from the beginning of the creation. For this they are willfully ignorant of, that the heavens were before,

> and the earth out of water, and through water, consisting by the word of God; whereby the world that then was, being overflowed with water, perished." (2 Peter 3:3-6)

Lyell's attempt to "free the science [geology] from Moses" is reflected in their being "willfully ignorant" of Noah's Flood. Jesus foretold that just before his return, people would act like people did right before the flood, being unconcerned that something big was just about to happen:

> "And as in the days of Noah, so shall also the coming of the Son of man be. For as in the days before the flood, they were eating and drinking, marrying and giving in marriage, even till that day in which Noah entered into the ark, and they knew not till the flood came, and took them all away; so also shall the coming of the Son of man be." (Matt. 24:37-39)

This confirms that the flood was a global event that affected everyone on earth, because it is compared to the Second Coming of Christ, which will also affect everyone on earth. So it is clear that uniformitarianism is condemned by the Bible. But what does natural science have to say about it?

The basis of uniformitarianism is the interpretation of the rock strata. It is assumed that it was deposited one horizontal layer at a time over millions of years. But is there any contrary evidence?

Guy Berthault performed experiments at the University of Colorado in the 1980's on the deposition of sediment in moving water. What he discovered was that multiple layers of sediment could be deposited in moving water simultaneously, with the sediment sorted by particle size. He also discovered that these layers could be deposited on a slope; they did not have to be horizontal. He further discovered that the depth and velocity of the water had an effect on how the sediments were deposited.

This contradicts the basis for the uniformitarian interpretation of rock strata. Multiple layers can be deposited rapidly, and on a slope. The layers do not then represent millions of years of time.

Another hard piece of evidence against the theory of uniformitarianism is bent layers of sedimentary rock found in places like the Grand Canyon. Since hard rock does not bend very well, the bent layers must have become bent when they were still soft. It might be possible to soften hard rock by heating it, but that would affect the composition of the rock itself. The bent layers of sedimentary rock do not show signs of heating.

The lack of erosion between rock layers also indicates that they were deposited rapidly, with very little time occurring between them. The relatively small amount of scree, or rock fragments, at the base of many cliffs is yet another sign that they are not that old. The amount of scree that is visible at road cuts indicates that it can build up rapidly in a short period of time.

The amount of coal found in large deposits around the world, such as the Powder River Basin of Wyoming, would have required a much larger amount of vegetation than exists today. The thickness of the coal layer also indicates a catastrophic event must have occurred at one time in order to get that much vegetation in one place.

Another piece of evidence against uniformitarianism are tree fossils found protruding through several layers of rock. The trees did not stand there for millions of years while the rock strata formed around them. So all the layers around the trees must have been deposited rapidly, while the trees were still standing. Uniformitarians are forced to admit as much, but make the convenient excuse that it must have only been a local flood around the trees. They will do anything to avoid recognizing a Biblical, global flood.

There have been local floods that demonstrate the power of moving water. In 1983, Lake Powell on the Utah-Arizona border flooded and the water was nearing the top of the Glen Canyon Dam. It was decided to let water out through spillways to reduce the amount of water in the lake. When this was done, rumbling sounds were heard and chunks of concrete and rock started exiting the spillways.

What was happening was that bubbles were forming in the rapidly moving water and then collapsing, a process known as cavitation. This can produce large vibrating forces which pound on any structure in the water like a jackhammer. The concrete structure of the spillways around the dam was heavily damaged and even the rock under the spillways was exposed.

A similar event happened during the Missoula Flood near the end of the Ice Age. A large ice dam stopped up the Clark

Fork River and the level of the lake behind the dam continued to rise until it was about 2,000 feet deep. At that point the ice dam collapsed catastrophically and all the water came rushing out. The floor of the valley under the lake was then scoured out by the cavitation occurring in the rapidly moving water. The water and sediment ran over Dry Falls, creating perhaps the largest waterfall in history for a short time, and eventually reached the Pacific Ocean.

The process that carved out the Grand Canyon was likely similar to the Missoula Flood. If the canyon had been carved out a little at a time over millions of years there would be a large river delta where all the sediment was deposited. There is no such delta and so a short-duration catastrophic event is a much better explanation. There is also a large canyon along the Toutle River near Mt. St. Helens in Washington that is known to have been formed in less than one day due to a catastrophic flood event.

Scientists will accept the idea of a global flood, as long it does not confirm the authenticity of the Bible. The geological features on Mars are thought to have been formed by flowing water. The extent of the features is such that some scientists think that there was actually a global flood on Mars. Very similar features can be seen all over the earth, so if there could have been a global flood on Mars, there certainly could have been one on the earth.

The layers of rock around the world and the fossils in them appear in certain patterns. Generally speaking, marine fossils are in the bottom layers, amphibians and reptiles are found in the layers above that, and birds and mammals are found near the top. Certain types of rock are associated with the various layers. This is called the Geologic Column.

Since it is assumed that the layers near the bottom are older, it is assumed that the organisms fossilized in those layers lived prior in time to the organisms fossilized in the layers above. So it is assumed that marine organisms (fish) evolved into amphibians, which evolved into reptiles, which evolved into birds and mammals, and eventually man.

However, the layers are not in perfect order. In some places certain rock layers are missing, repeated, or reversed. Some objects have been found in rock where they should not be if evolutionary assumptions are correct. These have been called out-of-place artifacts (OOP's). For example: 1.) a bronze bell found in West Virginia in 1944 by Newton Anderson within a lump of coal, 2.) an iron pot discovered in another lump of coal in Thomas, Oklahoma in 1912 by Frank Kennard, 3.) a hammer known as the London Hammer embedded in limestone found in London, Texas in 1934 by the Hahn family, 4.) a small clay human figurine known as the Nampa Image found more than 300 feet below the surface while drilling a well in Nampa, Idaho in 1889 by Mark Kurtz, and 5.) a silver bell-shaped vessel known as the Dorchester Pot found in Boston, Massachusetts after blasting sedimentary rock in 1851. The assumed evolutionary age of the coal and rocks should eliminate the possibility of human artifacts, but they have been found. Additionally, there are many man-made tunnels that have stalactites in them. This indicates that under the right conditions, rock, coal, and minerals can form rapidly, therefore the assumed ages are wrong.

Some scientists like to point out that meteor craters and dinosaur nests in the rock layers prove that there is a large amount of time separating each layer. Although there are meteor craters, they are very few in number, and meteors could have fallen to earth during the flood. The dinosaur nests also could have been built during the flood. The Bible says that the water rose during 150 days. That would be enough time for many nests to be built. Fossilized dinosaur embryos are very rare which suggests that the fossilized eggs were all laid during a relatively short period of time.

The Geologic Column is really a record of Noah's Flood. Not all the layers of rock strata are directly associated with the flood, but most of the rock layers and fossils found throughout the world are a result of the flood. For example, there are rock layers at the bottom of the Grand Canyon which run at an angle to those above. These layers do not have fossils in them. So they probably were deposited before the flood and were tilted and eroded to a nearly horizontal surface at the start of the flood.

The fossils on the bottom flood layers are just what got buried first. Things in the oceans were already on the bottom, so that is where they ended up. Amphibians and reptiles may have been close to the oceans and have streamlined bodies, meaning they would sink faster, so they got buried next. The birds and mammals would have been able to escape the flood waters longest, so they got buried last. The marine fossils at the tops of mountains are an indication that Noah's Flood was a global event that covered all the mountains, just as the Bible says.

Dating methods are also cited as proof of an old earth, but there are many assumptions involved with dating methods. The only uncontested aspect of dating methods is that there is a ratio of radioactive to stable elements in samples. The radioactive elements will decay over time and so they are continually decreasing in amount. The stable elements do not decay so the amount does not change. A very small ratio of radioactive to stable element is thought to indicate old age.

However, the initial concentration of elements must be assumed. It is also assumed that no amount of either element was either added or subtracted other than through radioactive decay. It is further assumed that the decay rate was constant. If any of these assumptions are false, the age is wrong.

One popular dating method, carbon dating, involves C-14 and C-12 (isotopes of carbon). It is known that the ratio of these elements in the atmosphere has not stabilized, and so this would affect C-14 dates. Since the magnetic field of the earth is decreasing in strength, it was stronger in the past, and this may have prevented very much C-14 production. That would make C-14 dates look older. If any C-14 were washed out of a sample, as by a flood, that would also make the dates look older.

The maximum age for C-14 dating is around 50,000 to 80,000 years due to the ability to detect C-14 atoms and the decay rate of C-14. The half-life of C-14 – or the amount of time it takes for half of a sample to decay to its stable isotope (nitrogen, N-14) – is about 5,730 years. After 10 half-lives, any radioactive element will be almost completely gone.

In carbon dating, it frequently happens that the assumptions are adjusted to match the expected age. Many labs refuse to date dinosaur bones because they are assumed to be older than the maximum age for C-14 dating. Other dating methods are used on the rocks that have the dinosaur fossil in them and the fossils are assumed to be of the same age.

However, some dinosaur bones have been C-14 dated and they give dates in the tens of thousands of years. Fossils of large, extinct Ice Age animals give similar dates. This shows that these animals lived at about the same time, as you would expect if you read the Bible.

Soft tissue has been found in some large dinosaur bones. It would be impossible for this soft tissue to be preserved for millions of years. This is another indication of the young age of the earth.

Distant stars are cited as evidence of an old universe, but do they prove that the world is billions of years old? We know that even the closest stars are light-years away, which is still very far. It is assumed that the farthest stars are billions of light-years away. So does that prove the light coming from them is actually billions of years old?

That does not necessarily have to be the case. There is some evidence that light has travelled faster in the past because historical measurements of the speed of light indicate that it is slowing down. The speed of light can also be affected by the medium through which it is traveling. Light travels slower in water, which causes it to be refracted at an angle. If you put a straw into a glass of water, you can see this.

There are traditions that Adam named the original constellations, and that they appear now just about the same as they did then – 6,000 years ago. So he would have seen light from the distant stars immediately after creation was finished on the sixth day. Creation would have had the appearance of age in the beginning, but Adam was created as a mature adult and nature would likewise have had the appearance of maturity.

The book *The Gospel in the Stars* by Joseph Seiss explains that the constellations can be "read" to give an account of the promise of a savior. (There is an explanation of the star of Bethlehem in that book which attempts to relate it to a conjunction, but the Bible and Bl. Anne Catherine Emmerich both say that it was miraculous.) Each of the twelve constellations of the zodiac are interpreted in light of the Biblical Gospels. The constellation Virgo (Virgin) represents the Blessed Virgin Mary and the constellation Leo (Lion) can represent Jesus Christ, the Lion of Judah (Apoc. 5:5).

On September 23, 2017, an interesting alignment of planets within those two constellations seemed to indicate that perhaps a ruler was going to make an appearance. Jupiter (the king planet) had been in the constellation Virgo for nine months and began to exit that day, as if the Virgin was giving birth to a king. This alignment seemed to correspond to the passage in the Apocalypse of St. John regarding the woman clothed with the sun (Apoc. 12). The brightest star in the constellation Leo is Regulus, which means "Little King" in Latin. Three other planets were also in the vicinity: Mars (god of war), Mercury (messenger god), and Venus (goddess of love and beauty).

One month prior to that, on Monday, August 21, 2017, the "Great American Eclipse" occurred across the United States. The total eclipse was visible from seven different towns named Salem (like Jerusalem) which means "peace." It also passed over St. Louis, Missouri which was named after King St. Louis IX. The French Monarch who will reign during the Era of Peace is supposed to be a direct descendent of his. After passing through St. Louis, the eclipse passed through Southern Illinois – an area known as "Little Egypt." This recalls the Bible passage "Out of Egypt have I called my son." (Hosea 11:1 and Matt. 2:15) On Monday, April 8, 2024 the "Great North American Eclipse" will pass through Mexico, the US, and Canada, with the path crossing the 2017 eclipse path near the New Madrid fault. Stay tuned.

The Bible says that God stretched out the heavens (Isaiah 45:12). It does not say that the second day of creation – when the waters above the firmament were separated from the waters below – was "good" (it was a Monday, after all). This may indicate that God had not finished stretching out the heavens on day two, and continued the work of the second day into the third and fourth days. The sun, moon, and stars were created on the fourth day.

The Bible says that the world was created out of water (Genesis 1 and 2 Peter 3) and water has been found in the farthest parts of the universe. All of this suggests that God started creation from nothing with a big ball of water. He used some of the water to create the earth, and used the rest of it to create the other heavenly bodies. There is also no proof that the universe is expanding so it is probably about the same size now as it was after the sixth day of creation, when the new stars were visible to Adam.

Throughout history, God has repeatedly warned mankind when it is about to take a wrong turn. These warnings usually take the form of miraculous signs and prophetic utterances. If the warnings are not sufficient to change hearts and minds, then chastisements may follow, all in God's effort to get man back on the right path.

Mary's appearance at Guadalupe, Mexico in 1531 was a warning against placing too much emphasis on the sun which led to heliocentrism and a rejection of the Biblical geocentrism. The miraculous cloak of Juan Diego still stands as a testament. Countless people have been healed at the shrine.

Her appearance at Fatima, Portugal in 1917 was a warning against atheistic Communism and the relativism that were beginning to dominate the world. The miracle of the sun is perhaps the greatest miracle since the Resurrection of Our Lord. The most astounding part of the miracle was not that the sun appeared to move in the sky, but that the rain-soaked ground and people were made instantly dry. The amount of heat required to do that would have incinerated them, if it were not a miraculous event.

Our Lady's appearance at Lourdes, France in 1858 was a warning against the theory of evolution and the idea of millions/billions of years which was about to be foisted upon the world in 1859 by Charles Darwin. The 18 appearances of Mary to St. Bernadette correspond with the three theological virtues of faith, hope, and charity, and the 15 mysteries of the Rosary. The warning against the theory of evolution was given when the Blessed Mother told Bernadette: "I am the Immaculate Conception."

Our Lady did not say "I am an Immaculate Conception" but said that she was the one and only Immaculate Conception. (Jesus Christ was incarnated by the Holy Ghost and so he was not conceived naturally.) This is significant in that Adam and Eve were both created without Original Sin. If they were born of pre-human hominoids, as some people say, they would have been conceived immaculately. The Blessed Virgin affirmed in this way that Adam and Eve were not conceptions, but creations. The Bible confirms this in Ecclesiasticus Chapter 17: "God created man of the earth, and made him after his own image ... He created of him a helpmate like to himself ..." This is a heavenly rejection of the theory of evolution which started to take hold after Darwin published his *On the Origin of Species* in 1859. It is also a very good argument against extraterrestrials.

2.8 The Spirit World

Many people like to speculate about parallel universes. There is actually one parallel universe – the spirit world. The world of spirits consists of God, angels, demons, and human souls. These are all immortal. Human souls will eventually be reunited with their bodies. Jesus and Mary already have their glorified bodies united to their souls.

Plato and Aristotle argued for the existence of the soul. Plato argued, in part, that recollection was a power of the soul and not of the body. Aristotle wrote *De Anima*, a treatise on the soul, in which he argued that things which are alive must have souls. He further argued that man's ability to think abstractly proved that he had a rational soul. Augustine spoke of a rational soul (center of thought) and an irrational soul (center of appetites). Aquinas picked up where they left off and said that while plants and animals have natural, mortal souls which die with them, man has an immortal soul which is the essence of the human person.

Medical science has shown that different areas of the brain control various bodily functions, but that there is no single part of the brain responsible for religious beliefs. This indicates that the soul is the center of religious beliefs and is distinct from the body. Many people have had near-death experiences in which they have seen their own dead bodies, which would not be possible without the existence of a soul apart from the body. In fact, death can be defined as the separation of the soul and the body. Visions of angels and demons are common in near-death experiences.

Visions of demons are also common in people susceptible to them, only they are thought of as aliens or Yeti or Sasquatch. The Bible warns against this: "Put you on the armor of God, that you may be able to stand against the deceits of the devil. For our wrestling is not against flesh and blood; but against principalities and powers ..." (Ephesians 6:12)

According to many theologians and visionaries, God created the angels on the first day of creation. They were given infused knowledge about God. Venerable Mary of Agreda had extensive revelations on this subject. These are recorded in a four-volume work, *Mystical City of God*.

She saw God as Father, Son, and Holy Ghost, with the Son proceeding eternally from the Father, and the Holy Ghost proceeding from the Father and Son. God conceived of the creation of the world all at once, although she explains it in a series of instances. God first desired to communicate himself outwardly, filling his creatures with every good thing, for their own good and his greater glory. He next thought to make the Second Person of the Holy Trinity visible in human form. The rest of humanity would have a body and soul, would be able to know and love their Creator, and be able to choose between good and evil with a free will. God would then fill his creation with gift and graces, firstly Jesus Christ, and secondly his holy Mother Mary.

The thought of the nine choirs of angels came next, being created to know, love, and serve God. They would also serve the deified humanity of Christ as their exemplar and king, and honor Mary as their queen. In giving them a free will, God saw that some would obey him and some would not, due to their pride and disordered self-love.

According to the Bible and tradition, there are nine choirs of angels divided into three hierarchies: 1.) Messengers: Angels, Archangels, Virtues; 2.) Governors: Powers, Principalities, Dominations; 3.) Counselors: Thrones, Cherubim, Seraphim. Three angels in the Bible are named: Michael, Gabriel, and Raphael. There is a fourth angel named Uriel in the apocryphal book of 4 Esdras.

According to Ven. Mary, it was revealed to the angels that they were created to know and serve God, that Christ would take human form and they would recognize him as their head, and that Mary would be his Mother, whom they would serve as queen. Some angels accepted this, but others did not. Lucifer was the leader of the fallen angels and desired to have himself worshipped rather than Jesus Christ. This led to the expulsion of Lucifer and his followers from heaven. Traditionally, they amounted to about one-third of all the angels (Apoc. 12:4).

Lastly God thought of humanity, who would be made in the image and likeness of Christ to be his followers. The Fall of Adam was foreseen, and as a remedy, humanity was made capable of suffering. Ven. Mary gives a description of the followers of Christ and the followers of Satan (Volume I, The Conception, Book One, Chapter XI):

> "The elect cling to their leader by faith, humility, charity, patience, and all the virtues and in order to obtain victory, they are assisted, helped and beautified by the divine grace and the gifts, which the Redeemer and Lord of all merited for them. But the reprobate, without receiving any such benefits from their false leader, or earning any other reward than the eternal pain and the confusion of hell, follow him in pride, presumption, obscenity and wickedness, being led into these disorders by the father of lies and the originator of sin."

She also said, concerning free will, that (Volume I, The Conception, Book Two, Chapter III): "The whole ruin or salvation of souls depends upon the use of their free will; but since most men use it ill and damn themselves, the Most High has established religious life under the sacred vows." Intellectual beings – angels and men – have been given a choice. The angels had one choice to make and men have many. If there were no penalty for making a bad choice, then there would be less motivation for making a good choice.

Ven. Mary wrote several chapters in her book regarding how Mary possessed all the virtues to an eminent degree. In Volume I, The Conception, Book Two, Chapters V-XII, she records how Our Lady possessed infused knowledge of created things, along with infused virtues which she exercised continually throughout her life.

Blessed Anne Catherine Emmerich also had revelations of the creation, of the fall of the angels, and of the Fall of Adam. She said that humanity would increase until the places in heaven vacated by the fallen angels were filled by the souls of the elect. She also describes the Fall of Adam and Eve in detail, even describing the fruit that they consumed out of disobedience.

Both Bl. Anne and Ven. Mary describe the sin of Satan and Adam as coming from a disordered self-love. God's love is directed outwardly, toward his creation. Even the love within God is directed to the other. The Father is the lover, the Son is the beloved, and the Holy Ghost is the love between them. If we want to love like God, our mind and heart need to be directed to the other, not to the self.

3 HISTORY OF THE WORLD

3.1 Creation and Original Sin

In 1650 Protestant Archbishop James Ussher of Armagh, Ireland calculated the year of creation to be 4004 B.C. He used various historical sources and the Bible. He fixed the birth of Christ at 4 B.C. and the date of the completion of Solomon's temple at 3000 years after creation (1004 B.C.).

The Septuagint text of the Bible can be used to give a creation date of 5199 B.C., which was recorded in the old Roman Martyrology for Christmas Day. This date was supported by St. Jerome and Eusebius Pamphili, Bishop of Cæsarea, as well as Venerable Mary of Agreda, author of *Mystical City of God.* It is interesting that the Septuagint text adds exactly 100 years to the ages of various patriarchs in Genesis 5 and 11, compared to the Masoretic, Vulgate, and King James versions.

According to the revelations of Blessed Anne Catherine Emmerich, the year of creation was 4004 B.C. She said that Jesus was speaking to the Pharisees and told them that the world had been in existence for 4028 years (Vol. 1, p. 64). He was 31 years old at the time, so the world was created 3997 years before he was born. In her book of the life of the

Blessed Virgin Mary (p. 205), it is written that Bl. Anne stated that there has been confusion in dating the birth of Jesus, but that he was born seven years before our reckoning, or 7 B.C. That puts the date of creation at 4004 B.C., in agreement with Archbishop Ussher.

Bl. Anne and Ven. Mary of Agreda had revelations regarding the creation of the world. Various other saints have had them also. They all support a literal interpretation of Genesis, not an evolutionary interpretation. No saint would doubt the Word of God on this matter.

Since the Bible starts with the creation of the world, there really are no prehistoric times. Modern scientists like to think that the universe is billions of years old, that hominoids go back millions of years, and that civilizations go back at least 10,000 years. As has been shown, however, the millions and billions of years are based on erroneous assumptions. They are used as tools to erase in the minds of men the true history of the world, as recorded in the Bible.

The Bible records that Cain, the son of Adam and Eve, built the first city. So humanity was civilized from the beginning. At least modern scientists agree that civilizations have only existed for thousands of years. The cave men and primitive people that are thought to have existed long before are really just the drop-outs from early societies. Even today there are tribes living in jungles.

Ancient men were not necessarily primitive. The great stone monuments of antiquity, like the pyramids of Giza in Egypt, could not be duplicated today. There are carved stones at the ancient Baalbek temple site in Lebanon that could not be moved by any existing piece of equipment. There are Egyptian mummies with dental bridges. The Antikythera Mechanism is an ancient piece of complex machinery. The ancient Inca roads built in Peru are extensive, and some are even in use today. Those roads are one reason that the Spanish explorers were able to conquer that area so rapidly.

The Ica stones of Peru depict surgeries, and there are bones in ancient graves showing surgical work. There are graves near Peru that have surgical tools buried in them, like scalpels with blades made of obsidian that are sharper than steel. Some Ica stones depict dinosaurs interacting with men, indicating that they lived at the same time. Although there are modern forgeries of the Ica Stones, the original stones show signs of great age.

After God created Adam and Eve, the command that he gave to them was to "increase and multiply, and fill the earth, and subdue it" (Gen. 1:28). He gave them fruits and herbs to eat, except for the fruit of the tree of knowledge of good and evil, which he commanded them not to eat, warning them that they would die if they did (Gen. 2:16). Bl. Anne Catherine Emmerich gave a description of it that sounded like a banyan tree. The Second Chapter of Genesis describes in detail the creation of Adam, the plants and animals, and Eve.

A river was said to have flowed out of Paradise which divided into four other rivers: the Phison, the Gehon, the Tigris, and the Euphrates (Gen. 2:11-14). The Tigris and Euphrates rivers exist today. The Gehon was said to flow through Ethiopia or Cush, which is generally understood to be southern Egypt, so that would be the Nile river. The Phison was identified by Josephus to be the Ganges river in India. If you look at a map of the world today, you realize that there is a geographical problem with that. Although the headwaters of the Tigris and Euphrates are close together, the other two rivers are far from there. However, the original creation was destroyed in a flood, so the topography of today is quite different than it was then. Bl. Anne Catherine Emmerich said that the terrain before the flood had gentle rises and broad plains. The cave in which Seth, the child of Adam and Eve, was born was the same cave in which Jesus Christ was born, so that particular feature survived the flood.

Also, the way to Paradise was blocked after the Fall (Gen. 3:24) and according to Bl. Anne it was actually removed far from the earth where it is now inaccessible. Somehow, before it was removed, the river running out of it flowed into those other four rivers. Perhaps Paradise was hovering just above the earth in the beginning. She further said that Enoch and Elijah were taken alive to Paradise and will come back to earth to preach during the reign of Antichrist.

So God had given Adam and Eve life, and every good thing that they needed. He also gave them a free will with which they could choose to love him in return for his love, or reject him out of self-love. The angels had been given the same choice. Without the choice – without free will – our actions would be merely instinctive, like the actions of brute beasts.

The devil, out of malice and envy, tempted Eve to disobey God by eating the fruit of the tree of the knowledge of good and evil. Admiring the beauty of the fruit, she chose to believe the devil, rather than to obey the command of God given to her by her husband. Adam had been given the command before Eve was taken from his side.

The devil did not tempt Adam with the fruit directly, because he knew Adam could not be deceived as easily. Ven. Mary of Agreda says: "He [Lucifer] first approached the woman, and not the man, because he knew her to be by nature more frail and weak ..." (*Mystical City of God,* Volume I, The Conception, Book One, Chapter XI). Bl. Anne also has a detailed description of The Fall (Volume One of *The Life of Jesus Christ and Biblical Revelations*). The devil knew that Adam was attracted to Eve and would not want to lose her. So he got Eve to eat the fruit first and offer it to Adam, who then decided to disobey God by eating the fruit rather than to risk losing Eve by not eating it.

So rather than putting the love of God first, both Adam and Eve chose the love of self and ate the fruit. Immediately, they lost the full control of the intellect over the will and became aware of their nakedness. The sight of the uncovered body of the other created a desire that caused a loss in their peace of mind. So they decided to cover themselves with fig leaves.

A man is visually stimulated. That is why pornography sells. If women want men to treat them respectfully, they need to dress modestly. Men should avoid pornography if they do not want to be consumed by it. They need to practice the "custody of the eyes." St. Paul says to keep your thoughts on things above and not those below (Col. 3:1-5). Traditionally, Jewish men were not allowed to read the Song of Solomon until age 30, because of the sensual language which is used to describe the spiritual relationship between God and his Church, or between Jesus and Mary.

God created humans, as well as most animals, male and female (Gen. 1:27). A major contributing factor to gender confusion is cross-dressing. This is condemned in the Bible (Deut. 22:5). St. Paul even chastises men for wearing their hair long (1 Cor. 11:14-15). You cannot change your genes by changing your mind. If you have a Y chromosome, you are male; if not, you are female. It is not helpful to tell someone they are something that they are not.

Upon being questioned by God about their disobedience, Adam blamed Eve, and Eve blamed the serpent. Rather than taking their lives at that moment, God took the lives of animals and gave Adam and Eve clothes made from the skins (Gen. 3:21). That was the start of the requirement of animal sacrifice which continued until the perfect sacrifice of Jesus Christ on the cross.

God pronounced an expiatory curse upon Adam and Eve. Adam was to work out his salvation by the sweat of his brow. The earth was cursed to produce thorns and thistles. Eve was to work out her salvation by pain in childbearing and by obedience to her husband. They were driven out of the Garden of Eden, but given the promise of a future savior (Gen. 3:15).

God told Eve that childbearing would be difficult and this is reflected in maternal deaths, especially before the advent of medical technology. However, St. Paul says that women are also saved through childbearing (1 Tim. 2:15). It is a traditional Catholic teaching that women who die while giving birth are brought immediately to heaven, just like martyrs.

Adam and Eve witnessed the disorder in their own children with the death of Abel by the hand of Cain. Cain left, taking his wife – who would have been his sister (Gen. 5:4) – and founded the first city. Taking your sister as your wife was acceptable then since no other women were available, and since early on there were very few genetic defects. Humanity continued to propagate, with their disorder, until finally God decided that there was too much evil on the earth (Gen. 6:6-7).

You may have heard it said, "All I ever needed to know I learned in kindergarten." Well, just about all you need to know about human nature can be learned from the book of Genesis. The seven deadly sins – Pride, Lust, Anger, Covetousness, Envy, Sloth, and Greed – are demonstrated in a number of places. Rebellion against God's laws is evident. Noah's Flood, the Tower of Babel, and Sodom and Gomorrah are testaments to God's judgment on the sins of mankind.

George A. Kendall said in a December 7, 2017 *Wanderer* article on euthanasia, *The Fourth Commandment And The Next Holocaust*, that a former professor of his argued that there is only one real sociological law: "Most people, most of the time, follow the path of least resistance." Water always follows the path of least resistance; it flows downhill all the time. That is why society continually declines except when enough people decide to lead lives of virtue.

Society begins with the family, and disorders within the family are reflected in disorders in society. Although a single family forms a small society, a perfectly functioning society needs more members because there are many occupations. That is partly why God told Adam and Eve to fill the earth.

The family that God established had a man as the head and a woman as his help-mate. This is the pattern that was intended to be maintained for all time. St. Paul gives a good description of how the family should operate in the Fifth and Sixth Chapters of Ephesians – husbands love your wives, wives be subject to your husbands, children obey your parents. The Second Chapter of First Timothy and the Seventh Chapter of First Corinthians are even more explicit about the roles of men and women, and divorce.

When asked about divorce, Jesus responded that from the beginning of creation they were created male and female and what God joined together, let not man put asunder (Mark 10:9). The Old Testament also condemns divorce (Malachi 2:15-16), even if allowance was made for it. Although divorce is hard on the spouses, it is even harder for the children. A divorce in the family is a leading indicator for later problems in life.

Sexual relations are to be kept between a man and his wife. There are any number of Biblical warnings against adultery. The primary purpose of marriage is the begetting and the raising of children, although there are many secondary benefits as well. Both Adam and Noah were commanded to fill the earth. The practice of contraception is condemned in the Bible (Gen. 38:9-10). The first man to practice it, Onan, was killed directly by God.

Contraception used to be known as Onanism. It is also associated with witchcraft since potions and pills are used to prevent pregnancy and induce abortion. The book of Tobias records that the archangel Raphael said that the devil has power over those who practice contraception: "For they who in such manner receive matrimony, as to shut out God from themselves, and from their mind, and to give themselves to their lust, as the horse and mule, which have not understanding, over them the devil has power." (Tobias 6:17)

There is a lot of talk about overpopulation and some cities are certainly crowded. But all of the people in the world could actually fit inside the city of Jacksonville, Florida. If you travel outside the cities in the western United States, you wonder how anyone could think that the world is overpopulated. There are supposedly nearly 3,000 abandoned villages in Spain alone.

The replacement birthrate is just over 2.0. That is, married couples must have at least two children in order to replace themselves. The birthrate in most countries is less than 2.0, in some countries it is much less. Those countries are dying out by definition – since people do not live forever – even if their death rate has not yet surpassed their birthrate, as it has in Russia. Even an aging population creates serious social and political issues.

World population has increased significantly since the early 20th century. However, as one population expert put it, it is not because people are breeding like rabbits, it is because they are not dying like flies. This is mostly due to advances in available medical technology. However, the declining birthrates around the globe could cause the world population to actually decline in the next few decades.

Abortion, contraception, euthanasia, homosexuality, murder, and warfare are causing a serious population problem – the lack of it! Currently, there are about 40-50 million surgical abortions per year in the world – more than the population of a large country! And that does not include a probably greater number of chemically-induced abortions caused by abortifacients, which are in many contraceptive pills. Abortion is actually the number one cause of death worldwide. Could this be the annihilation of nations spoken about by Our Lady of Fatima?

Ironically, perhaps, chastity and virginity are highly praised in the Bible. Jesus, Mary, Joseph, and the two St. John's (Baptist and Evangelist) were virgins. Catholic priests and nuns are voluntarily celibate. It is said that St. Bridget of Sweden had a vision in which Our Lady told her that any pope who dispensed with priestly celibacy would be punished most severely in this life and then tortured eternally in hell. Those who do not know prophecy are doomed to fulfill it. Every believer is called to be chaste, even those who are married (remaining faithful to your spouse).

Although the Apostles were almost all married, they gave up marital relations with their wives when they were ordained by Christ to serve the Church. The early Church had married priests but it was expected that they would not have marital relations either. Ordained ministers of the Latin Rite Catholic Church are expected to follow this practice.

In the Eastern Rites of the Church, priests can have marital relations with their wives, but not the day before performing the Divine Liturgy. That is one reason why most Eastern Rite churches do not have daily Divine Liturgy. Tobias and Sara did not have marital relations for three days after their marriage in order to not be like heathens (Tobit 8:5). When the Israelites came to Mt. Sinai, they had to abstain from marital relations for three days before approaching God (Exodus 19:15). The Catechism of the Council of Trent required that same practice before receiving Holy Communion. Pope Pius X lifted the requirement, but it is apparent that sexual relations, even if legitimate, do not increase holiness.

Being chaste includes not arousing yourself sexually, which leads to spiritual blindness. The only legitimate sexual relations are between a man and his lawful wife, in a manner that does not prevent procreation. St. Paul recommends people who are single or widowed remain in that state so that they can be preoccupied with heavenly concerns instead of earthly ones (1 Cor. 7:8).

Before he converted, St. Augustine had a mistress and a son by her. Perhaps that is part of the reason why he had a more ascetic viewpoint later, saying: "This continence is more meritorious; it is no sin to render the marital debt, while to demand it beyond what is necessary for begetting children is a venial sin." (*On the Good of Marriage*, n. 6)

St. Thomas Aquinas said: "... there are only two ways in which married persons can come together without any sin at all, namely: in order to have offspring and in order to pay the marriage debt; otherwise it is always at least a venial sin." (*Supplement*, Question 49, article 5) When he says "to pay the marriage debt" (mutual spousal obligation to consent to legitimate requests – 1 Cor. 7:3) it is an admission that men and their wives are not required to intend procreation from each marital act, only that the act not be intentionally closed to procreation. Union of the spouses is one of the secondary purposes of matrimony, after all. The Bible actually mentions Isaac playing with his wife Rebecca (Gen. 26:8) and Proverbs 5:19 says: "… be thou delighted continually with her [your wife's] love."

God commanded Adam and Noah to "be fruitful and multiply," so the traditional Judeo-Christian view on sexual relations is that they are only legitimate when open to procreation. The law of Moses prohibits relations when the woman is in her menstrual period (Leviticus 18:19). From a more conservative view, relations are not acceptable when the wife is already pregnant. When Abraham was told that he would have a son in his old age, Sarah laughed, saying: "After I am grown old and my lord is an old man, shall I give myself to pleasure?" (Gen. 18:12) Obviously, they had given up sexual relations at that time.

It happened during the Middle Ages that married couples past the age of childbearing would part company and join monasteries. Other couples agreed to be married but to not have sexual relations. These were known as "Josephite marriages" after St. Joseph.

While the practice of Natural Family Planning (NFP – limiting marital relations to infertile times) is acceptable, it is only allowed for very serious reasons. Marriage is primarily for the begetting and raising of children. Proponents of the Theology of the Body who would like to raise the marital act to something sacred are deluded.

Sexual activity outside of marriage is sinful, partly because a pregnancy outside of marriage is problematic. Sexual activity or attempted marriage between persons of the same sex is a direct violation of the order established by God. What happened to Sodom is an example for all humanity. The sin of Sodom is clearly described in the book of Jude (Jude 1:7). St. Paul says this about such sins: "Who, having known the justice of God, did not understand that they who do such things, are worthy of death; and not only they that do them, but they also that consent to them that do them." (Romans 1:32) For that and certain other verses, some people would like to ban the Bible or at least rewrite it.

St. Peter Damien wrote a book in 1049 on this subject called the *Book of Gomorrah*. He was very harsh with clerical homosexuality saying, "Was it not for such crimes that Almighty God destroyed Sodom and Gomorrah, and slew Onan for deliberately spilling his seed on the ground?" He accused those of allowing such practices of being "partners in the guilt of others" by permitting "the destructive plague" of sodomy to continue. Of the sin of sodomy itself he said that it: "brings death to the body and destruction to the soul

… pollutes the flesh, extinguishes the light of the mind, expels the Holy Spirit from the temple of the human heart, and gives entrance to the devil, the stimulator of lust … violates temperance, slays modesty, strangles chastity, and slaughters virginity … defiles all things, sullies all things, pollutes all things … leads to error, totally removes truth from the deluded mind … opens up Hell and closes the gates of Paradise."

Our Lord told St. Catherine of Siena (d. 1380) that: "But they … do worse, committing that accursed sin against nature, and as blind and fools, with the light of their intellect darkened, they do not know the stench and misery in which they are. It is not only that this sin [sodomy] stinks before me, who am the Supreme and Eternal Truth, it does indeed displease me so much and I hold it in such abomination that for it alone I buried five cities by a divine judgment, my divine justice being no longer able to endure it." – *El diálogo*

Pope Pius V had this to say about priests caught in sodomy: "So that the contagion of such a grave offense [sodomy] may not advance with greater audacity by taking advantage of impunity, which is the greatest incitement to sin, and so as to more severely punish the clerics who are guilty of this nefarious crime and who are not frightened by the death of their souls … we establish that any priest or member of the clergy, either secular or regular, who commits such an execrable crime, by force of the present law be deprived of every clerical privilege, of every post, dignity and ecclesiastical benefit, and having been degraded by an ecclesiastical judge, let him be immediately delivered to the secular authority to be put to death, as mandated by law as the fitting punishment for laymen who have sunk into this abyss." – Constitution *Horrendum illud scelus*, August 30, 1568, in *Bullarium Romanum*

We do not have an absolute right to life because we are all going to die someday. This is a consequence of Original Sin and the expiatory curse of God (Gen. 2:17). Even though "thou shalt not kill" is one of the Ten Commandments, execution is authorized in the Bible for certain acts: "Whosoever shall shed man's blood, his blood shall be shed: for man was made to the image of God." (Gen. 9:6) and "Every soul that shall commit any of these abominations, shall perish from the midst of his people." (Leviticus 18:29) But only a recognized authority is allowed to make this determination (Romans 13:1-5 and John 19:11), and so vigilantism in this regard is not allowed. This is also the teaching of the Catholic Church (Denzinger #425). Respect for life includes acknowledgement that such actions require a forfeiting of life. Even today, heinous crimes are punished in many countries with the death penalty.

St. Thomas Aquinas defended capital punishment in certain cases:

> "Therefore, if a man be dangerous and infectious to the community, on account of some sin, it is praiseworthy and advantageous that he be killed in order to safeguard the common good."
> – *Summa Theologica*, IIa-IIae, q. 64, a. 2.

"It is permissible to kill a criminal if this is necessary for the welfare of the whole community. However,

this right belongs only to the one entrusted with the care of the whole community – just as a doctor may cut off an infected limb, since he has been entrusted with the care of the health of the whole body."
– *Summa Theologica*, IIa-IIae, q. 64, a. 3.

Communists and materialists are generally opposed to the death penalty and even life in prison, at least for people who agree with their philosophy. They see no value in expiatory suffering and no possibility of eternal life. Unfortunately, many Catholics have been influenced by their way of thinking and have come to oppose the Church's long-standing support of the death penalty in certain cases.

There are various reasons why people develop an intrinsically, objectively disordered attraction to persons of the same sex (#2357-2359, *Catechism of the Catholic Church*). The disorder itself is not necessarily sinful. But the acting out of the disordered passions certainly is. Jesus said that persons who die with unrepentant sins against chastity will be outside the gates of heaven in eternity, which is eternal death, or the second death, and is much worse than physical death (Apoc. 21:8, 22:15). Persons afflicted with such desires must work to overcome them so that they do not act on them.

Although Jesus taught us to love one another and that we are not to be judgmental of persons (although words and actions can be judged), he told the woman caught in adultery to "sin no more." (John 8:11) He also said "… repent, and believe the gospel." (Mark 1:15) Any sin is forgivable, as long as there is repentance. Mary Magdalene was a famous penitent.

The unforgivable sin against the Holy Spirit m the Bible (Mark 3:29) is basically unrepentant traditional sins against the Holy Spirit are: 1.) L Presumption, 3.) Impugning the known truth, 4.) Envy of another's spiritual goods, 5.) Obstinacy in sin, and 6.) Final impenitence. Some sins are more difficult to repent of than others. If you are freed of a sin and return to it, repentance is especially difficult (Matt. 12:45). In order to die in a state of grace and go to heaven, we must repent of sin.

People attached to sins of the flesh (all of which are serious sins because they involve a corruption of the process intended for the transmission of life) like to accuse anyone who questions their behavior of being hateful. Although we are not to hate persons, the Bible says: "You that love the Lord, hate evil ..." (Psalms 96:10), "Hate evil, and love good ..." (Amos 5:15), and "Hating that which is evil ..." (Romans 12:9) Evil is anything contrary to the order established by God. We can hate the demons and the damned souls, since they have irrevocably rejected God.

3.2 Flood

In order to bring an end to the evils being committed on the earth, God chose to destroy all life by a flood, except for the family of Noah and pairs of animals that would be preserved in the ark. God gave Noah specific instructions for the building of the ark. Its length was to be 300 cubits. A cubit can be anywhere between 17 and 22 inches, so the ark would have been between 450 and 550 feet long. A very large boat indeed!

Pairs of land-dwelling animals were to be taken on the ark in order to reproduce after the flood: seven pairs of "clean" animals and birds, and one pair of "unclean" animals. The exact distinction between clean and unclean is not certain. After the flood, Noah offered a sacrifice of clean animals.

The Bible says that Noah was 500 years old when he had his three sons (Gen. 5:31). It seems that God told him to build the ark shortly after that time. Noah was 600 years old when the flood started, so it appears that it took him about 100 years to build the ark. Bl. Anne Catherine Emmerich gave a fairly detailed description of the building of the ark and said that it took Noah a long time to complete it.

Rain started to fall at the beginning of the flood and lasted 40 days. The water continued to rise for 150 days. The Bible mentions that the fountains of the great deep were broken up, and the flood gates of heaven were opened (Gen. 7:11). Noah and his family were on the ark for about one year, although the ark landed on the mountains of Armenia after seven months (Gen. 8:4).

Some people cannot conceive of a global flood that lasted one year and like to imagine that it must have been a local flood. It seems they fail to understand that if it were merely a local flood, Noah and the animals could have just relocated.

Noah and the flood are mentioned several times by Jesus Christ in the Bible. He speaks of it as a literal, historical event. He even goes so far to say that the end of the world will be similar to the time of Noah (Matt. 24:37). Since the end of the world will be a global event, it makes sense that the flood was also a global event.

The Catholic Church speaks of the flood as a prefigurement of baptism. As baptism is necessary for salvation, so was it necessary to be on the ark to be saved from the flood. This is another support for the global nature of the flood.

Nearly all cultures have a tradition of a global flood. The *Gilgamesh Epic* has parallels to the Biblical account that are striking, including the sending out of a dove. The story of the flood is immortalized in ancient Chinese characters as well. The character for "large ship" is made up of the characters for eight, person, and boat – similar to the eight persons that the Bible mentions who were in Noah's Ark.

Some people would say that the writer of the Bible just borrowed from local cultural traditions in order to come up with the stories of creation and the flood. However, since most all cultures have a tradition of a flood, it is likely that they are all based on an historical event.

There is an overwhelming amount of scientific evidence for a global flood. There are many sedimentary rock layers containing fossils of plants and animals all over the earth. There are even marine fossils on the tops of high mountains. Human footprints have been found together with dinosaur footprints in the same rock in Texas. It is likely that most of these rock layers were deposited by one global flood.

Some people doubt that a flood could cover the entire earth. However, if mountains were lower and the seas shallower before the flood, the water in today's oceans could have covered the mountains. If the earth were a perfect sphere, the amount of water in the oceans would be enough to cover the surface to a depth of about a mile and a half.

In his 1929 excavations of the city of Ur – traditional home of Abraham, located in modern-day Iraq – archaeologist Leonard Woolley (1880-1960) discovered a very thick layer of clay devoid of human artifacts that was sandwiched between layers containing artifacts above and below it. His wife exclaimed, "Well, of course, it's the flood."

Excavations of other ancient sites in that area revealed a similar layer of clay. It was dated to about 2500 B.C., which is also close to the Biblical date of the flood using the 4004 B.C. creation date. The Sumerian King List is an extra-Biblical source indicating the occurrence of a great flood with lifespans much greater before than after, just as is told in Genesis. Ancient Sumer is recognized even by modern archaeologists as the site of the world's first civilization. It may have been the first place that the post-flood peoples built a city since it is downstream of Mt. Ararat, where the ark landed, near the headwaters of the Euphrates river.

Some people wonder how Noah could have gotten enough animals on the ark to account for all the species that we have today. Although it would probably not have been possible to get a pair of every species on the ark, it may have been possible to get a pair of every genus on board. For example, one pair of "dogs" could have had all the necessary genetic information to account for all the breeds that we have today. The same applies to cats and other kinds of animals.

Genetic studies of the Y chromosome show that all men are related. Similar studies on mitochondrial DNA have shown that all women today descended from one woman known as Mitochondrial Eve. That woman could have been Noah's wife, since only Noah's family was on the ark. A study of reproduction rates shows that it does not take very long for a large population to arise, especially with high rates of reproduction and low death rates.

John Woodmorappe wrote a book called *Noah's Ark: A Feasibility Study* which shows how Noah and his family could have maintained an ark-load of animals for their one-year stay in the ark. It is likely that juvenile pairs of the larger animals were on board. It is also likely that many of the animals entered into some type of hibernation during that time.

The "fountains of the great deep" mentioned in the Bible were likely subsea volcanos that erupted large quantities of water during the flood. So after the flood the oceans would have been very warm, which would have produced a very mild climate over much of the earth. This probably accounts for the massive mammals, such as mammoths and rhinos, that lived just after the flood.

As the flood-waters cooled, the climate would have slowly changed as well. The evaporation of the warm ocean water could have produced large amounts of snow in cold regions. This could account for the Ice Age. Some people estimate that the cooling lasted about 500 years and that it took about 200 years to recover to normal temperatures after that. This could partially account for the slow reduction in lifespan for succeeding generations – down to 70 years for King David.

As the earth cooled during the Ice Age, the climate would have become less hospitable. The larger animals would have had a harder time finding food. One can frequently see wooly mammoths depicted in natural history museums that are walking through snow. However, such large creatures need to eat large quantities of food in order to survive. An adult elephant can eat 500 pounds of food and drink 50 gallons of water every day. That amount of food and water would not be available in an arctic climate.

Several mammoths frozen in Siberia have been found in remarkably good condition. Even the contents of their stomachs have been preserved. Only a rapid burial and sudden cold conditions would allow that to happen, otherwise, at least part of the carcass would have rotted or have been eaten by a scavenger. They would have needed to be buried in a single event in order to be so well-preserved. This could have happened during a massive dust storm at the start of a major climate shift.

The fossil remains of very large mammals suggest that conditions right after the flood were very favorable to them at that time. The largest land mammal to have ever lived was an Indricotherium, a type of rhinoceros. Apparently, those conditions did not last very long.

Some might object to a young-earth flood model by noting that the glaciers of Antarctica are dated using ice cores to be hundreds of thousands of years old. But, it is assumed that one snow/ice layer is one year and not just one storm. Under the right conditions, snow can build up rapidly. A WWII P-38 known as *Glacier Girl* was recovered from Greenland after being buried in 250 feet of snow and ice in just 50 years. The world record annual snowfall is held by the Mount Baker Ski Area in Washington, which reported 1,140 inches (95 feet) of snowfall for the 1998-99 season. At that rate, Antarctica could have easily acquired all of its glaciers since 2500 B.C.

There are a couple of objects located in Istanbul associated with the flood: 1.) an adze which Noah is said to have used in the construction of the ark and is supposedly buried at the base of Constantine's porphyry column, along with the baskets from the loaves and fishes miracle, an alabaster ointment jar of Mary Magdalene and other objects, and 2.) the Emperor Door of Hagia Sophia which sources say was made from the door of Noah's Ark. It is interesting that some people who claim to have seen the ark say that its door is missing.

It appears that some dinosaurs were on board the ark and lived after the flood. These would account for the many dragon legends from around the world. The Bible mentions dragons many times and the description of behemoth and leviathan in Job appear to fit the description of a large sauropod and a Spinosaurus. The well-known legend of St. George involves a dragon. St. Columba is said to have encountered the Loch Ness Monster on August 22, A.D. 565.

The Ica stones found in Peru have many images of dinosaur-type creatures on them indicating that they were produced from direct observations. There are many dinosaur-type figurines found in Acambaro, Mexico that also seem to be made from observation of live animals. Other well-documented images and figures from around the world support this idea. There are even modern-day eye-witness sightings of supposedly extinct animals like plesiosaurs, pterosaurs, and other large reptiles.

3.3 The Tower of Babel

The Bible records that within a few generations of the flood, mankind gathered at a particular location, Babel, and decided to build a tower: "Come, let us make a city and a tower, the top which may reach to heaven: and let us make our name famous before we be scattered abroad into all lands." (Gen. 11:4)

God was not happy with the project and decided to confuse their language – there had only been one language until that time. Groups of people speaking the different languages then split up and migrated to the different parts of the earth.

Some people will say that this is a just-so story made up to explain different languages – an etiological myth. But the different languages did originate somewhere. The usual name given to the first language is proto Indo-European.

In order to learn a language, you must be taught, usually from a young age. The idea that ancient languages developed from grunting is nonsense. The more ancient languages are actually more grammatically complex. Latin has declensions and conjugations that English does not have. There have been a number of children who grew up in the wild who were later brought into society – feral children – and they only learned language with great difficulty.

One of the more ancient written languages is the traditional Chinese language. It is made up of tens of thousands of individual characters, although only about 5,000 are in regular use. Some of the complex characters are combinations of several simple characters.

The character for "tower" is made up of the characters for dust, grass, people, one, and mouth. The character for "confusion" is made of the characters for tongue and mystery. Both bring to mind the story of the Tower of Babel. It seems that the ancient Chinese characters preserve a similar history as what is recorded in the book of Genesis.

The cuneiform Borsippa inscription of Nebuchadnezzar II commemorates the reconstruction of Etemenanki (meaning "temple of the foundation of heaven and earth"), the ziggurat at Babylon. In part it reads "A former king built it, (they reckon 42 ages) but he did not complete its head. Since a remote time, people had abandoned it, without order expressing their words." This also sounds very much like the story of the Tower of Babel recorded in the Bible.

The Tower of Babel event is closely linked to another event, the division of the earth (Gen. 10:25). The name of one of the patriarchs, Phaleg/Peleg, actually means "division." This may be the same event that is accepted by many scientists as the break-up of continents. Fernand Crombette imagined that the original, single continent had a rose shape. It is possible that the Ice Age occurred during that time and locked up much of the available water in ice. That would result in lower ocean levels and perhaps would have allowed human and animal migrations across continents. This would explain how different languages, cultures, and ecosystems arose after the flood since geographic isolation leads to dialects and the expression of recessive genetic traits.

There are some tribes of native Americans that have more Asian characteristics, and some that are more European. It is quite likely that both Asian and European people arrived in the Americas well before Columbus. There is a significant amount of archaeological evidence to back that up, including the fact that there are many more pyramids in Central America than there are in Egypt!

3.4 Ancient History

Most ancient history books start with some hominoid living in a cave progressing up through various stages of more human creatures, finally arriving at modern man. We are told that this happened over millions of years, usually beginning in Africa.

However, true history starts with one man and one woman – Adam and Eve – and continues for 10 generations until Noah and the flood. At this point history resets and continues with Noah's descendants. Since there is very little if anything left of the pre-flood world, the oldest archaeological evidence exists in the Middle East near where the ark landed.

The book *Buried Alive* by orthodontist Jack Cuozzo describes his investigations into the fossil skulls of

Neanderthal Man. What he discovered is that those skulls show signs of great age – greater than 150 years. That would be more in line with Biblical genealogies than the current accepted modern estimates which are based on evolutionary theory. He noted that fossil skulls had been deliberately depicted to indicate young age, contrary to their actual appearance. That is reminiscent of the Piltdown Man hoax of the early twentieth century.

The book, *After the Flood* by Bill Cooper records the early post-flood history of Europe starting from Noah. In the appendices, the three sons and 16 grandsons of Noah are listed as well as the cultures associated with them. These are the men who repopulated the earth after the flood. So there is only one human race, descended from Adam and then Noah, but many cultures. One country with direct links to Noah is Armenia, which was also the first country in the world to adopt Christianity as a state religion in A.D. 301. Armenia is named after Armaneak, son of Hayk, son of Togarmah, son of Gomer, son of Japheth, son of Noah. There are place-names in Armenia today related to Hayk: Haykashen, and the Castle of Haykaberd.

Also in that book, there is a genealogical tree of the descendants of Noah which ends with Alfred the Great on pages 84-86. Another book *Ancient Post-Flood History* by Ken Johnson gives a similar list on page 62. It is the "short list" of names compared to the "long list" in other sources that adds 29 names after Noah. The "long list" suggests more plausible lifespans, if Adam was created in 4004 B.C. Most of the European royalty can trace themselves back to Alfred the Great. So if you can trace your family back to

European royalty, you will have a bloodline all the way back to Adam! My bloodline is shown in Figure 1. The first 25 names are straight out of the Bible. Note that two names of supposedly mythical characters, #53 Finn MacCool and #56 Odin, were considered to be historical persons by the European royalty.

The book of Genesis traces the bloodline of Adam through the sons of Joseph. The death of Joseph, son of Jacob/Israel, is the last recorded event in Genesis. The ages of the patriarchs are given at the birth of the next generation, and also the number of years they lived after that, so a timeline can be created from creation through the death of Joseph. The age of Jacob at the birth of Joseph takes a little calculation: the age of Jacob when he met Pharaoh was 130 (Gen 47:9) minus the 2 years of famine before Jacob entered Egypt (Gen 45:6) minus the 7 years of plenty (Gen 41:53) minus Joseph's age of 30 when he explained Pharaoh's dream (Gen 41:46) gives 91 years old.

The ancient Israelites understood the Genesis genealogies to be literal years. They also understood the relationships to be father-son. Some people point out that there is an extra generation in Luke 3 that is not in Genesis 11 or 1 Paralipomenon/Chronicles 1 – Cainan, son of Arphaxad – but that could have been a copyist's error. Apparently, the earliest known text of Luke 3 does not have that name (Sarfati, Jonathan D., *Cainan of Luke 3:36*, CEN Technical Journal, 1998, 12[1]:39-40). You can construct a chart of the ages of the Genesis patriarchs along a timeline from creation as shown in Figure 2. Each man is represented by a diamond marker with the flood at 2348 B.C.

What is notable is that the first 10 generations of men lived to be 900 or more years old, except for Enoch who was taken directly to heaven, and Lamech who died the same year as the flood. Adam was originally created to be immortal, but after getting kicked out of the Garden of Eden, that was apparently limited to just less than 1,000 years. After 10 generations, the sins of men grew to such an extent that God decided to limit it further to 120 years (Gen. 6:3).

The decrease in lifespan from over 900 years to 120 years or less can be explained by the effects of the global flood. The reason that you age is because of defects in your DNA. Radiation, notably cosmic radiation, can be a major factor in producing defects in your DNA, apart from the defects that you inherit from your parents. It could very well be that the pre-flood world had an atmosphere that protected the surface of the earth from cosmic radiation. The amount and size of the flora, as indicated by fossil plants, was much greater before the flood than after. Giant coal beds, such as those in the Powder River Basin in the US, would have required enormous amounts of plant material in order to form.

The amount and size of the fauna, as indicated by fossil graveyards, was also much greater before the flood. The size of the plants and animals suggests that the amount of oxygen and carbon dioxide, and the atmospheric pressure, was greater. Today, hyperbaric oxygen chambers are used as medical treatment. It is known that plants grow better with increased carbon dioxide. Older people feel less joint pain when the atmospheric pressure is higher. All of those factors would have made living easier before the flood.

1. Adam
2. Seth
3. Enosh
4. Kenan
5. Mahalalel
6. Jared
7. Enoch
8. Methuselah
9. Lamech
10. Noah
11. Shem
12. Arphaxad
13. Shelah
14. Eber
15. Peleg
16. Reu
17. Serug
18. Nahor
19. Terah
20. Abraham
21. Isaac
22. Jacob
23. Judah
24. Zerah
25. Darda
26. Erichthonius
27. Tros
28. Ilus
29. Laomedon
30. Priam
31. Troana
32. Thor
33. Vingener
34. Hloritha
35. Eiaridi
36. Vingethorr
37. Vingener
38. Moda
39. Magi
40. Seskef
41. Bedweg
42. Hwala
43. Athra
44. Itormann
45. Heremod
46. Sceaf
47. Scealdea
48. Beowa
49. Tecti
50. Geata
51. Godwulf
52. Flocwald
53. Finn MacCool
54. Freothelaf
55. Frithuwald
56. Odin
57. Balder
58. Brand
59. Frithugar
60. Freawine
61. Wig
62. Gewis
63. Esla
64. Elesa
65. Cerdic
66. Cynric
67. Ceawlin
68. Cuthwine
69. Cutha
70. Ceol
71. Ceolwald
72. Cenrad
73. Ingild
74. Eoppa
75. Eafa
76. Ealhmund
77. Egbert
78. Ethelwulf
79. Alfred the Great
80. Edward
81. Eadgifu
82. Louis
83. Mathilde
84. Gerberge
85. Gisele
86. Henry
87. Henry
88. Agnes
89. Frederick
90. Frederick
91. Henry
92. Frederick
93. Manfred
94. Constance
95. Frederick
96. Elizabeth
97. Stephen
98. Isabelle
99. Catherine of Valois
100. Jasper Tudor
101. Helen Tudor
102. William Gardiner
103. William Gardiner
104. Thomas Gardiner
105. Richard Gardiner
106. Luke Gardiner
107. Richard Gardiner
108. Luke Gardiner
109. Anne Gardiner
110. Luke Mudd
111. Elizabeth Mudd
112. Luke Cassidy
113. Martha Cassidy
114. Sarah Rhodes
115. Joseph Jarboe
116. Rachel Jarboe
117. Eric Bermingham

Figure 1: Bloodline of author from Adam. Data from *The Illinois Jarboe Family* by Michael Jarboe.

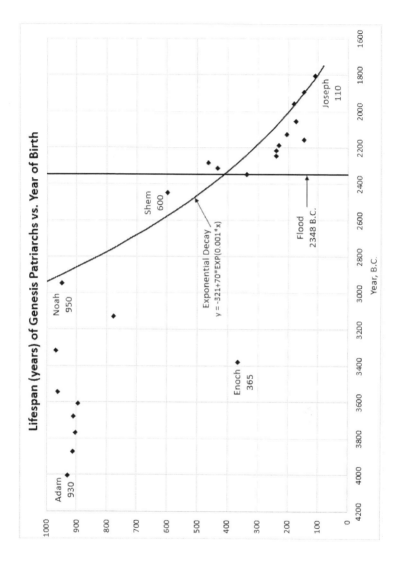

Figure 2: Lifespan in years of the Genesis patriarchs vs. their year of birth.

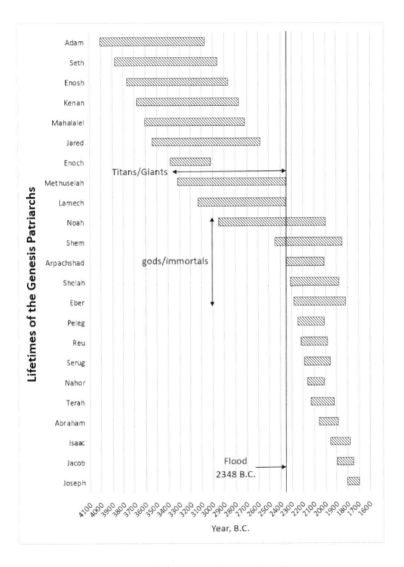

Figure 3: Lifetimes of the Genesis patriarchs.

The generations born after Noah had lifespans that dropped off exponentially after the flood. (Note line of exponential decay on Figure 2.) They finally flattened out after Joseph, who lived to be 110. Joseph's father Jacob said to Pharaoh: "The days of my pilgrimage are 130 years, few and evil, and they are not come up to the days of the pilgrimage of my fathers." (Gen. 47:9) He must have been feeling old, because he only lived 17 more years after that. He also must have been aware of the men who lived to much older ages not very many generations before him.

It took 13 generations after Noah for the lifespans to stabilize. It also appears that men matured faster during that time since their ages at the births of their sons were younger. Noah's son Shem lived to be 600, of which 500 years were after the flood. Two of the next three generations lived to be more than 400. After that, lifespans dropped to around 200 before finally settling after Joseph. One consequence of this was that the first several generations immediately after the flood outlived the next six generations. Shem outlived Abraham, who was born nine generations after him. Shem lived to see his nine-greats grandchild, Jacob! This can be seen visually on Figure 3, which shows the lifetimes of the Genesis patriarchs.

Since the generations born just after the flood lived so much longer than following generations, it would appear to those following generations that they were practically immortal, or even gods. Noah's son Japheth later became known as Jupiter or Jove, king of the Roman gods.

The Bible records that a race of giants was born shortly

before the flood: "Now giants were upon the earth in those days. For after the sons of God went in to the daughters of men, and they brought forth children, these are the mighty men of old, men of renown." (Gen. 6:4) The book of Baruch also mentions them (Baruch 3:26). The "sons of God" are taken by some people to be angels. Although angels are spiritual beings, they can produce physical effects. They could have obtained sperm from a man and impregnated women with it. Bl. Anne Catherine Emmerich said that the race of giants was fathered by Tubalcain, so it could have been him. Tubalcain (Gen 4:22) was the descendent of Cain, the sixth generation after. He lived at about the same time as Enoch. The "mighty men of old, men of renown" mentioned in the Bible could be what are known as the Titans, who are mentioned in the book of Judith (Judith 16:8). The mythological War of the Titans could have a basis in reality in that the giants/Titans existed before the flood, and the gods/immortals existed after. This recalls to the mind a quote from *The Lord of the Rings*: "And some things that should not have been forgotten were lost. History became legend. Legend became myth."

The book of Enoch records that the angels who had relations with women came to Enoch and asked him to pray to God that they not be punished so severely. The book of Enoch also says that the flood was largely brought on by this particular offense against God and nature. Among the Dead Sea Scrolls there is a Book of Giants which describes how one of the giants had a dream which indicated to him that his world was about to perish in a flood.

The best-known giant in the Bible is Goliath, who was killed by David: "And there went out a man baseborn from the camp of the Philistines named Goliath of Geth, whose height was six cubits and a span." (1 Kings/Samuel 17:4) A cubit is the length from a man's elbow to the tip of his middle finger – anywhere from 17 to 22 inches. A span is the length between the tip of the thumb and the tip of the little finger of an outstretched man's hand – about 9 or 10 inches. So Goliath would have been anywhere from 9 feet, 3 inches to 11 feet, 10 inches. Some people consider that to be ridiculous, but Robert Wadlow of Alton, Illinois (1918-1940) was within less than an inch of being 9 feet tall at his death at age 22, and he was still growing due to an over-active pituitary gland!

Other giants mentioned in the Bible are those seen by the Israelite spies who were sent into Canaan after Moses led them out of Egypt: "There we saw certain monsters of the sons of Enac, of the giant kind: in comparison of whom, we seemed like locusts." (Numbers 13:34) Also, King Og, who was apparently taller than Goliath: "For only Og king of Basan remained of the race of the giants. His bed of iron is shown, which is in Rabbath of the children of Ammon, being nine cubits long, and four broad after the measure of the cubit of a man's hand." (Deut. 3:11) If we allow one cubit for the length of the bed beyond his height, he still would have been 8 cubits tall, or between 11 and 14 and one-half feet tall! There are many stories from all over the world about giants, and although some are certainly exaggerations, there have definitely been some very tall people in history.

The Old Testament is primarily a history of the ancient Israelites. Of course, it mainly describes those cultures that interacted with them, most prominently the Egyptian since it was nearby and Moses was raised as an Egyptian. Abraham was born in Assyria and so they feature prominently as well. The prophecy of Daniel Chapter 2 is generally believed to indicate the Babylonian, Persian, Greek, and Roman empires.

Bible history can be broken up into epochs. One way to break it up is by 2,000-year periods which start with a creation event 6,000 years ago, and are delineated by the times of Abraham at 2,000 B.C., and Jesus, 2,000 years ago. These can be thought of as the time of the patriarchs, the time of the Israelites, and the time of Christ.

Abraham is key to those three epochs since he and Shem, the son of Noah, were contemporaries. Abraham's grandson Jacob was later renamed by God to be Israel, father of the Israelites (Gen. 32:28). Jesus Christ is called the seed of Abraham by St. Paul (Gal. 3:16).

The true religion – the system of worship of the One, True God – can also be broken up into these epochs. Adam spoke directly to God. His grandson Enosh is the first one that the Bible says called upon the name of the Lord (Gen. 4:26). God appeared to Noah and told him to build the ark. After the flood, Noah built an altar to the Lord and sacrificed animals on it (Gen. 8:20).

Abraham also called upon the name of the Lord and built an altar (Gen. 12:8). It was at this time that the promise of his "seed" was made, the promised originally given to Adam (Gen. 3:15). God appeared to Abraham several times, especially in regard to his descendants. God gave both him and his wife new names to signify their importance (Abram to Abraham and Sarai to Sara).

Abraham's nephew, Lot, lived in Sodom with his wife and two daughters just before the destruction of that city. His wife infamously turned into a statue of salt after looking back during their escape (Gen. 19:26). Lot and his daughters fled to a cave, and they got their father drunk and became pregnant by him. The cave is known today as Lot's Cave and is near the Dead Sea where Sodom is supposed to have been. The son of one of the daughters became the father of the Ammonites, from whom Amman, Jordan got its name.

The covenant of circumcision is first mentioned in the Bible with Abraham and his son Ishmael. (Gen. 17:10, 26). God tested Abraham's faith by asking him to sacrifice his son Isaac (Gen. 22:2). Melchizedek, the king of Salem (Jerusalem), priest of God, brought forth bread and wine in the presence of Abraham, signifying the later institution of the sacrifice of the Mass by Christ (Gen. 14:18). Bl. Anne Catherine Emmerich had a considerable amount to say about Melchizedek, claiming that he was an angel who laid out the outlines of future settlements shortly after the flood. St. Paul said that he was "without father, without mother, without genealogy" (Heb. 7:3). There is a Jewish tradition that identifies him with Shem, son of Noah, likely because he was still alive at the time of Abraham.

The covenant of circumcision starting with Abraham was continued by the Israelites. The laws of the Old Testament were given to Moses on Mt. Sinai, where he built an altar and was given the tablets of the law – the Ten Commandments. Joshua led the Israelites into the Promised Land. After that, a series of judges ruled Israel until King Saul, who was followed by King David. King Solomon, son of David, built the first Jewish temple at Jerusalem in about 1000 B.C.

God insinuated that the covenant of circumcision, the Old Testament, was not to be the last. The prophet Ezekiel said that God gave the Israelites some commandments that were not good (Ezekiel 20:25), perhaps indicating that the Old Testament system of law was not complete or the intended final form. Moses told the Israelites that another prophet would rise of their brethren and that they should listen to him (Deut. 18:15, Acts 7:37).

Jesus claimed to complete the old law when he said several times: "You have heard it said …" and then "But I say to you …" (Matt. 5). He also changed the law on divorce (Mark 10). At the last supper he made it clear the he was establishing a New Testament: "For this is my blood of the new testament, which shall be shed for many unto remission of sins." (Matt. 2:28)

3.5 Israel

Jacob, grandson of Abraham through Isaac, was renamed Israel by God. His son Joseph became a great leader in Egypt, a story well known from the Bible. The Bahr Yussef (the waterway of Joseph) is a canal which connects the Nile River with the Fayyum in Egypt. Bl. Anne Catherine

Emmerich said that Joseph and his wife Asenath became known as Osiris and Isis in Egyptian culture.

Many people doubt the historical truth of the story of Moses and the Israelites, and the journey from Egypt to Jericho, with the conquest of the land of Canaan by Joshua. They do not think that any archaeological evidence exists, or that the evidence for it is from the wrong time period.

You could say that modern archaeology started with Napoleon's campaign into Egypt. In 1799, a French soldier found the Rosetta Stone inscribed with Greek, Egyptian demotic, and Egyptian hieroglyphics. The text was identical in all three languages. This led to the deciphering of hieroglyphics, which up until that time had largely been a riddle. Egyptian monuments are full of history written in hieroglyphics.

One difficultly with Egyptian history is that years are measured by the start of dynasties, so the dates given are relative and not absolute. Another difficulty is that the dynasties were carried on from father to son, and it is possible that the father and son ruled at the same time. So the end of the father's reign would not necessarily be the start of the son's reign.

In the movie/book *Patterns of Evidence: Exodus*, Timothy Mahoney describes how Champollion – the man who originally decoded the Rosetta Stone – found the name Shoshenq on a wall in Karnak which he associated with Shishak in the Bible. This fixed the date for both of them at the Biblical 925 B.C. A careful reading of the Shoshenq account and the Shishak account makes it seem impossible that they were the same man. However, Egyptian chronology is fixed around this date, with much of ancient Middle Eastern chronology fixed to the Egyptian.

Additionally, the text of the Bible describing the slavery of the Israelites says that they built the city of Ramesses (Exodus 1:11). The reign of Pharaoh Ramesses II is dated from 1279 to 1213 B.C. That would put the Exodus at about 1250 B.C. Unfortunately, the events described in the book of Exodus and Joshua do not seem to line up with that timeline.

Kathleen Kenyon's estimate of the destruction of Jericho was about 1550 B.C. based on some pottery evidence, which was far removed from the assumed 1250 B.C. Exodus. Her dates cast doubt on the historic veracity of the Bible.

Mr. Mahoney did some investigation and found out that the ancient Egyptian city of Ramesses was built on top of another city, Avaris, as many cities were in ancient times. Furthermore, there was a house found in the city of Avaris which seemed likely to have been associated with Jacob and his sons. There were also twelve tombs nearby with one shaped like a pyramid and having a large statue in it with a coat of various colors. That fits the Biblical story of Jacob's son Joseph very well.

If Avaris was the city where the Israelites lived, then the time of the Exodus would have been earlier. The verse concerning the city of Ramesses in the Bible is an anachronism, that is, a place name is given with the name known at the time of the writing (or editing), but having a different name when the event occurred. Another example in the Bible of an anachronism is in Gen. 14:14. The city of Dan mentioned in that verse was originally called Laish, which we know from Judges 18:29.

Using the dating of Avaris as a basis, the estimate for the Exodus would be about 1450 B.C. That puts the destruction of Jericho at about 1410 B.C., which is a close fit to the actual evidence found there and fits the Biblical timeline. This understanding of time and events shows that the Bible is historically accurate.

In between the Exodus and the destruction of Jericho was the Israelite crossing of the Red Sea and the wandering in the desert. Lack of known evidence has caused modern scholars to question the Bible accounts in this case as well. However, the book *In Search of the Mountain of God: The Discovery of the Real Mt. Sinai* by Robert Cornuke shows that there is archaeological evidence of the Red Sea crossing and the desert wandering, if you look in the right place.

The location of the Red Sea crossing is very contentious, even among Biblical scholars. The description of the crossing itself has been given various interpretations: "And the children of Israel went in through the midst of the sea dried up: for the water was as a wall on their right hand and on their left." (Exodus 14:22) The scene in the movie *The Ten Commandments* shows this very dramatically. Modern scholars scoff at such a miraculous depiction of the event, however.

There is a sort of land bridge across the Gulf of Aqaba near the southern tip of the Sinai peninsula that may have been the site of the crossing. Some people claim to have found chariot wheels in that location.

Another point of contention among Biblical scholars is the location of Mt. Sinai. The traditional location is near the Monastery of St. Catherine in the Sinai Peninsula. That site does not seem to fit the Biblical descriptions of nearby places, however. Further, the Bible says that Sinai is a mountain in Arabia (Galatians 4:25). The Sinai Peninsula has always been considered a part of Egypt, so this seems to indicate that St. Paul believed that Mt. Sinai was not there.

There is a mountain called Jabal al Lawz in Saudi Arabia which seems to be a better fit to the evidence and to the Bible. The top of the mountain is dark, and when Robert Cornuke climbed to the top, the granite rocks there had the appearance of being burnt. The Bible records that when Moses when up to the top of Mt. Sinai, God appeared as fire.

On the path from the Gulf of Aqaba to Jabal al Lawz, Mr. Cornuke found various landmarks that seemed to fit the descriptions given in the Bible. Most striking was a very large rock with a crack down the middle and evidence of water activity at the base. This suggests the rock struck by Moses when the Israelites begged for water (Exodus 17:6).

Overall, there is plenty of archaeological evidence to support the literal interpretation of Biblical events. There is no need to question the accuracy of the Bible in this regard. Those who do question it seem to do so from more of a

The World from Beginning to End and the Era of

philosophical position than a scientific one.

Most scholars recognize that the building of Solomon's temple occurred in about 1000 B.C. Some question the existence of an historical King David, but the Tel Dan stela found in 1993 mentions the "House of David" so that would back him up. The events occurring after that are more or less accepted by scholars, or at least not disputed as much. The final destruction of the Temple in A.D. 70 is almost universally recognized as fact.

Ancient Hebrew society was always patriarchal. This is a reflection of God as Father (Ephesians 3:15). Before the flood, patriarchs governed society. Melchizedek was king of Salem (Jerusalem) during Abraham's time (Gen. 14:18). Although the Israelites did not have kings until Saul, other nations certainly had them. God was not happy with Saul (1 Kings 15:35), but he was happy with David, usually. In the Apocalypse, Jesus is called King of Kings (Apoc. 19:16).

So the governmental norm for the people of God has always been a patriarchal monarchy. Monarchs governed Western society up until the World Wars. It is said that Freemasons instigated those wars in order to rid society of monarchies. They also hate the papacy, which is a monarchy. There are prophecies that say that Antichrist will not come until the Roman Empire is finally ended. Even certain Jews believe that their secular messiah will not come until then.

Modern man has the idea that democracy is the best form of government. It certainly allows for a great deal of freedom, which can unfortunately be turned into a license to do just

Any idea can become law by a majority
)nal freedoms without reference to God's
to justify Satanism. History has shown that
I to be unstable, and they usually descend
ore finally being replaced by a dictatorship.
This is not how God intended society to be ordered.

3.6 Christendom

The life of Jesus Christ as recorded in the Bible, occurred
about 2,000 years ago. The oral traditions of the early
Christians have been handed down through the centuries (2
Thess. 2:14). There are not many extra-Biblical sources
concerning the life of Christ, but there are some.

Herod the Great appears in the Bible and is well known from
other sources. The name Pontius Pilate appears on a stone
found at Caesarea Maritima in 1961. Many relics of the life
of Christ are preserved in various churches throughout the
world, especially the Basilica of the Holy Cross in
Jerusalem, which is actually in Rome. The Holy House in
Loreto, Italy – miraculously transported from Nazareth – is
the house in which he grew up.

Most of the world accepts that Jesus Christ was a person who
lived about 2,000 years ago and that Christianity is based on
his teachings and those of his apostles. However, non-
Christians and naturalists/materialists tend to discount the
stories of miracles, especially when the morality associated
with Christianity interferes with their lifestyle choices.

The fact that Christians believed in one, true God in part

brought on the Roman persecution since the Romans worshipped many gods, as well as the emperor. Christians were also used as scape-goats when things were not going well in the empire, as was famously done by Nero.

The Roman persecution mostly ended when Constantine the Great became emperor and legalized Christianity with the Edict of Milan in A.D. 313. His mother, Helen, is known for discovering the true cross of Jesus Christ in Jerusalem and having various Christian churches built in the Holy Land. Constantine called the Council of Nicea in A.D. 325, which came up with the Nicene Creed as a way of formalizing the basic beliefs of Christians.

The Western Roman Empire degraded steadily after that until it fell in A.D. 476. However, the Eastern Roman Empire, headquartered in Constantinople (modern-day Istanbul), continued to exist until it fell much later in 1453. After the fall of Rome, Christian traditions were maintained in the East as well as in the monasteries of the West, particularly in the Benedictine monasteries. The line of popes was also kept intact.

The rise of Islam provided another challenge to Christianity. The violence and fanaticism of its followers allowed it to spread rapidly through the Middle East and north Africa, as well as into Spain and Europe. If it were not for the victory of Charles Martel at the Battle of Tours in A.D. 732, Europe may have been overrun and Christianity extinguished.

The Crusades were an attempt to protect Christian pilgrims against Muslim attacks. The Crusaders managed to hold parts of the Holy Land for a couple of hundred years starting in 1099 with the capture of Jerusalem by the First Crusade, and ending with the fall of Acre in 1291 – the same year that the Holy House of Loreto was miraculously translated to Tersatto in Dalmatia (Croatia) before being moved to Loreto in 1294. However, several key victories against the Muslims kept them mostly out of Christian Europe. Some of these were the Reconquista of Spain which ended in 1492, the Siege of Malta in 1565, the naval Battle of Lepanto in 1571, and the Battle of Vienna in 1683 – the end of which started on September 11, a date Muslims still remember.

The Holy Roman Empire started with the coronation of Charlemagne in the year A.D. 800. The role of the Holy Roman Emperor was essentially to maintain order in Christendom, in cooperation with the Christian kings and the Pope. Some thought that Charlemagne would marry Irene, the empress of Constantinople, in order to unite East and West, but it was not to be. In A.D. 988, Prince Vladimir I of Russia made Christianity the official religion of Russia.

The Schism of 1054 was the beginning of the East-West split. The second-brightest supernova explosion ever was witnessed that year (the brightest ever happened shortly before in 1006) forming the Crab Nebula – perhaps a sign in the heavens of God's displeasure. The end of the Holy Roman Empire effectively occurred when Napoleon crowned himself emperor in 1804.

There is a mistaken notion that the Middle Ages in Europe were "dark ages" in that the people were ignorant and oppressed. A serious study of history will show that many people at that time were well-educated. The language of scholars and of the Church was Latin, and so people from different countries could communicate with each other. The university system was established at that time; the University of Paris being established in about 1150.

The 13th century is thought by many to be the peak of the Middle Ages and Christendom. Various theologians, religious founders, and kings lived in that period including Sts. Aquinas, Bonaventure, Francis, Dominic, and Kings Louis IX of France and Ferdinand III of Castile. Christian art reached its peak with the construction of the cathedrals of Europe, like Chartres and Notre Dame. Christian philosophy and theology also peaked under St. Thomas Aquinas and his Scholasticism. Although there was not a lack of problems – the sack of Constantinople occurred in 1204 and Frederick II fought the Popes – society was relatively well ordered.

That did not last very long. Interestingly, the period between the deaths of Frederick II and Aquinas (1250-1274) is close to the 25 years of good harvests prophesied at La Salette, and is about the same time that Jesus spent in the Holy Land, if he was about eight years old after returning from Egypt.

You could argue that the end of the Middle Ages was brought on by the Black Death in 1346-1353. During that time, more than half of Europe's population died from the plague which first appeared in an area near the Don river in Russia. Things got so bad that in 1398 St. Vincent Ferrer had an apparition of Christ accompanied by St. Dominic and St. Francis, and was sent to preach penance and prepare men for the coming judgment, which was then averted.

3.7 Renaissance, Reformation, and Revolution

The European Renaissance of the 14th through 17th centuries followed the Black Death. It was a revival of ancient pagan philosophy and art. The work *De Rerum Natura* (On the Nature of the Universe) by Lucretius was rediscovered during that time. It is a work completely devoted to pleasure-seeking with a rejection of religion and morals. Similar materialistic ideas of Epicurus reappeared then also. Michelangelo's *David* was the first life-size freestanding nude statue created since ancient Roman times.

This period marked the beginning of a long line of wars and revolutions that have continued until our day. Whereas the Middle Ages were marked by cooperation between ecclesial and secular power, and between Faith/Religion and Reason/Science, the time since then has been marked by splits and contentions between them.

The Hundred Years' War between France and England lasted from 1337 to 1453. It was primarily fought over control of the region of Aquitaine and the succession to the French throne. It was one of the longest wars in history. During that time, Joan of Arc (1412-1431) managed to get Charles VII crowned king of France, hastening the departure of the English from French soil, and helping to bring an end to the war.

Unfortunately, while England and France were busy fighting each other, Constantinople was falling to the Ottomans. The East appealed for help from the West, but it came too little and too late. Constantinople finally succumbed in 1453, the same year that the Hundred Years' War ended.

The right to self-defense is only denied by strict pacifists. Jesus Christ was not a strict pacifist (Luke 22:36). Nations, likewise, have a right to defend their borders. A nation would commit suicide by allowing an invasion or unlimited immigration. A nation without borders is no nation. The just war theory applies to conditions of war within or between countries. Vigilantism is not justified. If France and England had followed the just war theory, the Hundred Years' War would have been shorter.

The original Catholic-Orthodox split in 1054 had been somewhat healed twice: firstly by the Second Council of Lyons in 1274, and secondly by the Council of Florence in 1439 – where the Byzantines, together with the Russian Orthodox, finally agreed to the Filioque clause in the Nicene Creed and to a definition of the primacy of the Pope. But neither agreement held very long in the East. The saying "Better the Turkish Turban than the Papal Tiara" was attributed to Loukas Notaras, which revealed the distaste of some Orthodox for any apparent subordination to the Western Pope.

In rejecting the primacy of the Pope, the claim of the Orthodox to be the one, true Church rests primarily on their belief that they are the true believers. Why is the Orthodox Church the one, true Church? Because they are the true believers. Who are the true believers? Those who belong to the Orthodox Church. Unfortunately, that is circular reasoning. Their other claim to being the one, true Church rests on supposed miracles like the Holy Fire. There would be many ways of faking that particular phenomenon, so it is hardly a solid foundation for an extraordinary claim. As long as the Greek and Russian Orthodox leaders would rather submit to the local secular ruler instead of the Pope, there is not much hope of an East-West reconciliation, unless the Pope capitulates and agrees to become the "first among equals," which regrettably has been suggested.

At about the same time as the Hundred Years' War, a political dispute in the Catholic Church resulted in the papal residence being moved to Avignon, France from 1309 to 1377. All seven popes at that time were French. Immediately after that, the Western Schism came about from 1378 to 1417. It started with the disputed election of Urban VI and the election of a second pope, Clement VII, who moved back to Avignon. A third pope was elected until finally the schism was ended by the Council of Constance (1414-1418) and the efforts of St. Vincent Ferrer. However, the wars and schisms scandalized many people and caused distrust in leadership.

With the end of the Reconquista in Spain in 1492 (the longest war in history – over 700 years), Isabella and Ferdinand were able to send Columbus on his voyage to the New World. The gold found in Central and South America enriched Spain and made it a world power. A considerable amount of gold was taken at one time when Inca chief Atahualpa paid Spanish conquistador Pizarro a ransom of a room full of gold. Francis Drake was able to pirate some of the Spanish gold for Britain to help build the Royal Navy, which later on defeated the Spanish Armada.

Another event that occurred at the end of the Reconquista was the Spanish Inquisition and the expulsion of Jews and Muslims from Spain. Catholicism was the state religion in Spain and so an attack on the Faith was considered to be an attack on the country as well. The traditional position of the Catholic Church regarding the Jews was that they should not be harmed, but also that they should not be allowed to do harm against Christian society. This was expressed in 1120 by Pope Callixtus II in *Sicut Judaeis*. Many Jews living in Spain converted to Catholicism, but their allegiances were questioned, especially because some of them favored the Muslims during the Reconquista and also because some of the converts continued to practice Judaism. The Inquisition was not nearly so bad as is generally believed, but there were certainly some abuses.

The primary motivation of Isabella in sending Columbus to the New World was to win converts for the Catholic Church. Unfortunately, some of the conquistadors did not have such good intentions. There were many instances of slavery and sexual exploitation. Although the Spanish brought much gold back to Europe, they also brought back syphilis. Isabella's plans were not completely foiled however, although she died in 1504 and did not live to see them realized.

Isabella was born in 1451, two years before the end of the Hundred Years' War and the fall of Constantinople. Spain was in miserable condition in her childhood, primarily due to the negligence of her step-brother, King Henry IV "The Impotent" of Castile. Christendom was not much better off because of the ravages of the war. The Catholic Church was beginning to splinter and would be split even further by Martin Luther in 1517. Eastern Europe was subject to persecution by the Ottomans. It was largely because of Isabella's efforts that Spain and Christendom were restored and the Catholic Faith brought to the New World.

The appearance of Our Lady of Guadalupe in 1531 to Juan Diego started the mass conversion of millions of the natives to the Catholic Faith, effectively replacing those lost to the Protestants in Europe. Up until that time the Americas were the land of the serpent, as evidenced by Serpent Mound in Ohio and extensive serpent imagery in Central and South America. The image of Our Lady still exists today in Mexico City. It has been examined many times and has proven to be miraculous – having no natural explanation. It is interesting that Columbus' ships were the *Nina*, the *Pinta*, and the *Santa Maria* which can be translated: young woman, painted, St. Mary.

During the time that Spain was exploring the New World, trouble was brewing back in Europe. On October 31, 1517, Martin Luther posted 95 theses on the door of the Castle Church in Wittenberg, Germany. There were certainly abuses going on at that time, but Luther went much farther than just correcting abuses. His ideas were a complete overturning of the Catholic Faith. Ideas like "Scripture Alone" (with no tradition or central authority) and "Faith Alone" (with works counting for nothing) are hallmarks of Protestantism, but are not supported by the Bible or by early Christian beliefs. They are just a catalyst for division, which is why there are thousands of Protestant sects today.

The invention of the printing press in the prior decades by Johannes Gutenberg went a long way in accelerating the spread of ideas, some of which were good and many of which were harmful. In fact, the Protestant Reformation probably could not have happened without the printing press. Somewhat ironically, the first book to be printed was the *Gutenberg Bible*, which was an edition of the Latin Vulgate – the Bible written by St. Jerome in the late fourth century and the official Bible of the Catholic Church until the 20th century.

Some people argue that the Catholic Church kept Bibles chained up and only written in Latin so that ordinary people could not read them and know what they really said. In actuality, Bibles were chained up because they were extremely valuable and written in Latin because that was the official language of the Church and the language of scholars. All Catholics were regularly taught lessons from the Bible so they were not ignorant of its contents.

Protestants made their own translations of the Bible which were more in line with their ideas. The King James Bible was completed in 1611 and is even used today by many Protestants. However, the Douay-Rheims Bible was a Catholic Church approved English translation which came out before that. So it cannot be rightly said that the Church was trying to hide the contents of the Bible from the people.

The Protestant rebellion might have passed into oblivion like so many of the early Christian heresies if it were not for Henry VIII (1491-1547). His desire for a male heir at any cost prompted him to proclaim himself head of the Church in England so that he could divorce his first wife, Catherine of Aragon (daughter of Isabella and Ferdinand), and marry another. Even at that, his daughter Mary (1516-1558) almost succeeded in keeping England Catholic. However, Henry VIII's other daughter Elizabeth (1533-1603) by Anne Boleyn, ensured that England remained Protestant.

The Catholic Church realized that all was not well within the Church and that the Protestant Reformation needed to be answered. The Council of Trent was called to do just that and started the Counter-Reformation in the Church. The *Catechism of the Council of Trent*, compiled by St. Charles Borromeo, was written in response to the council and became the handbook of Catholic teaching until the new Catechism came out in 1991. The Mass was also standardized under Pope Pius V and lasted in that form until 1969.

Pope Pius V said in *Quo Primum*, Promulgating the Tridentine Liturgy (1570) that: "Therefore, no one whosoever is permitted to alter this notice of Our permission, statute, ordinance, command, precept, grant, indult, declaration, will, decree, and prohibition. Would anyone, however, presume to commit such an act, he should know that he will incur the wrath of Almighty God and of the Blessed Apostles Peter and Paul."

Wars were fought between Catholics and Protestants until the end of the Thirty Years' War in 1648. Upheavals in religion and society caused many to question their beliefs. Even the natural order of things was called into question. Copernicus published his heliocentric ideas about the time of his death in 1543. Galileo picked up on these ideas and insisted that they must be true, unlike Copernicus who kept them to the hypothetical and thus avoided trouble.

Galileo went to trial in 1633 to answer for his insistence on heliocentrism. The Church was happy to entertain a heliocentric model of the solar system as long as it was just an idea that might produce a better way to determine the date for Easter. St. Robert Bellarmine was the prosecutor for the Church and was very familiar with Scripture and Science.

Bellarmine essentially told Galileo that if it could be proven that the earth revolved around the sun, then the understanding of certain passages of Scripture would have to be reconsidered. However, Bellarmine did not believe that Galileo had absolute proof, and even to this day it cannot be absolutely proven that the earth is moving. We would need an absolute reference frame to do that, and since we cannot view the universe from the outside, we cannot obtain one.

Affected by the disorders of the age, René Descartes (1596-1650) began to consider how one could know anything and ended up famously saying "I think, therefore I am." The Bible refers to God as the "I AM" (Exodus 3:14). Descartes was basically saying that he could determine his own reality in his head.

Thinking that at last they were free of the constraints of the Church and the Bible, forces began to reshape society to their liking. Freemasonry started with the founding of the first Grand Lodge of England in 1717. Started by businessmen, the goal of Freemasonry was essentially to get rid of the monarchies and the Pope, who stood in their way of global domination. During rituals at the highest degrees, a royal crown is stabbed while the inductee says "Down with tyranny!" Also, the papal tiara is stomped while saying "Down with imposture!" These people have an agenda, which has been recorded in *The Permanent Instruction of the Alta Vendita* by John Vennari. It is no wonder that Catholics in the past were automatically excommunicated for being Freemasons. Pope Leo XIII asked his fellow bishops in his encyclical *Humanum Genus*: "earnestly to strive for the extirpation of this foul plague …"

It is well known that the founders of the United States were Freemasons. The US was the first county to be founded without a state religion (Down with imposture!). Any idea of royalty was forbidden (Down with tyranny!). The American Revolution was the model for the French Revolution which had the motto "Liberty, Equality, Fraternity."

The 19th century was marked by wars in the US and Europe. Some people thought that the great meteor storm of the morning of Nov. 13, 1833 was an omen of the US Civil War, since it occurred over much of the area where that war was fought. One of the prophecies from La Salette was that: "In the year 1864, Lucifer, together with a large number of demons, will be unloosed from hell." That was the year that Thomas Huxley founded his subversive X Club. It was also the year that a prayer (see back of this book) was given to Blessed Fr. Louis-Édouard Cestac by the Holy Virgin Mary after seeing a vision of demons swarming over the earth.

The World from Beginning to End and the Era of Peace

On October 13, 1884, Pope Leo XIII had an apparition of God and Satan. The conversation went like this:

Satan: I can destroy your Church.

God: You can? Then go ahead and do so.

Satan: To do so, I need more time and more power.

God: How much time? How much power?

Satan: 75 to 100 years, and a greater power over those who will give themselves over to my service.

God: You have the time, you will have the power. Do with them what you will.

Pope Leo composed the St. Michael prayer after that and had it recited after all Low Masses. (Unfortunately, this practice was halted in 1964.) Thirty-three years to the day after the apparition, the great miracle of the sun occurred at Fatima. It might also be noted that in 1959, 75 years after the apparition and Satan's first estimate of the time he needed for the destruction of the Church, Vatican II was announced. It has been called the French Revolution in the Church. In 1984, 100 years after the apparition and Satan's second estimate, the first World Youth Day was celebrated. Maybe those were not such good ideas.

The wars and revolutions of the 19th century were only topped by those of the 20th century. World War I, the Great War and supposed to be the war to end all wars, caused the death of millions. Not very long after that WWII came along and killed millions more. (Jacinta of Fatima said that many people would die in WWII and that almost all of them would go to hell!) The US followed that up with the Korean War, the Vietnam War, the Gulf Wars, and the War on Terror.

All this time Communism was oppressing the Church and the world. The Bolshevik Revolution occurred in 1917, the same year Our Lady appeared in Fatima. The Cold War was an attempt by the US to contain the spread of Communism and nearly led to a nuclear war during the Cuban missile crisis in 1962.

Bishop Cuthbert M. O'Gara was a Catholic bishop in China during Mao's Communist Revolution which established the People's Republic of China in 1949. He said this about it:

> "When the Communist troops over-ran my diocese they were followed in very short order by the propaganda corps ... an organization, if anything, more disciplined, more zealous, more fanatical, than the People's Army of Liberation itself. The entire population ... was immediately organized into distinctive categories ... Everyone, for a week or more, was forced to attend the seminar specified for his or her proper category and ... in servile submission listen to the official Communist line.

> Now what ... was the first lesson given to the indoctrinees? ... The very first, the fundamental, lesson given was man's descent from the ape – Darwinism! This naturally shocked the Christian ... The non-Christians ... were equally antagonistic to the ape theory because from time immemorial the Chinese people in a nebulous sort of way had

believed in a Supreme Being, in a soul and in an existence after death.

Are you surprised that the Chinese Communists choose Darwinism as the corner-stone upon which to build their new political structure? At first this surprised me ... Later on, when in a Red jail the reason for this unanticipated tactic became very obvious to me. By that time, I knew very well that the primary purpose of the Peoples' Government in Peking was to extirpate all religious belief and practice from China – particularly to destroy utterly the Catholic Church ... The official policy, rigid and ruthless, was transparently clear ... Religion must be destroyed.

Darwinism negates God, the human soul, the after-life. Into this vacuum Communism enters as the be-all and the end-all of the intellectual slavery it has created. In the Red prison in which I was held, the slogan, 'Bring your mind over to us and all your troubles will end,' was hammered into the minds of the prisoners with brutal and numbing monotony. Nothing but a groveling holocaust of the human person can satiate the lust for dominance of Peking's Red regime."

The 1960's was a decade of revolution in the Church and in the world. At the start, in 1960, it was widely known among Catholics that the Third Secret of Fatima was supposed to be released by that year. Pope John XXIII opened it, but decided not to release it, saying that it did not apply to his pontificate. What it said (at least in part) was published on June 26, 2000 and reads as follows:

> The third part of the secret revealed at the Cova da Iria, Fatima, on July 13, 1917.
>
> I [Lucia] write in obedience to you, my God, who command me to do so through his Excellency the Bishop of Leiria and through your Most Holy Mother and mine.
>
> "After the two parts which I have already explained [vision of hell and request to establish devotion to the Immaculate Heart], at the left of Our Lady and a little above, we saw an angel with a flaming sword in his left hand; flashing, it gave out flames that looked as though they would set the world on fire; but they died out in contact with the splendor that Our Lady radiated towards him from her right hand: pointing to the earth with his right hand, the angel cried out in a loud voice: 'Penance, Penance, Penance!' And we saw in an immense light that is God: 'something similar to how people appear in a mirror when they pass in front of it' a bishop dressed in white 'we had the impression that it was the Holy Father.' Other bishops, priests, men and women religious going up a steep mountain, at the top of which there was a big cross of rough-hewn trunks as of a cork-tree with the bark; before reaching there the Holy Father passed through a big city half in ruins and half trembling with halting step, afflicted with pain and sorrow, he prayed for the souls of the corpses he met on his way;

having reached the top of the mountain, on his knees at the foot of the big cross he was killed by a group of soldiers who fired bullets and arrows at him, and in the same way there died one after another the other bishops, priests, men and women religious, and various lay people of different ranks and positions. Beneath the two arms of the cross there were two angels each with a crystal aspersorium in his hand, in which they gathered up the blood of the martyrs and with it sprinkled the souls that were making their way to God."

– Written at Tuy, Spain, January 3, 1944

It is no wonder that he thought, or hoped, that it did not apply to his pontificate! Fr. Malachi Martin (d. 1999) read the whole secret and commented in an interview that Pope John XXIII thought it would ruin his ongoing negotiations with Khrushchev and the Kremlin. It is known that special negotiations occurred between the Vatican and the Kremlin in order to secure the appearance of representatives of the Russian Orthodox Church at Vatican II. This was when communists were persecuting Catholics all over the world.

On October 11, 1962, when Pope John XXIII opened Vatican II, he said:

"We feel we must disagree with those prophets of gloom, who are always forecasting disaster, as though the end of the world were at hand. In the present order of things, Divine Providence is leading us to a <u>new order</u> of human relations which, by men's own efforts and even beyond their very expectations, are directed towards the fulfilment of God's superior and inscrutable designs." [emphasis mine]

Some people suspected the John XXIII was a Freemason, but even if he was not, the Freemasons were very enthused about his pontificate and mourned his death. He used the phrase "new order" – very similar to the Masonic "New Order of the Ages" – in his opening address, after dismissing the "prophets of gloom" who were, without doubt, the Fatima visionaries.

Some other things that Fr. Martin said about the Third Secret in interviews on the Art Bell Talk Show in 1995 and 1998 are: "What is in the secret is more horrible than what you've just read: essentially, the onslaught of natural powers ... terrible catastrophes, chastisements, and that's not the essence of the Third Secret; it's not the frightening one [probably referring to the apostasy in the Church] ... this will fill up the confessionals on Saturday evening. It will fill up the churches with worshippers striking their breasts." Regarding the "new order" he said: "Pope John Paul II is an ardent supporter of a one world government ... He wants to bring in his brand of Christianity, of course. To the UN he said, 'I am a member of humanity.' This is no longer Pius IX and Pius X [who said] 'I am the vicar of Christ.' Completely absent is the Kingship of Christ." He also said that the Third Secret: "... implies that the 'New World Order' now being installed ... is definitely something that will not last, and that is unacceptable to God ... The Third Secret implies this [the New World Order] is the very opposite of the Kingdom of God."

The World from Beginning to End and the Era of Peace

It has long been known that the Freemasons want to establish a world free from the influence of Christian kings and popes. The people behind the Freemasons have philosophies that are contrary to Christianity and they like to accuse anyone who opposes their plans of being racist, anti-Semitic, or homophobic. Charges of Islamophobia most likely stem from the idea that the enemy of my enemy is my friend. That, and the fact that the media never accuse anyone of being Christophobic, tells you who is controlling the media.

These same people control the UN, and by their collusion with non-governmental entities like the Council on Foreign Relations (read their publication *Foreign Affairs* if you want to know their ideas), they essentially control the US federal government as well. They were certainly involved with the 9-11 operation, as documented in *Solving 9-11* by Christopher Lee Bollyn. The Freemasons' "New Order of the Ages" or "New (Socialist) World Order" and its "Rule of Law" (their law, not God's law) is a rejection of the Old Order – Christendom. It is Luciferian in nature and a preparation for the coming of the Antichrist.

Vatican II was a prime opportunity to condemn Communism and consecrate Russia to the Immaculate Heart of Mary. There were efforts to do that, but they were suppressed by the liberals. The effects were disastrous for the Church as well as for society.

In Pope Benedict's farewell address to priests at the Vatican, as reported by L'Osservatore Romano on February 14, 2013, he said:

"And we knew that the relationship between the Church and the modern period was a bit in conflict, beginning with the error of the Church in the case of Galileo Galilei; we thought we could correct this wrong beginning and find the union between the Church and the best forces in the world in order to open up the future of humanity, to open true progress. So we were full of hope, of enthusiasm, and of the will to do our part for this thing." (*Pope Benedict XVI Says Vatican II Was Initiated Because of the 'Error in the Case of Galileo'* by Robert Sungenis, Ph.D.)

You would think that a pope would be more careful about admitting that the Church made an error, since if the Church made an error in the past, it could make an error in the future, and could even be wrong now. The movement of the earth cannot be scientifically proven in an absolute sense even now. We have no sense of the motion of the earth, and so it is a concept that has to be taught.

Anyway, if there were ever a case of misplaced enthusiasm, that remark from Benedict XVI was it. The very next day, Feb. 15, 2013, was the anniversary of Galileo's birth and also the very day a large meteor exploded above Chelyabinsk, Russia. Considering the warnings from Our Lady of Fatima, one should have taken notice.

Although it was distressing that the world seemed to be separating itself from the Church more and more, the solution should not have been to conform the Church to the modern world, but to strive harder to conform the world to the Church as Popes Pius IX, Leo XIII, and Pius X did. St. Paul said: "For I delivered unto you first of all, which I also received" (1 Cor. 15:3) The Church is conservative in nature, conserving that which has been handed down by the apostles. It is the progressives who refuse to understand that, and who are always wanting to change everything and make things "new." That is clear from the fact that their programs start with the word "new" – the New Order of the Mass (Novus Ordo), the New Evangelization, New American Bible, etc.

Ever since the 1960's, the world has scarcely known any peace. The Korean War never officially ended – they just agreed to stop fighting. Wars are continually going on around the globe. It is difficult to keep track of the wars between countries and within countries. Many nations are split between conservatives and liberals. The devil's strategy of "divide and conquer" is working well – for him.

Even within the Catholic Church there are many divisions. Never mind the thousands of Protestant sects. The aftermath of Vatican II was devastating. By just about every statistical measure, the Catholic Church has declined since then. The number of women religious fell drastically. Several cardinals admitted (with approval) that Vatican II was the French Revolution in the Church. They also admitted that the Roman Rite was destroyed. They would know since they instigated it. The bastions have been razed.

The mind of the Church was different at the time of the French Revolution. Pope Pius VI, in a secret consistory on June 17, 1793 (the year that Louis XVI was guillotined) said:

"To this false and mendacious name of liberty, those vaunted patrons of the human race have added the equally deceptive name of equality, as if among human beings who have come together in civil society, although they are subject to various emotions and follow diverse and uncertain impulses according to their individual whims, there ought not be one who by means of authority and force might prevail upon, oblige, moderate, and recall them from their perverse ways of acting to a sense of duty, lest society itself, from the reckless and contrary impetus of many desires, should fall into anarchy and be utterly dissolved."

One huge change in the Church was the innovation of the New Mass, introduced on April 4, 1969. What Catholics had practiced for centuries was forcibly replaced by a Mass that Pope Benedict XVI called "banal." Fr. Annibale Bugnini was the primary author of the New Mass and was suspected of being a Freemason. After the introduction of the New Mass, Catholic churches began looking like Freemasonic temples. Fr. Bugnini was quoted in a March 1965 *L'Osservatore Romano* article as saying: "We must strip from our Catholic prayers and from the Catholic liturgy everything which can be the shadow of a stumbling block for our separated brethren, that is, for the Protestants."

Pope Pius XII gave a warning about that in 1931 before becoming Pope (from pp. 52-53 of Msgr. Roche's biography of Pius XII, *Pie XII Devant L'Histoire* [as reported in *The Remnant* of November 30, 2017 by Christopher Ferrara in *Did Saint Francis Predict Pope Francis?*]):

"Suppose, dear friend, that Communism was only the most visible of the instruments of subversion to be used against the Church and the traditions of Divine Revelation ... I am worried by the Blessed Virgin's messages to Lucia of Fatima. This persistence of Mary about the dangers which menace the Church is a divine warning against the suicide of altering the Faith, in Her liturgy, Her theology and Her soul."

On June 5, 1969, Alfredo Cardinal Ottaviani presented *The Ottaviani Intervention: A Critical Study of the New Mass* to Paul VI, which pointed out serious flaws and deficiencies in the New Mass. In it, the New Mass was said to present "a striking departure" from the Old Mass representing a "grave break with tradition" causing an "agonising crisis of conscience" among the clergy. In justifying his complaints, Cardinal Ottaviani said:

"It has always been the case that when a law meant for the good of subjects proves to be on the contrary harmful, those subjects have the right, nay the duty of asking with filial trust for the abrogation of that law."

Somewhat ironically, the person perhaps most responsible for pushing Cardinal Ottaviani and his Holy Office aside was none other than Joseph Ratzinger, later the head of its replacement, the Congregation for the Doctrine of the Faith (CDF), and still later Pope Benedict XVI. The full name of the Holy Office was the Supreme Sacred Congregation of the Holy Office which used to be known as the Supreme Sacred Congregation of the Roman and Universal

Inquisition. No wonder they changed the name! Anyway, in 1985 Cardinal Henri de Lubac wrote that: "Joseph Ratzinger, an expert at the Council, was also the private secretary of Card. Frings, Archbishop of Cologne. Blind, the old Cardinal largely utilized his secretary to write his interventions. Now then, one of these interventions became memorable: it was a radical criticism of the methods of the Holy Office. Despite a reply by Card. Ottaviani, Frings sustained his critique … It is not an exaggeration to say that on that day the old Holy Office, as it presented itself then, was destroyed by Ratzinger in union with his Archbishop." (Reported by Hilary White on *The Remnant* website on March 12, 2018.)

Pope Paul VI in speaking about the New Mass admitted in a general audience on November 26, 1969 that this "liturgical innovation," this "novelty" would cause "pious persons [to be] disturbed most …" and that the Latin language and Gregorian chant were to be replaced – an action never intended by the Council Fathers:

> "It is here that the greatest newness is going to be noticed, the newness of language. No longer Latin, but the spoken language will be the principal language of the Mass. The introduction of the vernacular will certainly be a great sacrifice for those who know the beauty, the power and the expressive sacrality of Latin. We are parting with the speech of the Christian centuries; we are becoming like profane intruders in the literary preserve of sacred utterance. We will lose a great part of that stupendous and incomparable artistic and spiritual thing, the

> Gregorian chant. We have reason indeed for <u>regret</u>, reason almost for bewilderment. What can we put in the place of that language of the angels? We are giving up something of priceless worth. But why? What is more precious than these loftiest of our Church's values?
>
> The answer will seem <u>banal</u>, prosaic. Yet it is a good answer, because it is human, because it is apostolic. Understanding of prayer is worth more than the silken garments in which it is royally dressed. Participation by the people is worth more – particularly participation by <u>modern</u> people, so fond of plain language which is easily understood and converted into everyday speech." [emphasis mine]

Unfortunately, participation by modern people dropped off drastically after the New Mass was introduced. Clearly the New Mass did not have the intended effect – or did it? Partly for that, Fr. Luigi Villa wrote *Paul VI Beatified?* to stop his beatification, which only proceeded after Fr. Villa died.

Later, in a homily on June 29, 1972, Paul VI observed that: "It is as if … from some crack the smoke of Satan has entered the temple of God." Exorcists acknowledge that demons fear the Latin language. Apparently, the removal of Latin from the liturgy allowed demons to lose their fear of entering the sanctuary.

Belief in the Real Presence of Jesus in the Eucharist also declined after the changes to the Mass, especially after the introduction of the practice of Communion in the hand and the practical elimination of the Eucharistic fast. St. Paul said that anyone receiving Communion unworthily, without belief in the Real Presence, would be condemned, and that some people had become sick or died because of just that (1 Cor. 11:27-30). Persons living in a state of sin should not be receiving the Eucharist.

St. Jane of Chantal had this to say about belief in the Real Presence (taken from *The Divine Savior: A Pictorial Life of Christ*, Benziger Brothers, 1932):

> "So you don't believe that Jesus is present in the Blessed Sacrament! Yet, Christ has declared that He is, and the Church teaches He is. So you mean to say that Our Lord is a liar?! Well, if you said that to the King in my father's house, he perhaps would kill you. And will not God punish you for calling His Son a liar, and not believing what He tells you?"

It is said that "the corruption of the best is the worst." The closest most people can get to God in this life is by receiving Jesus in the Eucharist at the Mass. What was done to the traditional Latin Mass by Bugnini and Paul VI was very similar to what was done by Thomas Cranmer, Protestant Archbishop of Canterbury under Henry VIII in the 16th century. He turned the priest around from the altar and made him a presider at a table, rewrote the words of the Mass and introduced the Book of Common Prayer, and changed the sacrifice of the Mass into the Lord's Supper. The only difference is that Cranmer's goal was to destroy traditional Catholic beliefs and Paul VI's (stated) goal was to increase participation in the Mass and make it easier to understand.

They both had the same effect, however, of turning Catholics into Protestants.

There is a Latin saying: *Lex Orandi, Lex Credendi* (As you pray, so will you believe). The changes in the Mass had a destructive effect on the beliefs of Catholics. Those changes, together with lay participation in the Mass and the moving of tabernacles out of the center of the sanctuary, caused a precipitous drop in religious vocations, and caused many Catholics to stop attending Mass at all.

At the same time as these changes were happening, the form/wording of all the sacraments was changed, as well as the words used during blessings and exorcisms. In traditional baptisms, exorcism prayers are prayed over the infant, and the blessing over holy water traditionally had exorcism prayers. Sermons concerning the Four Last Things – Death, Judgment, Heaven, and Hell – were common before the changes. Absence of talk about hell and evil spirits caused many to doubt their existence. All this led to a drastic decline in the reception of the sacraments, especially Confession, and the acceptance of universal salvation.

Another enormous change in the Catholic Church was its approach to other religions. Throughout the centuries the Church has always declared that "Outside the Church there is no salvation." What that means is that Jesus Christ – in whose name only are we saved (Acts 4:12) – established the Catholic Church as the necessary means of salvation (Matt. 16:18). Joan of Arc said: "About Jesus Christ and the Church, I simply know they are just one thing, and we should not complicate the matter." Jesus Christ is the head of his body, the Catholic Church. If you are not a member of his body, you cannot be saved. This idea prompted a great missionary zeal in the Church (Matt. 28:19-20 – the Great Commission) from its inception until the recent change.

Perhaps the most obvious demonstration of the change in the missionary character of the Catholic Church (at least up until that time) was the first World Day of Prayer for Peace in Assisi, Italy on October 27, 1986. On that day representatives of many of the world's religions were invited by Pope John Paul II to pray to their own gods for peace in the world. This included pagan religions. Once, when asked for a synopsis of his pontificate, a nun replied to the effect that, "He taught us that all religions are equal." Although he never said that and even taught against that idea, she could be forgiven for thinking that, based on his actions.

The Bible says that the gods of the heathens are devils (Psalms 95:5 and 1 Cor. 10:20). Representatives of pagan religions were asked to pray to devils for peace on earth! The Basilica of Assisi was chosen by Pope John Paul II to be the center of the pan-religious meeting. The basilica was hit by an earthquake in 1997 and the table altar was substantially destroyed. God will not be mocked (Gal. 6:7).

Archbishop Marcel Lefebvre said on hearing about that meeting: "He who now sits upon the Throne of Peter mocks publicly the first article of the Creed and the first Commandment of the Decalogue. The scandal given to Catholic souls cannot be measured. The Church is shaken to its very foundations. If faith in the Church, the only ark of salvation, disappears, then the Church herself disappears.

All of her strength, all of her supernatural activity is based on this article of our faith."

It was largely because of Vatican II and its aftermath that Bl. Anne Catherine Emmerich could prophesy in the early 18th century that, "It was shown to me that there were almost no Christians left in the old acceptation of the word."

One excuse modernists give for wanting to make changes in the Church is to bring it back to a poorer, simpler time like it was before Constantine. Not only does that ignore almost 2,000 years of legitimate development, but it takes the world back to a time of paganism and the Church back to a time of persecution. We are experiencing that now.

Today, world leaders and even those in the Catholic Church are constantly tripping over themselves to defend practices that in the past were illegal, sacrilegious, or abhorrent. They seek to erase the past and replace it with their "new order." The duty to God has been replaced by the rights of man. Have they not read the Bible or paid any attention to the warnings given to them?

3.8 Warnings from Heaven

At various times throughout the centuries, mankind has been warned of coming calamities. These are usually associated with disordered behavior. Comets, earthquakes, volcanic eruptions, storms, famines, plagues, pestilences, and wars are all taken as signs of God's displeasure, even among pagans.

Since God does not desire the death of the living (Wisdom 1:13), he will warn mankind before sending disasters. Recently, in 2013, shortly after the resignation of Benedict XVI (February 11 – feast day of Our Lady of Lourdes), lightning stuck St. Peter's twice (February 11 – same day), there were two comets in the sky (Lemmon and Pan-STARRS), two large meteors appeared (2012 DA14 and one over Russia on February 15), and two earthquakes hit near Rome (February 16 and March 3). Many questions surround both the resignation of Benedict XVI and the election of Francis. Perhaps God was sending a message that he does not approve of two living popes. Never before in the 2,000-year history of the Church had a man assumed the title "pope-emeritus" as did Benedict XVI; all previously resigned popes went back to using their former titles and robes.

But God has been warning mankind for a long time. Twelve years before Copernicus published his *De Revolutionibus* (1543), describing his ideas about the motion of the earth around the sun, Our Lady appeared at Guadalupe, Mexico (1531). In the miraculous image left on the cloak of Juan Diego, she appears standing in front of the sun. This apparition occurred near the Temple of the Sun.

It could be understood that Mary appeared in order to warn the natives against the practice of worshipping the sun, since the most important of the Aztec gods was the sun god. There certainly was a mass conversion to the Catholic Church immediately after the apparition.

It could also be understood that Mary was warning mankind

against giving too much importance to the sun from the aspect of heliocentrism. Poet Johann von Goethe said: "But among all the discoveries and corrections, probably none has resulted in a deeper influence on the human spirit than the doctrine of Copernicus." To be displaced from the center of the world was a huge change of thought.

Since you have no sensation of motion while standing on the earth (usually), and the sun appears to move across the sky, to believe that we are moving around the sun is contrary to the senses and is only a mental construct. That kind of thinking leads to cognitive dissonance. Copernicus and Galileo probably caused a bigger change in the conception of the physical world than anyone before them. A change in the understanding of the age and size of the universe would come later with Charles Darwin and Edwin Hubble.

In Quito, Ecuador, both Jesus and Mary appeared to Venerable Mother Mariana de Jesus Torres, a Conceptionist nun from Spain. In 1582, as she was praying before the Blessed Sacrament, she heard a voice say: "This punishment is for the twentieth century." She then saw three swords hanging over Our Lord's head, each with an inscription. On the first was written, "I shall punish heresy"; on the second, "I shall punish blasphemy"; and on the third, "I shall punish impurity."

Mother Mariana had other revelations including:

> "In the nineteenth century a truly Christian president will govern Ecuador [Gabriel Moreno]. At the end of the nineteenth century and throughout a great part

of the twentieth, many heresies will be propagated in these lands."

"The Pope's infallibility will be declared a dogma of Faith by the same Pope chosen to proclaim the dogma of the mystery of my Immaculate Conception [Pius IX]. He will be persecuted and imprisoned in the Vatican through the usurpation of the Pontifical States and through the malice, envy, and avarice of an earthly monarch [Victor Emmanuel II]."

"Unbridled passions will give way to a total corruption of customs because Satan will reign through the Masonic sects, targeting the children in particular to ensure general corruption."

"Unhappy, the children of those times! Seldom will they receive the sacraments of Baptism and Confirmation. As for the sacrament of Penance, they will confess only while attending Catholic schools, which the devil will do his utmost to destroy by means of persons in authority. The same will occur with Holy Communion. Oh, how it hurts me to tell you that there will be many and enormous public and hidden sacrileges!"

"In those times, the sacrament of Extreme Unction will be largely ignored. Many will die without receiving it, being thereby deprived of innumerable graces, consolation, and strength in the great leap from time to eternity."

"The sacrament of Matrimony, which symbolizes the

union of Christ with the Church, will be thoroughly attacked and profaned. Freemasons, then reigning, will implement iniquitous laws aimed at extinguishing this sacrament. They will make it easy for all to live in sin, thus multiplying the birth of illegitimate children without the Church's blessing."

"Secular education will contribute to a scarcity of priestly and religious vocations. The holy sacrament of Holy Orders will be ridiculed, oppressed, and despised, for in this both the Church and God himself are oppressed and reviled, since he is represented by his priests."

"The devil will work to persecute the ministers of the Lord in every way, working with baneful cunning to destroy the spirit of their vocation and corrupting many. Those who will thus scandalize the Christian flock will bring upon all priests the hatred of bad Christians and the enemies of the One, Holy, Roman Catholic, and Apostolic Church."

"The small number of souls who will secretly safeguard the treasure of Faith and virtues will suffer a cruel, unspeakable, and long martyrdom. Many will descend to their graves through the violence of suffering and will be counted among the martyrs who sacrificed themselves for the country and the Church."

"In those times the atmosphere will be saturated with the spirit of impurity which, like a filthy sea, will engulf the streets and public places with incredible license. Innocence will scarcely be found in children, or modesty in women. He who should speak seasonably will remain silent."

"There shall be scarcely any virgin souls in the world. The delicate flower of virginity will seek refuge in the cloisters. Without virginity, fire from heaven will be needed to purify these lands."

"To be delivered from the slavery of these heresies, those whom the merciful love of my Son has destined for this restoration will need great will-power, perseverance, courage, and confidence in God. To try the faith and trust of these just ones, there will be times when all will seem lost and paralyzed. It will then be the happy beginning of the complete restoration. Then will the Church, joyful and triumphant like a young girl, reawaken and be comfortably cradled in the arms of my most dear and elect son of those times. [most likely the Great French Monarch]"

Our Lady asked that a statue of her with the child Jesus be made in her honor. That miraculous statue exists today and twice a year, in February and October, the statue of Our Lady of Good Success is displayed for public veneration.

The revelation that modesty would scarcely be found in women is surely an indictment the latter half of the twentieth century. The standards set by the Church were expressed in a directive issued by the Cardinal-Vicar of Pope

Pius XI, Cardinal Pompili on September 24, 1928 and are as follows: "In order that uniformity of understanding prevail ... we recall that a dress cannot be called decent which is cut deeper that two fingers' breadth under the pit of the throat, which does not cover the arms at least to the elbows, and scarcely reaches a bit beyond the knees. Furthermore, dresses of transparent materials are improper." Even as late as the 1950's, many women followed those standards and were given much more respect.

Women used to cover their heads in church, or even just in public. In St. Paul's First Epistle to the Corinthians, he says that a woman should have a head covering. Catholic Canon Law used to state that women should cover their heads in church. Although the 1983 Canon Law does not mention it, the law has not been abrogated.

The sexes were also more separated in the past, especially before the twentieth century. Our fallen human nature makes us only too prone to illicit relationships. A healthy separation would be beneficial, especially at the pool or at the beach, or at least in the bathroom! Separate schools for boys and girls used to be common. How many affairs have gone on in the workplace?

Our Lady of Fatima revealed that, "The sins which lead most souls to hell are sins of the flesh!" She specifically revealed to Jacinta that: "Certain fashions are going to be introduced which will offend Our Lord very much. Those who serve God should not follow those fashions. The Church has no fashions; Our Lord is always the same ... Woe to women wanting in modesty." Actresses like Katherine Hepburn,

Greta Garbo, and Marlene Dietrich were the first to wear pants in the movies. Women would do well to avoid wearing pants if they do not want to follow those fashions.

St. Padre Pio would not hear the confession of a man dressed in less than a shirt and trousers, or of a woman with a dress shorter than eight inches below the knees. St. Bridget of Sweden had very severe things to say about women who dressed immodestly or even wore makeup. In the West, as late as the early 1900's, makeup was mostly worn by prostitutes. It was made fashionable by companies such as Maybelline (founded by Tom Lyle Williams, the sodomite who invented mascara) so that now most women wear it.

The revelation that innocence would scarcely be found among children reflects the fact that modern children have been exposed to sex education and erotica on television, in the movies, and on the internet from an early age. In past times, children below the age of puberty were not exposed to such things and enjoyed a quiescent period during which time they were free from interests in sexuality. Children today do not enjoy this freedom and have lost their innocence. It is hardly surprising that virginity is disparaged because of the lack of modesty and innocence.

One Bible story in particular teaches a lesson about being properly clothed. The Eighth Chapter of the Gospel of Luke records that when Jesus went to the country of the Gerasens, he met a man who was naked and possessed by a legion of devils. Jesus drove the devils out of the man into a herd of swine, after which the man was found, "sitting at his [Jesus'] feet, clothed, and in his right mind." (Luke 8:35) That suggests people who run around naked are possessed and out of their minds.

Ven. Mary of Agreda (1602-1665) received a series of revelations from the Blessed Virgin Mary concerning various subjects. These revelations are recorded in *Mystical City of God.* In Volume III, The Transfixion, Book Two, Chapter XXIII, there is described a council held in hell by Lucifer and the demons after the death of Jesus Christ. During the council, they discussed how to get more souls to reject God and be sent to hell. Part of what was revealed to Ven. Mary of Agreda was this:

> "They [the demons] resolved to continue to propagate idolatry in the world, so that men might not come to the knowledge of the true God and the Redemption. Wherever idolatry would fail, they concluded to establish sects and heresies, for which they would select the most perverse and depraved of the human race as leaders and teachers of error. Then and there was concocted among these malignant spirits the sect of Mahomet, the heresies of Arius, Pelagius, Nestorius, and whatever other heresies have been started in the world from the first ages of the Church until now ..."

This was a clear warning against religious indifferentism and corruption of the One, True Faith. People who want to "dialogue" with a "religion of peace" should take notice.

Our Lord Jesus Christ appeared to St. Margaret Mary Alocoque in 1689 and asked for the consecration of France to his Sacred Heart. King Louis XIV refused to do it as did his successor, Louis XV. King Louis XVI apparently wrote out a personal vow to the Sacred Heart, but only after the French Revolution started. The monarchy had already fallen, exactly 100 years to the day of the original request on July 16, 1689 (feast of Our Lady of Mt. Carmel).

The modern age of Marian apparitions started in 1830 with revelations to St. Catherine Labouré in Paris. She was given the Miraculous Medal with an image of Mary on it and the inscription: "O Mary, conceived without sin, pray for us who have recourse to thee." This was shortly before Pius IX dogmatically defined the doctrine of the Immaculate Conception of Mary in 1854. It was also the same year that Charles Lyell published his *Principles of Geology* which espoused uniformitarianism, in conflict with the catastrophism of the Biblical Flood.

Our Lady appeared to two shepherd children, Maximin and Melanie, in 1846 at La Salette, France. Individual messages were given to the children, which they were requested to write down for Pope Pius IX. The messages were found in the archives of the Vatican in 1999. It is possible that Melanie received additional messages or did not write the complete message at that time.

The message given to Maximin speaks of the loss of faith in France and of persecution of the Pope. An era of peace is mentioned when all nations would become Catholic with the help of a northern European country. The peace would be short and be ended by a monster, assumed to be the Antichrist.

The message of Melanie was longer but similar. Paris and Marseilles were threatened with destruction and there would be disorder all over the world. Then a great king would help spread religion and a period of peace would occur. The period of peace would be short and be ended with the rise of the Antichrist, born of a religious sister. Later versions of Melanie's message are controversial.

In 1858 the Blessed Virgin appeared at Lourdes, the third approved Marian apparition in France in less than 30 years. She appeared 18 times to St. Bernadette, the first time on February 11, and the last time on July 16, feast of Our Lady of Mt. Carmel. During the third apparition, Our Lady requested Bernadette to come for 15 days, each corresponding to a mystery of the Rosary. Our Lady requested that a chapel be built at Lourdes and revealed that she was the Immaculate Conception. She did not say much to Bernadette, but she did say: "Penance, Penance, Penance. [The same message given by the angel in the Third Secret of Fatima.] Pray to God for sinners. Kiss the ground as an act of penance for sinners." She also said: "I do not promise you happiness in this world, but in the next."

This was one year before Darwin's publication of *On the Origin of Species* in 1859. As if anticipating that, Mary's revelation that she was the Immaculate Conception indicated that she was the only human person conceived without sin. This eliminated the possibility that Adam and Eve were conceived, since they were created sinless, and giving the lie to the evolution of man from apes.

Evolution – the change of one organism into another kind of

organism – has never been observed either in the lab (barring genetic manipulation), in nature, or in the fossil record. Stephen Gould admitted as much in coming up with his "punctuated equilibrium" theory – also called the "hopeful monster" theory – which says evolution happens so fast that it cannot be observed. Is not science supposed to be based on observation?

Two major floods occurred at Lourdes in recent years; one in October of 2012 and another in June of 2013. The one in 2012 occurred when the relics of Pope John Paul II were at Lourdes. At the time, it was noted by Salvatore Pagliuccia, president of UNITALSI, that: "the presence of the reliquary of the blessed on the pilgrimage is a very significant sign, because it represents the presence of his ideas and his sentiments." His ideas and sentiments on evolution and ecumenism would seem to clash with those of Our Lady of Lourdes. The flood in 2013 occurred just before the decree announcing the upcoming canonization of John Paul II was signed. Although he and Ratzinger were thought to be arch-conservatives during their time together as #1 and #2 at the Vatican, they both were known to be quite liberal before Vatican II. What most Catholics do not realize is that their ideas never changed, it was just that the positions of everyone around them shifted to the left after the Council.

In October of 1859, Our Lady of Good Help appeared to Adele Brice near Green Bay, Wisconsin with this message:

"I am the Queen of Heaven, who prays for the conversion of sinners, and I wish you to do the same. You received Holy Communion this morning, and that is well. But you must do more. Make a general confession, and offer Communion for the conversion of sinners. If they do not convert and do penance, my Son will be obliged to punish them."

Twelve years later on October 8, 1871, the most deadly fire in the history of the United States occurred in that area, which is known as the Peshtigo Fire. It was the same night as the more well-known Chicago Fire. The church where Adele fled to from the fire was miraculously spared, however. Apparently, sinners did not convert and do penance. If voluntary penance for sins is not done, it will have to be done involuntarily. That is true in this life as well as in the next.

On January 17, 1871, Our Lady appeared at Pontmain, France in a completely silent apparition lasting three and one-half hours (5:30 PM – 9:00 PM) and occurring in several phases. The vision was perhaps the most visually complex Marian apparition of all time, and had various eschatological themes including the three and one-half hours being the same number of years as the reign of Antichrist. In the vision, Mary appeared inside an oval with three bright stars on the outside and four candles inside, reminiscent of an advent wreath – the time before the end of the world can be called the Second Advent. As the apparition unfolded, the four candles were lit one-by-one, indicating that we may be near the end of the period of the Second Advent.

Our Lady's robe was covered in stars, and the stars in the background of the apparition fell to her feet. This is evocative of the Bible verse (Matt. 24:29) concerning the end times: "… the stars shall fall from heaven …" Messages on a banner also appeared which said, "But pray, my children. God will soon grant your request. My Son allows himself to be moved." 1871 was the same year that Charles Darwin published *The Descent of Man* which speculated that man descended from the apes. The Franco-Prussian War of 1870 ended shortly after this apparition.

The 1871 apparitions in Pontmain occurred in the same year that George Biddell Airy (UK) performed his famous experiment with a water-filled telescope. He attempted to demonstrate the speed of the earth through the ether by filling a telescope with water and comparing observation of starlight between that and a telescope without water. His failure to measure the expected difference is what is known as "Airy's Failure." This troubled Einstein and was part of his motivation to develop his Relativity theories.

It could be argued that the three bright stars on the outside of the oval in the Pontmain apparition indicate that only the Holy Trinity knows the true operation of the universe, since only God can view it from the outside. As late as the early 1900's, many scientists still believed in heliocentrism. Our Lady's message could also be interpreted in English as: "My sun allows himself to be moved." This could be considered as a direct answer from heaven as to whether it is the earth or the sun that moves.

Our Lady appeared at Knock, Ireland on August 21, 1879. It was a completely silent apparition where she appeared with St. Joseph and St. John the Evangelist, with an altar having a lamb on it surrounded by angels. St. John was dressed as a bishop standing on the gospel side of an altar and held open a book. It occurred on the same day that a coronation of Our Lady of La Salette was happening in France. This seemed to be a verification of the earlier messages of La Salette, which had been suppressed.

It is interesting that the image of St. John holding a book on the gospel side of the altar was so prominent, considering that the last Gospel of St. John was removed from the Novus Ordo Mass in 1969. It has been suggested that the last Gospel was removed because it has the phrase, "He came unto his own, and his own received him not." (John 1:11) which could be offensive to Jews – just like the Good Friday prayers for the conversion of the Jews were modified for the same reason. One part of the message of Our Lady of La Salette to Maximin was: "Before all that arrives [the conversion of nations], great disorders will arrive, in the Church, and everywhere." Might not some of the great disorders in the Church be related to the changes to the Mass? The place where the Knock apparitions happened makes one think of the verse, written by St. John: "Behold, I stand at the gate, and knock. If any man shall hear my voice, and open to me the door, I will come in to him, and will sup with him, and he with me." (Apoc. 3:20)

In 1917 Mary appeared to three children in a series of six apparitions in Fatima, Portugal. At the time, WWI was being fought and the Bolshevik Revolution in Russia was brewing. Our Lady of Fatima told Jacinta, one of the children, that "wars are punishments for sins of the world."

Before the six apparitions of Mary, the children had three

apparitions of an angel. Just before the second apparition of the angel, the children were outside playing. Suddenly, the angel appeared and said: "What are you doing? Pray! Pray a great deal! The Sacred Hearts of Jesus and Mary have merciful designs concerning you. Offer prayers and sacrifices constantly to the Most High!"

It is said that the sins of the modern age are the loss of the sense of sin and the wasting of time, mostly with sports and electronic media. Our Lord asked the apostles in the Garden: "Could you not watch one hour with me?" (Matt. 26:40) If people spent as much time in prayer as they did with sports or other entertainment, the world would be a much better place. St. Paul says to work out your salvation with fear and trembling (Phil. 2:12). The Fatima children certainly did not waste any more time after the second apparition of the angel!

At the first apparition of Fatima, Lucia asked the Blessed Virgin if a recently deceased girl was in heaven. Our Lady said that she was with her. She asked about a second girl and Our Lady said that she would be in purgatory until the end of the world. If we waste the time given to us on earth to atone for our sins, we will have to make up the time in purgatory, assuming that we avoid going to hell. At the fourth apparition of Fatima, the Blessed Virgin said: "Pray, pray very much and make a sacrifice for sinners, because many souls are going to hell because no one offers sacrifices for them." So we are our brother's keeper.

The message of the apparitions of Our Lady was that people needed to amend their lives. Our Lady specifically recommended reciting the Rosary, and by way of her appearance as Our Lady of Mount Carmel, the wearing of the brown scapular. (Our Lady told St. Simon Stock: "Whosoever dies clothed in this habit [scapular] shall not suffer the fires of hell."). She said during the third apparition of July 13, 1917, after a vision of hell during which the visionary Lucia said she would have died if she had not already been promised by Our Lady to be taken to heaven:

"You have seen hell where the souls of poor sinners go. To save them, God wishes to establish in the world devotion to my Immaculate Heart. If what I say to you is done, many souls will be saved and there will be peace. The war is going to end: but if people do not cease offending God, a worse one will break out during the Pontificate of Pius XI [name of future pope]. When you see a night illumined by an unknown light [occurred January 25, 1938], know that this is the great sign given you by God that he is about to punish the world for its crimes, by means of war [WWII], famine, and persecutions of the Church and of the Holy Father. To prevent this, I shall come to ask for the consecration of Russia to my Immaculate Heart, and the Communion of reparation on the First Saturdays. If my requests are heeded, Russia will be converted, and there will be peace; if not, she will spread her errors throughout the world, causing wars and persecutions of the Church. The good will be martyred; the Holy Father will have much to suffer; various nations will be annihilated. In the end, my Immaculate Heart will triumph. The Holy Father will consecrate Russia to me, and she shall be converted, and a period of peace will be granted to the world. In Portugal, the dogma of the faith will always be preserved, etc."

This vision of hell verified that it is a place that you can go and that it is not empty, contrary to those who would wish otherwise. It was also a stark reminder that God is offended by sin and does punish people in order to get them to amend their lives, if they will not do it otherwise. Jacinta was obsessed with this vision of hell for the rest of her life. It seemed to be a warning against the relativism that would soon permeate the world, in no small part because of the propagation of Einstein's Theory of Relativity.

Einstein did not believe in a personal God. He had very little respect for the Bible or the Church. He said in an address to Princeton Theological Seminary: "For example, a conflict arises when a religious community insists on the absolute truthfulness of the Bible. This means an intervention on the part of religion into the sphere of science; this is where the struggle of the Church against the doctrines of Galileo and Darwin belongs." Obviously, Einstein favored the doctrines of Galileo and Darwin over the doctrines of the Catholic Church, probably because of his multiple mistresses. You can bet that if he thought the Church and Bible with their sexual morality could have been proven wrong by geocentrism and a young earth, he would have been very favorable to those concepts.

The apparitions at Fatima were confirmed by a miracle announced months in advance, on October 13, 1917. That day, about 70,000 people had gathered to witness the miracle, and they were soaked by a downpour of rain.

As predicted, Our Lady appeared and requested a chapel be built in her honor. She foretold the end of WWI and said that people must amend their lives and ask forgiveness for their sins. She added, "Let them offend Our Lord no more for he is already much offended." After that, there occurred the famous miracle of the sun and three scenes, representing the Joyful, Sorrowful, and Glorious mysteries of the Rosary, which only the children saw.

In the first scene, the Holy Family appeared (Jesus, Mary, and Joseph). In the second scene, there appeared a vision of Our Lady of Sorrows and of Our Lord as a man of sorrows (Isaiah 53:3). In the third scene, Our Lady of Mount Carmel appeared crowned as Queen of heaven and earth, holding the child Jesus near her heart.

The rest of the people present saw the sun dancing in the sky, shooting off various colors. It also appeared to plunge toward the earth which prompted many to openly confess their sins. Even the atheists present had to acknowledge that something supernatural had occurred.

One of the most amazing aspects of the event was that, even though the miracle only lasted a few minutes, the ground and the clothes of the people were completely dry right after it was over. Someone estimated the energy required to do that on a natural basis. If that amount of energy had been released in such a short time, ordinarily the people would have been incinerated. Anyone doubting the miracle would have a hard time coming up with an explanation of that.

After the apparitions and the death of visionaries Jacinta and

Francisco, Mary appeared again to Lucia in Tuy, Spain on
June 13, 1929 and requested the consecration of Russia:

> "The moment has come in which God asks the Holy
> Father to make, in union with all the bishops of the
> world, the consecration of Russia to My Immaculate
> Heart, promising to save it by this means. So
> numerous are the souls which the justice of God
> condemns for sins committed against Me, that I come
> to ask for reparation. Sacrifice yourself for this
> intention and pray."

Some people who give importance to 100-year periods think
the year 2029 (1929 + 100) might be significant in this
context. Unfortunately, the consecration of Russia was not
done in 1929 and Jesus appeared to Lucia in Rianjo, Spain
in 1931 to complain of it. Lucia wrote that Our Lord told
her:

> "Make it known to My ministers, given that they
> follow the example of the King of France in delaying
> the execution of My command [the request to
> consecrate France to the Sacred Heart in 1689], they
> will follow him into misfortune. It is never too late to
> have recourse to Jesus and Mary."

In another description of the event, Lucia wrote that:

> "They did not wish to heed My request! Like the
> King of France they will repent of it, and they will do
> it, but it will be late. Russia will have already spread
> its errors in the world, provoking wars and
> persecutions against the Church. The Holy Father

The World from Beginning to End and the Era of Peace

will have much to suffer."

One may wonder why Our Lord was so insistent that Russia be consecrated to the Immaculate Heart of Mary. It seems that he wants Our Lady to receive the recognition due to her for being worthy to be his Mother. Also, Russia is the largest country on earth and was once Catholic, before the Orthodox split. Additionally, it is the country which was most instrumental in spreading atheistic Communism.

Various popes since the apparition have attempted to consecrate Russia as requested by Our Lady. The most recent consecrations were done by Pope John Paul II at Fatima in 1982 and 1984. Russia was not mentioned by name, however. There have been many arguments about whether or not that sufficed, but without a mention of Russia by name and participation by the all bishops of the world, it does not seem like it has fully been done. Even a child must be baptized by name, so naming Russia would seem to be a requirement. At Fatima on May 13, 2010, Pope Benedict XVI said that: "We would be mistaken to think that Fatima's prophetic mission is complete."

It is interesting to note that in 1982 and 1984, Apollo 15 astronaut Jim Irwin made expeditions to Mt. Ararat to search for Noah's Ark. Ed Davis claimed to have sighted Noah's Ark in the summer of 1943, the year after Pope Pius XII consecrated the human race to the Immaculate Heart of Mary. In 1929, the Blessed Virgin Mary requested that Russia be consecrated to her Immaculate Heart, which was the same year that Woolley found the "flood layer" at the city of Ur. Perhaps when the Pope and the bishops consecrate Russia by name to the Immaculate Heart of Mary as requested, the location of Noah's Ark will become generally known. That could change the worldview of many, to the degree of Columbus' discovery of America.

Although the Pope and the bishops are the ones who would have to consecrate Russia in order to fulfill the first half of Mary's request, any Catholic can help fulfill the other half – the Communion of reparation on the First Saturdays. This can be accomplished by doing the following on the first Saturday of five consecutive months: 1.) Receiving Holy Communion worthily, 2.) Going to sacramental Confession within eight days; before or after, 3.) Praying at least five decades of the Holy Rosary, and 4.) Meditating for fifteen minutes on the mysteries of the Rosary. Perhaps when enough reparation is done, the consecration will happen.

This must be done with the intention of making reparation for offences against the Immaculate Heart of Mary. Our Lady promised to anyone who would make the five First Saturdays that she would assist them at the hour of their death, with the graces necessary for salvation.

Our Lord revealed to Lucia the reason why the devotion was to be carried out on five consecutive Saturdays: "My daughter, the reason is simple. There are five types of offences and blasphemies committed against the Immaculate Heart of Mary: 1.) Blasphemies against the Immaculate Conception, 2.) Blasphemies against her virginity, 3.) Blasphemies against her divine maternity, in refusing at the same time to recognize her as the [spiritual] Mother of men, 4.) Blasphemies of those who publicly seek to sow in the hearts of children, indifference or scorn or even hatred of this Immaculate Mother, and 5.) Offences of those who outrage her directly in her holy images."

There have been various apparitions of Mary in the world since 1917, although not many have been approved by the Church. Two happened in the year 1933 in Belgium: at Beauraing (last apparition in 1933) and at Banneux. The repeated message given by Our Lady at Beauraing and Banneux was to "Pray much." The rise of the Nazi party, or German National Socialism began in 1933, when Adolf Hitler was named chancellor of Germany.

Near Rome itself, Our Lady of Revelation appeared in 1947 to a fallen-away Catholic who had made himself an enemy of the Church, Bruno Cornacchiola (d. 2001). Although the messages are not officially approved, two popes (Pius XII and John Paul II) have blessed statues of Our Lady of Revelation, and Masses are permitted on the spot of the apparition, near the Church of St. Paul at the Three Fountains. In 1997, Pope John Paul II approved the renaming of the place to "Holy Mary of Third Millennium at Three Fountains."

The earth of the grotto there is reported to have miraculous healing properties. On the evening of April 12, 1980 (thirty-third anniversary of the apparition) thousands of faithful gathered at Three Fountains and watched a miracle of the sun similar to what had happened in Fatima on October 13, 1917. This was repeated in 1986.

A book recently came out about that apparition: *The Seer –*

The Secret of the Three Fountains, by Saverio Gaeta, publisher Salani, Milan, 2016. Some of the messages are:

> Before Russia is converted and leaves the path of atheism, a tremendous and severe persecution will be unleashed. Pray it can be stopped.

> From the east a strong people, but far from God, will launch a terrible attack, and will break the most sacred and holy things. The world will go into another war, the most ruthless of all.

> Outside the Apostolic and Roman Catholic Church there is no salvation.

> The shepherds of the flock are not fulfilling their duty. Too much of the world has entered into their souls, giving scandal to the flock and diverting them from the path.

> False prophets, who seek by all means to poison souls, changing the doctrine of Jesus into satanic doctrines, they will take away the sacrifice of the cross that is repeated on the altars all over the world.

> Satan now reigns in all the highest command posts. Satan will enter in the leading places of the Church.

> You must offer yourself as a victim for the conversion and the sanctification of priests and religious, who have abandoned the path of doctrine and of morality, losing the strength of salvation; because of them, many souls go to hell.

An approved apparition occurred in Akita, Japan in 1973, the same year that abortion was legalized in the United States. Our Lady appeared to Sr. Agnes Sasagawa with several messages that seemed to be a confirmation of previous apparitions. Howard Dee, former Philippine ambassador to the Vatican, stated that "Cardinal Ratzinger [future Pope Benedict XVI] personally confirmed to me that these two messages, of Fatima and Akita, are essentially the same." (*Inside the Vatican* magazine, 1998)

A message on August 3, 1973 contained these words:

> "My daughter, my novice, do you love the Lord? If you love the Lord, listen to what I have to say to you. It is very important ... You will convey it to your superior.

> Many men in this world afflict the Lord. I desire souls to console him to soften the anger of the Heavenly Father. I wish, with my Son, for souls who will repair by their suffering and their poverty for the sinners and ingrates.

> In order that the world might know his anger, the Heavenly Father is preparing to inflict a great chastisement on all mankind. With my Son, I have intervened so many times to appease the wrath of the Father. I have prevented the coming of calamities by offering him the sufferings of the Son on the cross, his Precious Blood, and beloved souls who console him forming a cohort of victim souls. Prayer, penance and courageous sacrifices can soften the

Father's anger."

On October 13, 1973 – the anniversary of the miracle at Fatima – Our Lady told Sr. Agnes this:

"As I told you, if men do not repent and better themselves, the Father will inflict a terrible punishment on all humanity. It will be a punishment greater than the deluge, such as one will never have seen before. Fire will fall from the sky and will wipe out a great part of humanity, the good as well as the bad, sparing neither priests nor faithful.

The survivors will find themselves so desolate that they will envy the dead. The only arms which will remain for you will be the Rosary and the sign left by my Son. Each day recite the prayers of the Rosary. With the Rosary, pray for the Pope, the bishops and priests.

The work of the devil will infiltrate even into the Church in such a way that one will see cardinals opposing cardinals, bishops against bishops. The priests who venerate me will be scorned and opposed by their confreres ... churches and altars will be sacked; the Church will be full of those who accept compromises, and the demon will press many priests and consecrated souls to leave the service of the Lord.

The demon will be especially implacable against souls consecrated to God. The thought of the loss of so many souls is the cause of my sadness [her statue

wept]. If sins increase in number and gravity, there
will be no longer pardon for them … Pray very much
the prayers of the Rosary. I alone am able still to
save you from the calamities which approach. Those
who place their confidence in me will be saved."

This message testifies to the historical fact of Noah's Flood
(deluge). It is also a confirmation of the hatred of the devil
for the Church and religious. We see disagreements between
bishops and cardinals today. The Communist Party has
worked against the Catholic Church from its inception.

Bella Dodd, who was a Communist before converting to the
Catholic Faith said in a 1950 lecture at Fordham University
that: "In the 1930's we put eleven hundred men into the
priesthood in order to destroy the [Roman Catholic] Church
from within." She also said that: "Right now they [the
Communist infiltrators] are in the highest places in the
Church." She further said that the changes planned by the
Communists for the Church would be such that when they
were done: "You will not recognize the Catholic Church."
This is confirmed by the book *AA-1025*.

In 1995 at Civitavecchia, Italy, a statue of Our Lady Queen
of Peace started weeping blood. The local bishop, Girolamo
Grillo, was favorably disposed toward the apparitions,
although official approval seemingly was not given. The
visionary Jessica Gregori was given messages including the
Third Secret of Fatima, which she was able to confirm in a
conversation with Sr. Lucia. The message of July 30 was:
"Satan controls all of humanity and is now trying to destroy
the Church of God with the help of many priests."

We have heard many times about the mercy of God, but these messages and those of Fatima are a stark reminder of His justice, which made the Redemption necessary. If the sacrifice of Jesus on the cross was necessary for the reconciliation of all mankind with God, then the followers of Jesus would have to expect to imitate their Lord: "If any man will come after me, let him deny himself, and take up his cross, and follow me." (Matt. 16:24)

3.9 Power of the Rosary

In the midst of so many warnings, you would think that people would eventually get the point and respond. At Fatima and at Akita the recommended prayer to God was the Rosary. At Fatima, Our Lady promised to take the visionary Francisco to heaven, but that he first must say many Rosaries. He responded by saying that he would say as many Rosaries as she wanted.

Tradition holds that St. Dominic (1170-1221) devised the Rosary as we know it, with three sets of mysteries of the Christian Faith (Joyful, Sorrowful, and Glorious) composed of five decades each (10 Hail Mary "Ave Maria" prayers). It was a development of prayers recited in the Middle Ages. Monks used to say all 150 Psalms each day, but that was reduced to 150 Our Father ("Pater Noster") prayers. Strings of beads were used to count them which became known as Paternosters. Eventually, the Ave Maria prayer became associated with the Psalms and the events of the lives of Jesus and Mary, which led to it being referred to as a Rosarium ("rose garden") or "Mary's Psalter."

In 2002, Pope John Paul II wrote a letter
(*Rosarium Virginis Mariae*) with a "prop
the Luminous Mysteries of the Rosary, fou
lifetime of Jesus between his baptism and death.
popes throughout the centuries have heartily recommende
the recitation of the Rosary, noting the appropriateness of the
150 Ave's. It was suggested to Pope Paul VI to update the
Rosary, but he responded that the "faithful would conclude
that 'the Pope has changed the Rosary,' and the
psychological effect would be disastrous ..." Some things
are better left alone.

The 150 Ave's in a full Rosary, with the standard three Ave's
at the beginning, is reminiscent of the 153 fish caught by the
apostles as recorded at the end of John's Gospel. The 15
days that St. Bernadette was requested to visit the grotto at
Lourdes, France are evocative of the 15 mysteries. There are
15 promises of Our Lady made to St. Dominic and Bl. Alan
de la Roche corresponding to the 15 mysteries:

1.) To all those who shall recite my Rosary devoutly, I
promise my special protection and very great graces.

2.) Those who shall persevere in the recitation of my Rosary
shall receive some signal grace.

3.) The Rosary shall be a very powerful armor against hell;
it will destroy vice, deliver from sin, and dispel heresy.

4.) The Rosary will make virtue and good works flourish,
and will obtain for souls the most abundant divine mercies;
it will substitute in hearts love of God for love of the world,
and will lift them to the desire of heavenly and eternal things.

ow many souls shall sanctify themselves by this means!

5.) Those who trust themselves to me through the Rosary, shall not perish.

6.) Those who shall recite my Rosary devoutly, meditating on its mysteries, shall not be overwhelmed by misfortune. The sinner shall be converted; the just shall grow in grace and become worthy of eternal life.

7.) Those truly devoted to my Rosary shall not die without the sacraments of the Church.

8.) Those who recite my Rosary shall find during their life and at their death the light of God, the fullness of his graces, and shall share in the merits of the blessed.

9.) I shall deliver very promptly from purgatory the souls devoted to my Rosary.

10.) The true children of my Rosary shall enjoy great glory in heaven.

11.) What you ask through my Rosary, you shall obtain.

12.) Those who propagate my Rosary shall be aided by me in all their necessities.

13.) I have obtained from my Son that all the members of the Rosary Confraternity shall have for their brethren the saints of heaven during their life and at the hour of death.

14.) Those who recite my Rosary faithfully are all my beloved children, the brothers and sisters of Jesus Christ.

15.) Devotion to my Rosary is a great sign of predestination.

The Rosary devotion is so powerful in part because the meditations on the mysteries unite us with the lives of the only two completely sinless people to walk the face of the earth – Jesus and Mary. In order to be pleasing to God, we should imitate those who were most pleasing to him. St. Louis de Montfort wrote the book *True Devotion to Mary* to describe the appropriate devotion that we should have.

St. Dominic is attributed with saying: "One day, through the Rosary and the [brown] scapular, Our Lady will save the world." Pius IX, the much-embattled Pope, exclaimed: "Give me an army saying the Rosary and I will conquer the world!" When looking for his rosary beads, St. Padre Pio is known to have said: "Where is my weapon?"

Various events of the past demonstrate the power of the Rosary. One of the most famous was the Battle of Lepanto in 1571, the battle that saved the Christian West from defeat at the hands of the Ottoman Turks.

Selim II (1524-1574), known as "Selim the Sot", was the son of Suleiman the Magnificent. He was looking for a military victory to carry on the tradition of his father. He first turned to Cyprus, which was quickly overrun. Next was Italy.

Pius V was Pope at the time. During his six-year reign (1566-1572), he promulgated the Council of Trent, published the works of Thomas Aquinas, issued the *Roman Catechism* and a new missal and breviary, created 21 cardinals, and excommunicated Queen Elizabeth I of England. Concerned about the survival of Christendom, he called upon the princes of Europe and founded the Holy League on March 7, 1571. The man chosen to lead the Holy League in battle was Don John of Austria. After assembling a fleet of ships, they sailed out to meet the Turks.

Pope Pius V, realizing that the Muslim Turks had a clear military advantage, called upon all of Europe to pray the Rosary for victory. Every man in the Christian fleet was given a rosary to pray. The Archbishop of Mexico had an exact copy of the image of Our Lady of Guadalupe sent to King Philip II, who in turn gave it to Andrea Doria, one of the three admirals of the fleet, who placed it in his cabin.

At dawn on October 7, 1571, the Holy League rowed down the west coast of Greece and turned east into the Gulf of Patras. When the morning mist cleared, the Christians, rowing directly against the wind, saw the squadrons of the larger Ottoman fleet arrayed like a crescent from shore to shore, bearing down on them under full sail. Apparently with divine intervention, the wind shifted 180 degrees.

The battle began at midday and lasted about five hours. During the battle, Pope Pius V, accompanied by many faithful, was praying the Rosary in the Basilica of Saint Mary Major. The result was that all but 13 of the nearly 300 Turkish vessels were captured or sunk and over 30,000 Turks were slain. Not until WWI would there again be so many casualties in a single battle. Pius V saw in a vision the victory of the Christians saying, "Let us return thanks to God for victory over the Turks."

In thanksgiving for the victory at Lepanto, on the first

The World from Beginning to End and the Era of Peace

Sunday of October 1571, Pope Pius V ordered that the Rosary should be commemorated on that day. This was later extended to the Universal Church, and is celebrated as the feast of Our Lady of the Holy Rosary on October 7.

Miguel de Cervantes, a Spanish soldier wounded in the battle, was so inspired by the event that he incorporated elements of it in his novel, *Don Quixote*. G. K. Chesterton wrote the poem *Lepanto* about it. Hilaire Belloc called it Chesterton's greatest poem and the greatest poem of his generation.

Even today, at the Royal Monastery of Santa Maria of Guadalupe, a large warship lantern captured from the Turkish ships at Lepanto can be seen. In Rome, the ceiling of Santa Maria in Aracoeli is decorated with gold taken from the Ottoman galleys. A large Turkish flag from Lepanto is kept as a trophy in the Doges Palace in Venice. In Rome at Saint Mary Major Basilica, there used to be a captured flag close to the tomb of Pope Pius V. This flag was returned to Turkey in 1965, as a friendly gesture.

Other victories associated with the Rosary are:

1.) The Victory of Muret (1213): A vastly outnumbered Count Simon de Montfort defeated the Albigensians on Sept. 12, while St. Dominic and his friars prayed the Rosary.

2.) La Rochelle, France (1627): When King Louis XIII went to war against the Huguenots, he asked his subjects to pray the Rosary with the victory of France as their intention.

3.) The Battle of Vienna, Austria (1683): The battle started on September 11. King Jan III Sobieski of Poland led the Christians to victory over Pasha while many people prayed the Rosary. This was the last time the Turks seriously threatened Europe until now. Pope Innocent XI set the feast of the Holy Name of Mary to September 12 in memory of the battle. The croissant was invented to celebrate it.

4.) The Battle of New Orleans (1815): Gen. Andrew Jackson led a small American army to victory against the British at the end of the War of 1812. During the battle, many of the soldiers' families gathered and prayed the Rosary.

5.) Bombing of Hiroshima, Japan (1945): A priest and seven other men living near ground zero survived the blast. They attributed their survival to living the message of Fatima.

6.) Communists leave Austria (1955): A Franciscan priest named Father Petrus remembered the story of Lepanto and launched a Rosary crusade. On May 13, 1955, the anniversary of the first apparition of Our Lady at Fatima, the Russians left Austria without a shot being fired.

7.) Philippine's People Power Revolution (1986): Ferdinand Marcos was ruling the Philippines as a dictator when political rival Benigno Aquino returned in 1983. His assassination sparked outrage. Jaime Cardinal Sin urged the people to prayer and peaceful resistance. Tanks were met with Rosaries. In 1986, Marcos fled the country.

4 THE ERA OF PEACE

4.1 Prelude – Minor Chastisement

The cycles of history are marked by decline and restoration, since those who do not know history are doomed to repeat it. The world has been in a precipitous moral decline ever since the 1960's – the era of sexual promiscuity, hallucinogenic drug usage, and Rock and Roll music. We are at the point where things that were previously considered evil are now put forth as good. Consensual sexual relations of any type are considered to be legitimate. The killing of a child is considered to be a woman's choice. Killing of the sick and elderly is considered to be "mercy." Marriage between persons of the same sex is considered to be a matter of equal rights. Gender confusion is rampant.

The Bible warns against this:

> "Woe to you that call evil good, and good evil: that put darkness for light, and light for darkness: that put bitter for sweet, and sweet for bitter." (Isaiah 5:20)

> "You have wearied the Lord with your words, and you said: Wherein have we wearied him? In that you say: Every one that does evil is good in the sight of the Lord, and such please him: or surely where is the

God of judgment?" (Malachi 2:17)

The technology that can send words and images around the world in an instant is mostly not being used to spread the gospel, but instead is being used to corrupt the morals of society. Much of what is available on the internet is pornographic or erotic. The same technology is being used for global surveillance.

Music can even be used to bad effect. The term "Rock and Roll" is actually a term for sexual intercourse. The tritone ("Chord of Evil") was thought to be evil in the early days of music. In the book *Heaven is for Real*, Colton Burpo asked the angels to sing the song *We Will Rock You* (by Queen) but they refused. It is known that drumbeats can be used to summon devils.

Those wanting to control the world by force or bribery know that the quickest way to enslave a population is to corrupt religion and morals. The strongest religious and moral force of the last 2,000 years has been Christianity. That is why the greatest efforts of those wanting to dominate the world are directed against the Catholic Church and traditional Christian values.

The Bible predicts efforts against Christianity will one day culminate in the form of the Antichrist. He will reign for three and one-half years, immediately before the end of the world. His reign will be the Major Chastisement as the Bible says: "And unless the Lord had shortened the days, no flesh should be saved: but for the sake of the elect which he has chosen, he has shortened the days." (Mark 13:20)

What we are experiencing now, and is about to come to a climax, is the Minor Chastisement. It will end with an event that has been called the "Three Days of Darkness." This will mark the end of the penultimate cycle of history and the start of the Era of Peace. Only a minority of mankind will survive this event. It has been foretold by several visionaries.

One of the most complete descriptions of events to take place until the end of the world was given to Melanie Calvat – the visionary of La Salette. Our Lady appeared to her on September 19, 1846 as she was tending cattle with Maximin Giraud. She appeared to them dressed in royal garments and a crown of roses, while weeping as she told them of future calamities to befall the world because of the sinfulness of mankind:

> "Come, my children, fear not, I am here to proclaim great news to you. If my people do not wish to submit themselves, I am forced to let go of the hand of my Son. It is so heavy and weighs me down so much I can no longer keep hold of it. I have suffered all of the time for the rest of you! If I do not wish my Son to abandon you, I must take it upon myself to pray for this continually. And the rest of you think little of this. In vain you will pray, in vain you will act, you will never be able to make up for the troubles I have taken over for the rest of you." [emphasis mine]

> "I gave you six days to work, I kept the seventh for myself, and no one wishes to grant it to me [Jesus' complaint]. This is what weighs down the arm of my

Son so much. Those who drive carts cannot speak without putting the name of my Son in the middle. These are the two things which weigh down the arm of my Son so much."

At the time, various nations of Europe were caught up in revolutions that even threatened the papacy of Pius IX. It was revealed by Our Lord to Fr. John Edward Lamy in 1931 that WWI was a punishment specifically for "blasphemy, Sunday labor, and the desecration of marriage."

To paraphrase the rest of the words of Our Lady to Melanie:

On account of the sins of men, a famine was to strike France. She also complained of the wicked lives of the priests and how none were capable of making a spotless sacrifice of the Holy Mass to appease the wrath of God. She said that in 1864 (founding year of Thomas Huxley's X Club), Lucifer together with a large number of demons would be unleashed from hell. God would abandon mankind to itself.

Our Lady further related that the Pope and the Church would be persecuted and that civil governments would attempt to do away with any sort of religious principle. Righteous people would suffer greatly and would plead to God for justice.

Suddenly, God would act and have all his enemies put to death (during the Three Days of Darkness). Peace would reign, men would be reconciled with God, and Jesus Christ would be worshipped. This peace would only be short-lived. After 25 years of good harvests, men would forget that sin is the cause of disorder in the world. The Antichrist would rule at this time. (If the Antichrist begins his reign at the age of 30, like Jesus Christ, he may have been born near the end of the Minor Chastisement.) Rome would lose the Faith and become the seat of the Antichrist. The Church would be in eclipse, but Enoch and Elijah would return to preach repentance to the world.

After Enoch and Elijah were put to death, pagan Rome would disappear, and the sun would begin to darken. The Antichrist would attempt to rise into heaven, but would be struck down by St. Michael the Archangel. After the Antichrist was thrown into hell, the world would then be renewed, and God would be served and glorified in eternity.

Note that the Blessed Virgin started her conversation with Melanie and Maximin in this approved apparition by telling her that she had "great news." If the Mother of God says that she has "great news" then we should be attentive. The French bishops unfortunately attempted to suppress this news. But this prophecy is critical if we are to understand the events to transpire before the end of the world.

Our Lady told Melanie of La Salette that, "… there will be a kind of false peace in the world. People will think of nothing but amusement [like sports, television, movies, and social media]. The wicked will give themselves over to all kinds of sin." We seem to be living that now.

Our Lady complained to visionary Marie-Julie Jahenny that her words at La Salette were ignored. In a vision on September 19, 1901 she said:

> "My children, when I remember, ever since that day when, on the holy mountain [La Salette], I brought my warnings to a threatened land ... when I remember the harshness with which they received my words, not all, but many, and those who should have passed them in the hearts of my children, with an immense confidence and a penetration profound, they have not made the case. It despised them, and for the most part, they have refused their confidence. Ah well! I assure you that all these promises, my intimate secrets, will come true. They must pass visibly. When I see what awaits the earth, my tears flow again. When the earth has been purified, by the chastisements, of its crimes and all the vices with which it is coated, the beautiful days will return with the savior [French Monarch] chosen by us, unknown to our children so far."

On September 19, 1896 (50th anniversary of the apparition at La Salette, France) Our Lord told Marie-Julie this: "Remember my serious words about the mountain of La Salette. The priest is no longer humble and is no longer respectful." Compare this to what Our Lady told Melanie at La Salette: "The priests, ministers of my Son, the priests, by their wicked lives, by their irreverence and their impiety in the celebration of the holy mysteries, by their love of money, their love of honors and pleasures, the priests have become cesspools of impurity."

In the early 1800's, shortly after the French Revolution, Our Lord appeared to Blessed Elizabeth Canori Mora and told her that the crimes in the world and in the Church had reached a peak and that he was going to send a chastisement. Elizabeth pleaded for mercy, in part by agreeing to spend nine days in hell as an act of reparation, and Our Lord relented saying that he would send several holy Popes who would be firm in the teaching given to the Apostles. However, he also said that Freemasonry would rise again and that it would be so successful that he would have to then send the chastisement so that all would not be lost.

It was also revealed to Bl. Elizabeth that an ecclesiastical crisis would occur in the future and would progress to the point where it would seem that the Church had disappeared. A small number of lay persons and clergy would defend it against a larger number trying to destroy it by introducing devastating changes. At the peak of the crisis there would be two popes. The true Pope would be forced to leave Rome and would be murdered in exile, leaving the Church without a head. Shortly after that time, the chastisement (Three Days of Darkness) would be sent to eliminate the enemies of God. The minority of mankind who were left would then be led by a pope, born near Rome, appointed by St. Peter himself, and known as "Peter the Roman" (the last pope in the line of the prophecy of St. Malachy).

Marie-Julie Jahenny, also saw that at the height of this crisis, "there will not remain any vestige of the Holy Sacrifice, no apparent trace of faith. Confusion will be everywhere." We are certainly living in an era of unprecedented confusion now. In a message given to Marie-Julie on September 29,

1882, she said: "The Church will have its seat vacant for long months ... There will be two successive antipopes that will reign all this time over the Holy See ..."

Supposedly, just before the death of St. Francis, he gathered his followers and told them this (from the *Works of the Seraphic Father, St. Francis of Assisi*, R. Washbourne, London, 1882, pp. 248-250 [as reported in *The Remnant* of November 30, 2017 by Christopher Ferrara in *Did Saint Francis Predict Pope Francis?*]):

"At the time of this tribulation, a man not canonically elected will be raised to the Pontificate, who by his cunning, will endeavor to draw many into error and death. Then scandals will be multiplied, our Order will be divided, and many others will be entirely destroyed because they will consent to error instead of opposing it."

Pope Pius X had two visions regarding a fleeing pope. In 1909, he said of one vision: "What is certain is that the Pope will leave Rome and, in leaving the Vatican, he will have to pass over the dead bodies of his priests!" Then just before he died, he had a second vision: "I have seen one of my successors, of the same name, who was fleeing over the bodies of his brethren. He will take refuge in some hiding place; but after a brief respite, he will die a cruel death." The first name of Pope Pius X was Joseph, which is the same as the first name of Pope Benedict XVI, Joseph Ratzinger.

These prophecies are very much in line with some given by Bl. Anne Catherine Emmerich, who was a contemporary of

Bl. Elizabeth. Blessed Anne mentions a dark or false church being built with the help of those inside the Church, in accordance with human reason. The true Church was being persecuted by a sect (Freemasons) and the Pope had a great desire to leave Rome, which would lead to a terrible crisis. Finally, a new, young, Italian pope was elected who would be very firm. Together with a Catholic Emperor named Henry, he would restore the Church and society.

The revelations of Bl. Anne Catherine Emmerich (1774-1824, buried at Holy Cross Church in Dülmen, Germany) were recorded by Clemens Brentano and are arranged by date. Many of them correspond with the traditional liturgical calendar of the Catholic Church. Some of them are quite startling, such as:

April 12, 1820: "I have had another vision on the great tribulation everywhere reigning. It seemed as if something were exacted of the clergy, something that could not be granted. I saw many aged priests, some of them Franciscans, and one in particular, a very old man, weeping bitterly and mingling their tears with those of others younger than themselves. I saw others, tepid souls, willingly acceding to conditions hurtful to religion. The old faithful in their distress submitted to the interdict and closed their churches. Numbers of the parishioners joined them; and so, two parties were formed, a good and a bad one."

August 10, 1820: "I see the Holy Father in great anguish. He lives in a palace other than before and he admits only a limited number of friends near him. I fear that the Holy Father will suffer many more trials before he dies. I see that the false church of darkness is making progress and I see the dreadful influence it has on the people."

August 25, 1820: "Then I saw an apparition of the Mother of God, and she said that the tribulation would be very great. She added that people must pray fervently with outstretched arms, be it only long enough to say three Our Fathers. This was the way her Son prayed for them on the cross. They must rise at twelve at night, and pray in this manner; and they must keep coming to the church. They must pray above all for the church of darkness to leave Rome ... She (the Holy Mother) said a great many other things that it pains me to relate: she said that if only one priest could offer the bloodless sacrifice as worthily and with the same disposition as the Apostles, he could avert all the disasters (that are to come)."

September 12, 1820: "I saw again the strange big church that was being built there (in Rome). There was nothing holy in it. I saw this just as I saw a movement led by Ecclesiastics to which contributed angels, saints and other Christians. But there (in the strange big church) all the work was being done mechanically (i.e., according to set rules and formula). Everything was being done according to human reason."

October 4, 1820: "When I saw the Church of St. Peter in ruins and the manner in which so many of the clergy were themselves busy at this work of destruction – none of them wishing to do it openly in front of the others – I was in such distress that I cried out to Jesus with all my might, imploring His mercy ... It was shown to me that there were almost no Christians left in the old acceptation of the word."

October 22, 1822: "I saw in Germany among worldly-wise ecclesiastics and enlightened Protestants plans formed for the blending of religious creeds, the suppression of Papal authority ... which projects found abettors in many of the Roman prelates ... Very bad times will come when non-Catholics will lead many people astray. A great confusion will result. I saw the battle also. The enemies were far more numerous, but the small army of the faithful cut down whole rows of enemy soldiers. During the battle, the Blessed Virgin stood on a hill, wearing a suit of armor. It was a terrible war. In the end, only a few fighters for the just cause survived, but the victory was theirs ..." (This seems to refer to the "Birch Tree Battle" where the King of France will defeat the Russian forces.)

April 22, 1823: "I saw that many pastors allowed themselves to be taken up with ideas that were dangerous to the Church. They were building a great, strange, and extravagant church. Everyone was to be admitted in it in order to be united and have equal rights: Evangelicals, Catholics, sects of every description. Such was to be the new church ... But God had other designs ... The Jews shall return to Palestine, and become Christians toward the end of the world."

A similar set of events was foretold as far back as the sixth century by St. Columba of Iona, Ireland (521-597). (extracted from the book, *The Prophets and Our Times*, by Fr. Gerald Culleton, 1941, pages 128-130, Imprimatur):

> "Hearken, thou, until I relate things that shall come to pass in the latter ages of the world. Great carnage shall be made, justice shall be outraged,

multitudinous evils, great suffering shall prevail, and many unjust laws will be administered. The time will come when they shall not perform charitable acts, and truth shall not remain in them. They will plunder the property of the Church, they will be continually sneering at each other, they will employ themselves at reading and writing.

They will scoff at acts of humanity, and at irreproachable humility; there shall come times of dark affliction, of scarcity, of sorrow, and of wailing in the latter ages of the world's existence, and monarchs will be addicted to falsehood. Neither justice nor covenant will be observed by any one people of the race of Adam; they will become hard-hearted and destitute, and will be devoid of piety.

Judges will administer injustice, under the sanction of powerful, outrageous kings; the common people will adopt false principles. Oh, how lamentable shall be their position! Doctors of science shall have cause to murmur, they will become miserly in spirit; the aged will mourn in deep sorrow, on account of the woeful times that shall prevail.

Cemeteries shall become all red, in consequence of the wrath that will follow sinners; wars and contentions shall rage in the bosom of every family. Excellent men shall be steeped in poverty, the people will become inhospitable to their guests, the voice of the parasite will be more agreeable to them than the melody of the harp touched by the sage's finger. In consequence of the general prevalence of sinful practices, humility shall produce no fruit.

The professors of science shall not be rewarded, amiability shall not characterize the people; prosperity and hospitality shall not exist, but miserliness and destitution will assume their place. The changes of seasons shall produce only half their verdure, the regular festivals of the Church will not be observed; all classes of men shall be filled with hatred and enmity towards each other. The people will not associate affectionately with each other during the great festivals of the seasons; they will live devoid of justice and rectitude, up from the youth of tender age to the aged.

The clergy shall be led into error by misinterpretation of their reading; the relics of the saints will be considered powerless, every race of mankind will become wicked! Young women will become unblushing, and aged people will be of irascible temper; the cattle will seldom be productive, as of old; lords will become murderers. Young people will decline in vigor, they will despise those who shall have hoary hair; there shall be no standard by which morals may be regulated, and marriages will be solemnized without witnesses.

Troublous shall be the latter ages of the world, the dispositions of the generality of men I will point out, from the time they shall abandon hospitable habits with the view of winning honor for themselves, they will hold each other as objects for ridicule. The professors of abundance shall fall through the multiplicity of their falsehoods; covetousness shall take possession of every glutton, and when satiated their arrogance will know no bounds.

Between mother and daughter anger and bitter sarcasms shall continually exist; neighbors will become treacherous, cold, and false-hearted towards each other. The gentry will become grudgeful, with respect to their trifling donations; and blood relations will become cool towards each other; Church livings shall become lay property. Such is the description of the people who shall come in the ages to come; more unjust and iniquitous shall be every succeeding race of men.

The trees shall not bear the usual quantity of fruit, fisheries shall become unproductive and the earth shall not yield its usual abundance. Inclement weather and famine shall come and fishes shall forsake rivers. The people oppressed for want of food, shall pine to death. Dreadful storms and hurricanes shall afflict them. Numberless diseases shall then prevail. Fortifications shall be built narrow during those times of dreadful danger [think open borders].

Then a great event shall happen [the Three Days of Darkness]. I fail not to notice it: rectitude shall be its spacious motive, and if ye be not truly holy, a more sorrowful event could not possibly happen."

4.2 Three Days of Darkness

The end of the Minor Chastisement will be marked by the Three Days of Darkness. Our Lord revealed to Marie-Julie Jahenny on January 4, 1884:

> "There will be three days of physical darkness. For three days less one night, there will be a continual night. The blessed wax candles will be the only ones that give light in this terrible darkness: only one will suffice for three days, but in the homes of the wicked, they will not give any light. During these three days and two nights, the demons will appear under the most hideous forms. You will hear in the air the most horrible blasphemies. The lightning will enter your homes, but will not extinguish the candles; neither wind, nor the storm can put them out ... The famine will be great. Everything will be in turmoil and three-quarters of men will perish."

There is a small book devoted to the prophecies concerning the Three Days of Darkness (*The Three Days' Darkness*, by Albert J. Hebert) and what individuals can do to be prepared for and survive those days. In that book, various details surrounding the event are given such as:

- A Russian invasion of Europe will precede the event.

- A red cross in a blue sky will appear the day before.

- It will be extremely cold the night before.

- There will be a continual earthquake; few buildings will survive – mostly single-story houses.

‫‪you must stay inside with doors and windows
d drapes or blinds shut.

is in hell will be let loose on the earth.

- Looking outside will cause instant death.
- Demons will imitate voices of loved ones in an attempt to lure you outside.
- Only one-quarter to one-third of mankind will survive.
- The event will last 72 hours, including the night after.
- The only available light will be from a blessed candle.
- The atmosphere will burn; it will be hell on earth.
- Crops will be destroyed; a famine will follow.
- It will be as springtime immediately afterward.
- The earth will be purified and will later become very fertile.
- People will then lead agrarian lifestyles; closer to God and nature.

Marie-Julie Jahenny said that it would occur on a Thursday, Friday, and Saturday. It would be preceded 37 days by two days of darkness. Before that time, there would be one day of darkness, and another day with a period of darkness. This might indicate that the sun is burning out. Isaiah 30:26 says that the sun will burn seven times brighter during a time of peace, perhaps its final burst before the end of the world.

It was also requested of Marie-Julie Jahenny, on August 23, 1878, that a new scapular be created offering protection during times of chastisements – the purple scapular.

The Three Days of Darkness are indicated in Biblical prophecy:

Exodus 10:22: (prefigured)
"And Moses stretched forth his hand towards heaven: and there came horrible darkness in all the land of Egypt for three days."

Joel 2:31:
"The sun shall be turned into darkness, and the moon into blood: before the great and dreadful day of the Lord comes."

Isaiah 13:9-11:
"Behold, the day of the Lord shall come, a cruel day, and full of indignation, and of wrath, and fury, to lay the land desolate, and to destroy the sinners thereof out of it. For the stars of heaven, and their brightness shall not display their light: the sun shall be darkened in his rising, and the moon shall not shine with her light. And I will visit the evils of the world, and against the wicked for their iniquity: and I will make the pride of infidels to cease, and will bring down the arrogance of the mighty."

Ezekiel 39:12: (This may indicate the large number of dead.)
"And the house of Israel shall bury them for seven months to cleanse the land."

4.3 Era of Peace Foretold in the Bible

The end of the Three Days of Darkness signals the beginning of the Era of Peace. There are several prophecies in the Bible that foretell of an age of peace. The Apocalypse of St. John,

Chapter 20, speaks of a thousand-year reign of Christ during which time Satan is bound. Many people take this literally, but the Apocalypse is mostly symbolic/spiritual so the 1,000 years are likely symbolic. It could be that the goodness of a normal 1,000 years will be compressed into 25 years of peace – "For better is one day in thy courts above thousands." (Psalms 83:11)

Isaiah 11:6 suggests an era of peace which is often depicted by a lion and a lamb lying down next to each other: "The wolf shall dwell with the lamb: and the leopard shall lie down with the kid: the calf and the lion, and the sheep shall abide together, and a little child shall lead them." Isaiah 65:25 has a similar verse: "The wolf and the lamb shall feed together; the lion and the ox shall eat straw; and dust shall be the serpent's food: they shall not hurt nor kill in all my holy mountain, says the Lord."

Micah 4:3 says: "And he shall judge among many people, and rebuke strong nations afar off: and they shall beat their swords into ploughshares, and their spears into spades: nation shall not take sword against nation: neither shall they learn war anymore." This is very similar to Isaiah 2:4.

4.4 Promised at Fatima and La Salette

During the third apparition of Our Lady to the children of Fatima on July 13, 1917, she promised that: "In the end, my Immaculate Heart will triumph. The Holy Father will consecrate Russia to me, and she will be converted, and a period of peace will be granted to the world."

The Third Secret of Fatima was also given at this time. Sr. Lucia wrote: "In Portugal the dogma of the Faith will always be preserved, etc." What the "etc." contains is a matter of great speculation. It obviously has to do with the preservation of the Catholic Faith. Cardinal Ratzinger admitted in the *Ratzinger Report* (1984) that it had to do with: "dangers threatening the faith and the life of the Christian and therefore of the world."

The message given to Melanie of La Salette also mentioned an era of peace: "Suddenly, the persecutors of the Church of Jesus Christ and all those given over to sin will perish and the earth will become desert-like. And then peace will be made, and man will be reconciled with God. Jesus Christ will be served, worshipped and glorified. Charity will flourish everywhere. The new kings will be the right arm of the holy Church, which will be strong, humble, and pious in its poor but fervent imitation of the virtues of Jesus Christ. The gospel will be preached everywhere and mankind will make great progress in its faith, for there will be unity among the workers of Jesus Christ and man will live in fear of God."

There are not many details about what exactly the Era of Peace will be like, other than to say it will be like the original Paradise. Many saints have had visions of heaven, but they were not very specific about what they saw other than to say that it was too wonderful to be described. Some were not even permitted to say what they saw or heard (Apoc. 10:4). St. Paul said this about a vision of heaven:

"I know a man in Christ above fourteen years ago (whether in the body, I know not, or out of the body,

257

I know not; God knows), such a one caught up to the third heaven. And I know such a man (whether in the body, or out of the body, I know not: God knows), That he was caught up into paradise, and heard secret words, which it is not granted to man to utter." (2 Cor. 12:2-4)

4.5 Other Prophecies

According to various other prophecies, during the Era of Peace a French Monarch and a Pope appointed directly by Sts. Peter and Paul will reign. This Pope will reform the Church according to the traditional disciplines. Prophecies say that he will be an Italian and may have or take the name Peter. The confusion in the Church will stop under his direction.

The French Monarch will be a direct descendant of King St. Louis IX. All French kings have been anointed at the Cathedral of Rheims with oil from the Holy Ampulla. He supposedly will have the name Henry, or a form of it. He will walk with a limp. It could be that he will put an end to the civil war that is supposed to ravage France. Along with 12 kings, he will govern the world. Just laws will be enforced. Society will be well-ordered. These secular rulers will support the Church, not persecute it.

Ven. Barthalomew Holzhauser said this about the Era of Peace:

"There will rise a valiant monarch anointed by God. He will be a Catholic, a descendant of Louis IX, yet a descendant of an ancient imperial German family, born in exile. He will rule supreme in temporal matters. The Pope will rule supreme in spiritual matters at the same time. Persecution will cease and justice shall rule. Religion seems to be suppressed, but by the changes of entire kingdoms it will be made more firm."

"He will root out false doctrines and destroy the rule of Islam. His dominion will extend from the East to the West. All nations will adore God their Lord according to the Catholic teaching. There will be many wise and just men. The people will love justice, and peace will reign over the whole earth. Peace will reign over the whole earth because God will bind Satan for a number of years until the days of the Son of Perdition."

"No one will be able to pervert the Word of God since, during the sixth period, there will be an Ecumenical Council which will be the greatest of all councils. By the grace of God, by the power of the Great Monarch, by the authority of the Holy Pontiff, and by the union of all the most devout princes, atheism and every heresy will be banished from the earth. The Council will define the true sense of Holy Scripture, and this will be believed and accepted by everyone."

A final Marian dogma is also supposed to be defined proclaiming the Blessed Virgin Mary as Co-Redemptrix, Mediatrix, and Advocate.

4.6 Retransformation of Society

During this time society will become more agrarian. There might not be electricity or gasoline for cars, especially just after the Three Days of Darkness. It is interesting that Nikola Tesla, not a religious man and inventor of the AC electric motor that transformed the way people live, saw the plans for the motor in a dream. He apparently had various dreams and visions, and heard voices that made him very uneasy. Where do you suppose those voices came from? And if there is no fuel for vehicles to run, and perhaps no passable roads after the earthquake during the three days, goods will not be able to be easily transported. The shelves of Walmart will be empty. At least that way family-run businesses might be able to make a comeback.

Nature, including human nature, is basically the same today as it was after the Fall of Adam. The way most people have lived throughout history was very much the same, at least until the late 17th century and the Industrial Revolution. The invention of the steam engine, the internal combustion engine, and the jet engine have greatly changed transportation. The distribution of electricity led to another huge change in daily life – thanks to the irreligious Thomas Edison – together with the invention of refrigeration and air conditioning. Radio, television, movies, and the internet have radically changed the way people spend their time.

The pace of change in society was never more dramatic than in the 20th century. The World Wars had a tremendous impact in many different ways including destroying the monarchies, mechanizing transportation and production, and removing women from the home (glorification of "Rosie the Riveter"). In 1953, Sir Edmund Hillary became the first man to reach the summit of Mt. Everest. But just 16 years later in 1969, Neil Armstrong became the first man on the Moon. Ironically, America's claim to being the greatest country ever rests largely on this feat which is denied by many Americans today. But the Apollo hardware is still up there, including a red Bible left on a lunar rover by Apollo 15 Commander David R. Scott.

If for some reason all that technology were taken away, man would be back to nature. An agrarian society is more in tune with nature and natural cycles. Farmers are attuned to the weather and to seasons – their lives revolve around them. The religious practices of the past were also in harmony with nature. Society is more stable with regularity.

A woman's work week was very regular in times past: Monday, washday; Tuesday, ironing; Wednesday, mending; Thursday, upstairs cleaning; Friday, baking; Saturday, downstairs cleaning; Sunday, church. There might have been variations on that, but it was consistent.

Agrarian societies are more self-sufficient and follow the principle of subsidiarity. You raise your own food, sew your own clothes, build your own houses and barns, chop your own wood, educate your own children, take care of your own relatives, etc. This allows everyone the greatest freedom to live a productive, virtuous life. St. Paul said: "… if any man will not work, neither let him eat." (2 Thess. 3:10)

Although capitalistic societies provide an abundance of

material goods, you only need so much, and an excess of material wealth provides an obstacle to a healthy spiritual life. Jesus told the rich young man to sell what he had, give it to the poor, and follow him, if he wanted to become perfect (Matt. 19:21). Jesus also said: "It is easier for a camel to pass through the eye of a needle, than for a rich man to enter into the kingdom of heaven." (Matt. 19:24)

The early Church lived in community and held everything in common – a form of pure, voluntary communism (Acts 4:34-35). St. Paul told them: "In this present time let your abundance supply their want, that their abundance also may supply your want, that there may be an equality. As it is written: 'He that had much, had nothing over; and he that had little, had no want.'" (2 Cor. 8:14-15) However, forced communism, especially the atheistic variety, is not charitable.

Today, agrarian societies like the Amish are criticized on the one hand for creating too much carbon dioxide – a "greenhouse gas" – with their farm animals, and on the other hand for having too many children who will damage the earth. However, one volcanic eruption can produce more carbon dioxide than humans can in a year. In about 535, during Justinian the Great's building of Hagia Sophia, Mt. Krakatoa erupted and darkened the world's skies for more than one year. The 1815 volcanic eruption of Mt. Tambora was one of the most powerful in modern history. The following year it caused what is known as "The Year without a Summer." This just shows that the global climate is affected more by the sun and volcanic eruptions than by human-generated carbon dioxide emissions.

A global cooling period known as the "Little Ice Age" occurred between the early 14th and the late 19th centuries. The Spanish explorers crossed the Rio Grande River on ice during that time. The Ohio River was regularly frozen over in the winters during the Civil War, allowing slaves to escape to the North. A period of very low solar activity known as the "Maunder Minimum" occurred in the middle of that time.

Just before the Little Ice Age, from about A.D. 950 to 1250, a much warmer period occurred called the "Medieval Warm Period." It was a period of higher solar activity. The island of Greenland was inhabited at that time, when it was actually green. Coincidently, the Middle Ages and Christendom peaked spiritually and economically at that time. Perhaps if people behaved themselves, things would go better all the way around.

Ignoring those facts, global warming alarmists and the ultra-rich want to herd everyone into cities so that society can be controlled at every level; all decisions being made by a small elite who have no interest in true freedom. It can be expected that the Antichrist will act similarly during his brief reign.

Conversely, in a society practicing subsidiarity, decisions are made at the lowest level. The federal government does not do what the states can do, the states do not do what the counties can do, the counties do not do what the villages can do, and the villages do not do what families can do. It does not take a village to raise a child.

In the early days of America, there was no standing army in

times of peace. However, each man had a weapon and could be called upon to use it on short notice. Historically, sports have been used for military training, and only men participated.

Women in sports is a recent development. This goes hand-in-hand with women dressing like men. Because of their advantage in strength and their aggressive nature, almost all sports records are held by men. Although the Greeks and Romans had stadiums, they were not built much after the fall of Rome until the 1800's. In the Biblical story of the Machabees, the Greek corrupted the Jews and got them to build a gymnasium, thus directing their attention away from God: "And they built a place of exercise in Jerusalem, according to the laws of the nations." (1 Mac. 1:15)

Now practically every national capital has a soccer stadium. It is said that soccer was designed as a sport in which both men and women could participate, since the advantage men have in upper body strength is not as critical. Now women are seen more as competitors than help-mates to men, to the detriment of children and society.

Roles traditionally held by men, such as military, policemen, firefighters, and construction workers, are now allowed to be filled by women. Due to their disadvantage in upper-body strength and stamina, the presence of women weakens these institutions. Men have an innate sense of duty to protect women and children, and to be leaders. Having women in positions of leadership in traditionally male-dominated institutions causes conflict in men.

Even in politics and the judiciary, the fact that women are more influenced by emotion and concern with safety leads to issues being driven more by feelings and sentimentality than by good judgment ("The government should do something." "It's for the children." "It wasn't his fault, society is to blame."). The first woman appointed to the US Supreme Court, Sandra Day O'Connor, believed in the constitutional right of a woman to kill her unborn child. How ironic!

Feminist Gloria Steinem supposedly said, "We are becoming the men we wanted to marry." It is true that through conditioning and hormones, women can become more masculine. Men can also become more like women in the same way. In the Age of Chivalry during the Middle ages, the roles and dress of men and women were much more defined. We can now say, for the most part, that "Chivalry is dead."

Women used to be more concerned about duties in the home. Domestics skills were passed from mother to daughter. Colleges even taught courses in home economics not very long ago. With women essentially forced into the workplace, domestic skills have suffered.

In ages past, women thought it their duty to bear and raise children. Before Christ, Jewish woman especially had this duty because they could have been the mother of the Messiah. A woman's entire physiological composition is designed for the conception, bearing, and raising of children. It is the tragedy of modern times that women have given this up in order to be more like men. They have been deceived by those wanting to destroy the family and society. Karl Marx said that in order for Communism to succeed, private property, religion, and the family would have to be destroyed. A big part of Communism's strategy is to get the woman out of the home and into the workplace.

Children suffer the most when warehoused in daycares or separated from a mother (or father) in a divorce. It has been said, "The hand that rocks the cradle is the hand that rules the world." Many famous people were highly influenced by their mothers. That will not happen if children spend more time in daycares than with their mothers.

Roles for men and women were more structured in the past. Men were the providers and protectors, women bore the children and stayed in the home, providing care and comfort for the family. Celebrations involved extended family and churchgoing was part of life. It can be expected that life will be like that during the Era of Peace.

At the end the Era of Peace, prophecies say that the French Monarch will go to Mt. Olivet in Israel to oppose the Antichrist and will lay down his crown – probably meaning he will die there – right next to the Valley of Josaphat. At that point will begin the reign of the Antichrist.

5 LAST THINGS

5.1 Reign of Antichrist – Major Chastisement

The end of the Era of Peace, as indicated by the death of the great French Monarch on Mt. Olivet, will mark the start of the reign of the Antichrist. By that time the charity of the world will once again have grown cold. The generation that grew up during the Era of Peace, not being content with a simple life of following the Commandments, will be looking for a leader to free them from such constraints and will find him in the Antichrist.

The message of Our Lady of La Salette to Melanie was that, "Twenty-five years of plentiful harvests will make them forget that the sins of men are the cause of all the troubles on this earth." It could be that the reign of the Antichrist will not begin exactly 25 years after the start of the Era of Peace, but apparently at least some troubles will start after 25 years of peace – enough time for one generation to grown up.

The word "Antichrist" only appears in the Bible in the letters of First and Second John. He is described as a liar, a seducer, and as a spirit whose presence was already in the world:

> "Who is a liar, but he who denies that Jesus is the Christ? This is Antichrist, who denies the Father,

and the Son." (1 John 2:22)

"Little children, it is the last hour; and as you have heard that Antichrist comes, even now there are become many antichrists: whereby we know that it is the last hour." (1 John 2:18)

"And every spirit that dissolves Jesus, is not of God: and this is Antichrist, of whom you have heard that he comes, and he is now already in the world". (1 John 4:3)

"For many seducers are gone out into the world, who confess not that Jesus Christ is come in the flesh: this is a seducer and an antichrist." (2 John 1:7)

Anyone denying that Jesus is the Christ is an antichrist, or a precursor to the Antichrist, and there will be many of those. There have been some notable antichrist figures in history like Marx, Lenin, Stalin, Mao, and Hitler. However, there will be a single man who will reign just before the end of the world who is the one and only Antichrist. St. Paul uses the term "man of sin" and "son of perdition" for this man:

"Let no man deceive you by any means, for unless there come a revolt first, and the man of sin be revealed, the son of perdition, who opposes, and is lifted up above all that is called God, or that is worshipped, so that he sits in the temple of God, showing himself as if he were God. Remember you not, that when I was yet with you, I told you these things? And now you know what withholds, that he may be revealed in his time. For the mystery of iniquity already worketh; only that he who now holds, do hold, until he be taken out of the way." (2 Thess. 2:1-7)

What St. Paul refers to as holding back the Antichrist is traditionally believed to be the Roman Empire. The fourth and last kingdom in the visions of Daniel the prophet is traditionally believed to be the Roman Empire. When the ancient Roman Empire fell, the Eastern empire continued to exist until the fall of Constantinople in 1453. The Holy Roman Empire existed until Napoleon Bonaparte put an end to it in 1804, although Roman laws exist today. Some commentators hold that this refers to Christendom, which is almost extinct but which still exists in the remnant of the Catholic faithful and in traditional Catholic institutions.

John, writing in the Apocalypse, refers to the Antichrist as the Beast. He gets his power from the dragon, who is the Devil or Satan, and he is accompanied by a second beast, or false prophet. The false prophet may be a religious figure or even a false pope. He makes men worship an image of the first beast and receive a mark on their hand or forehead.

The number identified with the Antichrist is 666. Many prophecies state that he will kill the two witnesses (Apoc. 11:3), understood to be Enoch and Elijah, after their three and one-half year period of speaking against him. During this same period, he will persecute those faithful to God (Apoc. 12:14). There is a prophecy of St. Vincent Ferrer that says anyone not having received the sacrament of Confirmation at that time will apostatize, or reject the Catholic Faith.

Jesus spoke of the Antichrist in a veiled way in the parable of the unjust judge (Luke 18:1-5), and as one who would come in his own name and be received by the Jews: "I am come in the name of my Father, and you receive me not: if another shall come in his own name, him you will receive." (John 5:43)

There are also Old Testament prophecies relating to the Antichrist in the book of Daniel in Chapters 7-12. The "little horn" of the fourth beast is believed to refer to him. He will be allowed to persecute Christians for three and one-half years before his power is finally taken away:

> "And he shall speak words against the High One, and shall crush the saints of the most High: and he shall think himself able to change times and laws, and they shall be delivered into his hand until a time, and times, and half a time.

> And judgment shall sit, that his power may be taken away, and be broken in pieces, and perish even to the end. And that the kingdom, and power, and the greatness of the kingdom, under the whole heaven, may be given to the people of the saints of the most High: whose kingdom is an everlasting kingdom, and all kings shall serve him, and shall obey him." (Daniel 7:25-27)

Many things have been written about the Antichrist. He will be a child prodigy and claim to be born of a virgin, although some prophecies say that his mother will be a Jewish nun and his father a bishop. The message of Our Lady of La

Salette said that his father would be a bishop. He will be a very charismatic leader. He will fake his own resurrection. He will get people to worship him as God ("abomination of desolation" in Daniel).

He is said to be of the tribe of Dan and will be accepted by Jews as their worldly Messiah. He will rebuild the Temple in Jerusalem and destroy the Church of the Holy Sepulcher. He will persecute Christians using every means.

His life will mimic the life of Christ in many respects. He will have power to work wonders that will convince many that he is divine (2 Thess. 2:1-4 and Mark 13:22). However, his reign will be only three and one-half years, corresponding to the public life of Christ.

The period of tribulation before the Era of Peace in which we are now living has been called the Minor Chastisement. It is difficult, but not impossible, to practice the Faith openly in these times. The period of time during the reign of the Antichrist has been called the Major Chastisement. It will no longer be possible to practice the Catholic Faith openly at that time.

St. Benedict (d. 543) said: "During the three and one-half year reign of Antichrist, God will send Henoch and Elias to help the Christians." And also: "In the last times, the Benedictines will render the Church the truest service and fortify many in the faith."

St. Michael the Archangel is said to arise at the end to rescue the Christians immediately before the general resurrection (Daniel 12:1). After the Antichrist kills Enoch and Elijah, the two witnesses, their bodies will be taken up into heaven after three and one-half days (Apoc. 11:7). After 30 days, the Antichrist will attempt to follow them, only to be struck dead by St. Michael on Mt. Olivet. The end of the world and the Final Judgment follow very shortly after:

> "And from the time when the continual sacrifice shall be taken away, and the abomination unto desolation shall be set up, there shall be a thousand two hundred ninety days. Blessed is he that waits and comes unto a thousand three hundred thirty-five days." (Daniel 12:11-12)

These verses indicate that the Holy Mass, the continual sacrifice, shall be suppressed by the Antichrist and that he, the abomination of desolation, shall set himself up to be worshipped instead. The difference between the number of days mentioned, 1335 - 1290, or 45 days, is taken by some to be the time between the death of the Antichrist and the Second Coming of Jesus Christ.

5.2 End of the World

The end of the world or the end of time, and the Second Coming of Jesus Christ with the General Resurrection and Final Judgment, is prophesied many times in the Bible. Not all cultures have a concept of the end of time. Some eastern religions hold the belief that we are continually reincarnated. But, St. Paul said: "And as it is appointed unto men once to die, and after this the judgment." (Heb. 9:27) Nature itself points to a final end. Given enough time, all of the stars in the sky would someday burn out and could not be reconstituted in a natural way.

The genetic load of humanity is at such a high level today, and the number of genetic diseases are multiplying so rapidly, that it does not seem possible that very many more generations of men will be able to be born. This is documented in the book, *Genetic Entropy*, by John Sanford (2005). Many other species are also quickly becoming extinct. The end of life and of humanity seems relatively near from just a natural point of view.

However, Jesus Christ promised that humanity would be in existence until the end of the world: "Amen I say to you, that this generation shall not pass, till all these things be done." (Matt. 24:34) That is to say, the generations of mankind will not pass away until the end of time. It was privately revealed to Bl. Anne Catherine Emmerich that when the number of places in heaven vacated by the fallen angels had been filled by human souls, the end of the world would occur.

St. Peter said that: "But of this one thing be not ignorant, my beloved, that one day with the Lord is as a thousand years, and a thousand years as one day." (2 Peter 3:8) The traditional interpretation of this verse is that just as the world was created in six days, so it would last about 6,000 years. St. Irenaus said: "For in as many days as this world was made, in so many thousand years shall it be concluded." (*Adversus haereses*, Book V, Chap. XXVIII) If the world was created in 4004 B.C., then we would be near the end.

St. Peter also said that although the original creation perished in a flood (2 Peter 3:6), the current world would end in fire: "But the day of the Lord shall come as a thief, in which the heavens shall pass away with great violence, and the elements shall be melted with heat, and the earth and the works which are in it, shall be burnt up." (2 Peter 3:10) After that, the "new Jerusalem" will be brought down from heaven (Apoc. 21:2), and the original Paradise might be brought back to the earth.

Further support for the idea that Paradise will be brought back to earth is that Jesus told John during his vision on Patmos that the tree of life was currently in Paradise (Apoc. 2:7), but that it would exist in eternity (Apoc. 22:2, 14). Additionally, a river of water of life (Apoc. 22:1, 17) is present in eternity which may be the same river that ran out of Paradise in the beginning.

St. Paul said that people living during the reign of Antichrist would be deceived because they did not love the truth: "And in all seduction of iniquity to them that perish; because they receive not the love of the truth, that they might be saved. Therefore, God shall send them the operation of error, to believe lying." (2 Thess. 2:10-11)

Our Lord questioned whether there would be faith upon his return: "But yet the Son of man, when he comes, shall he find, think you, faith on earth?" (Luke 18:8) The implication is that no, he would not. The people of that time would be generally unaware that the end was upon them, just like the people before Noah's Flood: "And as in the days of Noah, so shall also the coming of the Son of man be. For as in the days before the flood, they were eating and drinking, marrying and giving in marriage, even till that day in which Noah entered into the ark, and they knew not till the flood came, and took them all away; so also shall the coming of the Son of man be." (Matt. 24:37-39)

Jesus foretold various signs that would occur before his return. Chapter 24 of Matthew, Chapter 13 of Mark, and Chapter 21 of Luke describe some of them: false prophets and messiahs, the abomination of desolation (the Antichrist), wars, pestilences, famines, earthquakes, persecutions, powers of heaven being moved (stars falling), and signs in the sun, moon, and stars. The return of the Jews to Israel shortly before the end of the world seems to be prophesied: "Jerusalem shall be trodden down by the Gentiles; till the times of the nations be fulfilled." (Luke 21:24)

Immediately before the end, the sun, moon, and stars would no longer give their light and the sign of the cross would appear in the sky. Some saints have said that the actual cross of Christ will be reassembled and shown to all men for their consideration. At this point the angels would be sent out through the world to gather people for the Final Judgment.

The apocryphal book of Fourth Esdras gives several signs of the end of time not recorded in the Bible, especially in the Sixth Chapter. The archangel Uriel and God himself tell Esdras many things about the end times, and of the small number of the saved. The book mentions women giving birth to beasts, children being born prematurely, and infants speaking. It also mentions the sound of a trumpet and the disappearance of food in the final few days, and says that the Final Judgment will last seven years!

St. Patrick said that Ireland would sink into the sea exactly seven years to the day before Judgment Day. This is probably to protect it from the influence of the Antichrist. St. Patrick's prophecy is mentioned by St. Columba and St. Nennius. So if Ireland sinks into the sea, mark your calendar!

St. Paul says that those who are alive at the end of the world will be taken up: "Then we who are alive, who are left, shall be taken up together with them in the clouds to meet Christ, into the air, and so shall we be always with the Lord." (1 Thess. 4:16) Protestants refer to that event as the Rapture, even if they have the timing wrong. However, the penalty for Original Sin is death, and so everyone must undergo a certain type of death, even those who live until the end of the world. This can be inferred by another passage:

> "Now this I say, brethren, that flesh and blood cannot possess the kingdom of God: neither shall corruption possess incorruption. Behold, I tell you a mystery. We shall all indeed rise again: but we shall not all be changed. In a moment, in the twinkling of an eye, at the last trumpet: for the trumpet shall sound, and the dead shall rise again incorruptible: and we shall be changed." (1 Cor. 15:50-52)

5.3 Final Judgment

At the end of time all the dead will be brought back to life for the Final Judgment. The Bible says that it will take place in the Valley of Josaphat, which is just east of the old city of

Jerusalem: "Let them arise, and let the nations come up into the valley of Josaphat: for there I will sit to judge all nations round about." (Joel 3:12) There are many graves there, in part because of the anticipation of the Final Judgment.

Jesus proclaimed a number of times that you will be judged according to your works. Several parables are similitudes of the Final Judgment including the parable of the talents, of the 10 virgins, and of the king who went on a journey. The phrase "kingdom of heaven" appears more than 30 times in the Gospel of Matthew, each time describing an aspect of heaven or the requirements for admittance there.

The Final Judgment is described as a separation of the sheep and the goats, or the sorting of good fish and bad fish. There are several lists in the Bible of people who will not be admitted into heaven. One appears in 1 Cor. 6:9-10:

> "Know you not that the unjust shall not possess the kingdom of God? Do not err: neither fornicators, nor idolaters, nor adulterers, nor the effeminate, nor liers with mankind, nor thieves, nor covetous, nor drunkards, nor railers, nor extortioners, shall possess the kingdom of God."

The book of the Apocalypse has two similar lists:

> "But the fearful, and unbelieving, and the abominable, and murderers, and whoremongers, and sorcerers, and idolaters, and all liars, they shall have their portion in the pool burning with fire and brimstone, which is the second death." (Apoc. 21:8)

"Without are dogs, and sorcerers, and unchaste, and murderers, and servers of idols, and every one that loves and makes a lie." (Apoc. 22:15)

So do not be on those lists if you want to enter heaven! Note that sins of the flesh appear in all three lists, emphasizing what Our Lady of Fatima told Jacinta about them leading more people into hell than any other sins.

Conversely, Our Lady has revealed that people can avoid hell by wearing the brown scapular, by reciting the Rosary daily, or by making the five First Saturdays. Our Lord also promised that those who made the nine First Fridays would not suffer the fires of hell. Those fulfilling the requirements of the Sabbatine Privilege are promised to be taken into heaven by Our Lady on the first Saturday after their death.

The Bible emphasizes a judgment based on works, so obviously it matters what we do in this life: "… and the dead were judged by those things which were written in the books, according to their works." (Apoc. 20:12) "Behold, I come quickly; and my reward is with me, to render to every man according to his works." (Apoc. 22:12)

Those who are admitted into heaven are the ones who perform good works:

> "Then shall the king say to them that shall be on his right hand: Come, ye blessed of my Father, possess you the kingdom prepared for you from the foundation of the world. For I was hungry, and you gave me to eat; I was thirsty, and you gave me to drink; I was a stranger, and you took me in: naked,

and you covered me: sick, and you visited me: I was in prison, and you came to me. Then shall the just answer him, saying: Lord, when did we see thee hungry, and fed thee; thirsty, and gave thee drink? And when did we see thee a stranger, and took thee in or naked, and covered thee? Or when did we see thee sick or in prison, and came to thee? And the king answering, shall say to them: Amen I say to you, as long as you did it to one of these my least brethren, you did it to me." (Matt. 25:35-39)

The motivation for good works should be charity and not self-seeking: "And if I should distribute all my goods to feed the poor, and if I should deliver my body to be burned, and have not charity, it profits me nothing." (1 Cor. 13:3) Those passing the judgement are about one third of mankind: "And I will bring the third part through the fire ..." (Zach. 13:9)

5.4 Revelation / Apocalypse of St. John

The Book of Revelation, otherwise known as the Apocalypse of St. John, contains prophecies of end-time events written in symbolic language. One common error of many interpreters is to assume that the events described will take place literally and in the sequence in which they are recorded. If we line up what is written with historic events and private revelations, we will see that this is not the case.

Apocalypse: Chapters 1-3

The book starts off with St. John having a vision of Jesus Christ while in exile on the island of Patmos. The vision describes future events. Jesus has a message for the seven churches of Asia, or modern-day Turkey (Ephesus, Smyrna, Pergamus, Thyatira, Sardis, Philadelphia, and Laodicea), each headed by a bishop described as a star or angel. He commends the churches for what they are doing well, and corrects them for their faults. That covers the first three chapters of the book.

It is notable that none of those churches exist today. The house of Mary where she lived with John exists in Ephesus, however. One of the churches, Pergamus or Pergamon, is said to have the seat of Satan. The Pergamon Museum in Berlin contains the altar of Pergamon which was excavated from the ruins of that city in Turkey in the early 20th century. It is a large temple structure decorated with marble friezes of Greek gods, most notably Athena and Zeus.

St. Paul says that the gods of the pagans are devils (1 Cor. 10:20). The chief of the Greek gods is Zeus. The chief of the devils is Satan, so it follows that a very large temple dedicated to Zeus would be the seat of Satan. This temple was taken from Pergamon to Berlin just before the rise of Hitler. Albert Speer, Hitler's architect, modeled the speaker's platform at the Zeppelin field in Nuremberg, Germany after the Pergamon Altar. This was where Nazi rallies were held. Coincidence?

Apocalypse: Chapter 4

The Fourth Chapter of the Apocalypse describes 24 thrones and the four creatures around them. The 24 thrones are traditionally believed to be the 12 thrones of the apostles, who were promised them by Christ (Matt. 19:28), and the 12 thrones of the apostles of the last days. The four creatures: the man, the lion, the calf/bull, and the eagle, represent the four gospel writers: Matthew, Mark, Luke, and John, respectively.

St. Vincent Ferrer (d. 1419) is supposed to have been one of the twelve apostles of the last days. So he gets one of those thrones. The story is told of how he claimed that he was the angel of the Apocalypse (Apoc. 14:6). To prove this, one time he asked a dead person "Am I the angel of the Apocalypse?" and the dead person got up and replied "You are the angel of the Apocalypse!"

Obviously, the world did not end during St. Vincent's time, so was he wrong? The response of the people to his preaching was such that he claimed that the Blessed Virgin Mary was able to obtain a delay in the Final Judgment. He performed innumerable miracles included raising more than 30 people from the dead. He converted many Jews and Muslims to the Catholic Faith. It is believed by some that he performed more miracles than any other saint.

Apocalypse: Chapter 5

The Fifth Chapter of the Apocalypse describes a book with sevens seals. Only the lamb that was slain is worthy to open the book. The lamb is an obvious reference to Jesus Christ, the Lamb of God. The book is most likely the book of life, wherein the names of all those worthy to enter heaven are written. By his sacrificial death, Jesus opened the way to eternal life for us.

Apocalypse: Chapter 6

The Sixth Chapter of the Apocalypse explains what happens when six of the seven seals are opened. Upon opening the first four, horses are released: a white horse with Christ on it, a red horse signifying war, a black horse signifying famine, and a pale horse signifying plague. After the opening of the fifth seal, the martyrs of the Church cry out for revenge and are given white robes.

It is commonly taught by the saints that disturbing events will occur in the last days. War, famine, and plague are such events. The rise of militant Islam has led to the persecution of Christians in our time. In the end, Antichrist will be accepted as the Jewish Messiah and Christians will be persecuted again.

At the opening of the sixth seal, there is a great earthquake, the sun and moon turn dark, the stars fall from the sky, the heavens are rolled up, and the people hide from God because it is the great day of his wrath. This is a description of the end of the world and Judgment Day.

The rest of the 22 chapters of the Apocalypse are further descriptions of end-time events, but the final event – Judgment Day – has already been mentioned. That clearly means that the book is not written in sequential order since the final event of history is mentioned early in the book. So we cannot expect the following events to happen in order of appearance, although they are all closely related.

The World from Beginning to End and the Era of Peace

Apocalypse: Chapter 7

The Seventh Chapter of the Apocalypse describes the sealing of the servants of God upon their foreheads. From each of the 12 tribes, 12,000 people are signed. That makes for a total of 144,000 people. That number is mentioned again in Chapter 14.

Some people have the idea that 144,000 people are all that will be admitted into heaven. These same people are usually convinced that they are part of that 144,000. However, that number is only symbolic of a very large number. This is obvious from the following verse: "After this I saw a great multitude, which no man could number, of all nations, and tribes, and peoples, and tongues, standing before the throne, and in sight of the Lamb, clothed with white robes, and palms in their hands." There will be many more than 144,000 people in heaven.

Apocalypse: Chapter 8

The Eighth Chapter of the Apocalypse describes what happens upon the opening of the seventh of the seven seals. Immediately, there is a period of silence in heaven of one half-hour. That could be coincident with a similar event on earth. Some prophecies speak of an "Illumination of Conscience" that will happen just before the Era of Peace. It will serve as a warning to mankind of events to follow.

Upon the opening of the seventh seal, seven angels with trumpets begin to blow them and various events take place. The events following the first four trumpets are mentioned in this chapter. The three trumpets after that are said to be woes (Woe, woe, woe …).

Ven. Magdalene Porzat (d. 1850) said that the world would cry "Woe, woe, woe" when Easter fell on the feast of St. Mark (April 25). St. Bridget of Sweden (d. 1373) said essentially the same thing. That is the latest possible date for Easter in the Catholic Church calendar. It happens about once per century. It happened in 1943, at the peak of the WWII Axis powers, right after Pope Pius XII consecrated the world to the Immaculate Heart of Mary. So it could be said that this prophecy has already been fulfilled. However, Easter does fall on April 25 in 2038, but not again until 2190.

After the first trumpet, a third of the earth is burnt with the grass and trees. After the second trumpet, a mountain is cast into the sea and a third of the sea turns to blood. A third of the creatures in the sea die, and a third of all the ships on the sea are destroyed. After the third trumpet, a star called Wormwood falls on the rivers and springs which turn bitter. Interestingly, Chernobyl means wormwood in Russian. The wormwood plant grows in the Ukraine, the site of the 1986 Chernobyl nuclear disaster. Various end-times prophecies speak of a great comet (falling star) that will come very close to the earth and possibly even hit it.

After the fourth trumpet, a third part of the sun, moon, and stars are struck, and a third of the day and night are darkened. Note that back in Chapter 6, the sun, moon, and stars are completely dark, so Chapter 8 would seem to refer to events that happen before that. Again, the book is not written in sequential order.

Apocalypse: Chapter 9

The Ninth Chapter of the Apocalypse refers to events that occur upon the blowing of the fifth and sixth trumpets. After the fifth trumpet, a pit is opened and locusts come out of the pit to harm men who do not have the sign of God on their foreheads, which is mentioned in Chapter 7. This likely means that people who do not have God foremost in their thoughts will be subject to dark forces.

After that, a great battle is mentioned and the leader of the forces coming out of the pit is given several names: Abaddon, Apollyon, and Exterminans. These can mean "The Destroyer." Upon the blowing of the sixth trumpet, four angels are let loose from the Euphrates river in order to kill one-third of men. The name Saddam means Destroyer in Arabic. Saddam Hussein was the leader of Iraq, a country through which flows the Euphrates river.

An army of twenty thousand times ten thousand (200,000,000) is mentioned. The horses described sound more like battle tanks. It is thought by some people that China could field an army of 200 million men. There are prophecies that mention a large army from the East invading Europe.

Even though one-third of all men are killed in this scenario, the rest of mankind do not repent: "Neither did they penance from their murders, nor from their sorceries, nor from their fornication, nor from their thefts."

Apocalypse: Chapter 10

The Tenth Chapter of the Apocalypse describes a mighty angel who declares: "That time shall be no longer." That clearly means the end of time, or the end of the world. He also says that when the seventh trumpet begins to sound, it means "the mystery of God shall be finished" – another sign of the end of the world. Again, we are presented with events leading up to the end of the world, but not in sequential order. There have been trumpet sounds heard in the air around the world in recent years which may have a connection with the trumpets mentioned in the Apocalypse.

The apostle John is then handed a book by the mighty angel, and he is instructed to eat it. John is told that it will be sweet in his mouth, but sour in his belly. He is also told that he will prophesy to "many nations, and peoples, and tongues, and kings." The book is a reference to the gospel of Jesus Christ which will be pleasant for John to proclaim by his mouth. However, his evangelizing efforts would lead to persecution, like his exile on the island of Patmos, signified by the sourness in his belly.

Apocalypse: Chapter 11

In the Eleventh Chapter of the Apocalypse, John is instructed to measure the temple. He is also told about two witnesses who will prophesy for three and one-half years before finally being killed by the beast. Their bodies would lie exposed for three and one-half days in "the city where their Lord also was crucified" which is obviously Jerusalem. After that, they would be taken into heaven.

These witnesses are mentioned in several private revelations as being Enoch and Elijah, the two men who were taken up to God without dying (Gen. 5:24 and 4 Kings 2:11). They will appear near the end of time to preach during the reign of the Antichrist – the "beast." During that time, they will have the power "to shut heaven, that it rain not in the days of their prophecy: and they have power over waters to turn them into blood, and to strike the earth with all plagues as often as they will." (Apoc. 11:6) When he lived on earth the first time, Elijah prayed that it would not rain on earth for three and one-half years (3 Kings 17:1 and James 5:17). So it appears that he will have a repeat performance. After Enoch and Elijah are taken up into heaven, the Antichrist will attempt to follow them, only to be struck down by St. Michael the Archangel, according to other prophecies.

John then hears voices in heaven proclaim that: "The kingdom of this world is become our Lord's and his Christ's, and he shall reign for ever and ever." – as immortalized in the Hallelujah Chorus of Handel's *Messiah*. Also mentioned is a judgment, meaning the Final Judgment. The book of Daniel seems to indicate that there are 45 days between the death of the Antichrist and the Final Judgment at end of the world (Daniel 12:11-12).

Apocalypse: Chapter 12

The last verse of Chapter 11 of the Apocalypse could really be the first verse of Chapter 12 – "And the temple of God was opened in heaven: and the ark of his testament was seen in his temple, and there were lightnings, and voices, and an earthquake, and great hail." The first verse of Chapter 12 is a continuation of this: "And a great sign appeared in heaven: A woman clothed with the sun, and the moon under her feet, and on her head a crown of twelve stars."

The original ark of testament, or ark of the covenant, was the box that Moses ordered to be made that contained the tablets of the Ten Commandments. The new testament, or new covenant, is embodied in the person of Jesus Christ. Mary, the Mother of Jesus, held Jesus in her womb so she was in effect the ark of the new testament. So the ark of the covenant and the woman seen by John in heaven were the same thing. He saw an apparition of the Blessed Virgin Mary.

A similar apparition was given to St. Juan Diego in Guadalupe, Mexico in 1531. Interestingly, the Indian name of St. Juan, "Cuauhtlatoatzin," means "the talking eagle" and Juan is the Spanish version of John. St. John the Evangelist, who wrote the Apocalypse, is associated with the eagle among the four beasts in the Fourth Chapter. Both men were well-advanced in years at the times of the apparitions.

Proof of the apparition was given in the form of an image on the cloak of St. Juan. The image clearly depicts a woman clothed with the sun with the moon at her feet. There is an angel with wings in the image which parallels the description of "two wings of a great eagle" in verse 14. There is no crown in the image on the cloak, as described in the Bible verse, but it is there in a certain sense.

If you line up the stars on the mantle of the woman in the image with a star map of the constellations which would have been in the sky at the time of the apparition, the constellation Corona Borealis (Northern Crown) appears over the head of the woman. That is her crown! The great red dragon mentioned in the Bible also appears as constellation Draco. The woman is looking directly at the head of the dragon with a look of composure. This seems to signify that Mary is not intimidated by the dragon.

The woman of the Apocalypse is also a representation of the Church, and the twelve stars on her crown can represent the twelve apostles. Her crying out with pain signals the painful efforts made by those bringing people into the Church – the birth of spiritual children.

Some might think that the woman crying out in labor represents the Blessed Virgin Mary giving birth to Jesus. However, several saints have had visions of a miraculous birth involving no pain where Jesus passed through the womb of Mary in the same way he passed through doors after his resurrection. The dogmatic teaching of the Catholic Church is that Mary was a virgin before, during, and after birth.

The description of the great red dragon represents Satan and his kingdom of this world. The heads, crowns, and horns can be thought of as evil rulers. The third of the stars that he sweeps away with his tail are traditionally thought to be the third of the clergy who fall away from the Church.

St. Michael the Archangel has a fight with the dragon or Satan, and he and his fellow angels are cast out of heaven – another representation of the third of the stars. It is traditionally thought that the angels were created on the first day of creation and immediately had a choice to serve God or not. Lucifer, or Satan, decided not to serve and he and his followers were cast out by Michael and the good angels. Certain visionaries say that the world will end when the places in heaven vacated by the demons are filled with men.

Satan and the demons now reside inside the earth, as attested to by any number of visionaries, and they continually attempt to bring the souls of men down with them. The demons' hatred for God is implacable, and they are incapable of love or repentance, as are also the damned.

The woman is taken out into the desert for three and one-half years (1260 days, or a time, times and half a time) – the length of time of the reign of the Antichrist. The river coming out of the dragon's mouth represents the evil that sometimes floods the earth, but the earth swallowing the river indicates that Satan cannot do all that he wishes.

Ven. Mary of Agreda has a detailed description of this chapter in *Mystical City of God*, Volume I, The Conception, Book One, Chapters XIII-X. As to the woman crying out with pain, she says this did not mean the pain of childbirth, but "because it was to be a great sorrow for that Mother to see that divine infant come forth from the secrecy of her virginal womb in order to suffer and die as a victim for the satisfaction of the sins of the world."

Apocalypse: Chapter 13

The Thirteenth Chapter of the Apocalypse concerns two beasts and a dragon. The dragon is clearly Satan, or the devil. The first beast refers to the Antichrist, who was mentioned back in Chapter 11 as being the one who killed the two witnesses. He is described as having seven heads, ten horns and ten crowns, whereas in Chapter 12 he had the same number of heads and horns, but seven crowns. Somehow, in the space of one chapter, the beast picked up three crowns.

The beast is also described as being like a leopard with the feet of a bear and the mouth of a lion. He is given the power of the dragon. One of the heads of the beast which appears to be dead is healed, and the world adores the dragon and the beast. One of the goals of Satan is to have himself worshipped, rather than God. The verse that says "And they adored the dragon …" indicates that he will be worshipped at that time by most of the people in the world.

Even today Satanism is on the rise in America. The satanic creed – "Do what thou wilt shall be the whole of the law" – seems to be established in American law. Supreme Court Justice Anthony Kennedy said in the 1992 *Planned Parenthood v. Casey* decision on abortion that: "At the heart of liberty is the right to define one's own concept of existence, of meaning, of the universe, and of the mystery of human life."

Russia is often referred to as the bear. Russia was also mentioned by Our Lady of Fatima as being the chosen instrument of God for the persecution of the world. Some think that the head which appears to be dead and is healed represents the resurgence of Russia. The supposed fall of Communism in 1989 and the current rise of Russia in the

Ukraine would seem to reflect that. It could also refer to the reappearance of evil during the reign of the Antichrist, after the Era of Peace.

The three and one-half year reign of the Antichrist is mentioned again (42 months), and his persecution of Christians. Those who are not written in the book of life are those who adore the beast.

A second beast is then described as having two horns like a lamb while talking like the dragon. He does signs, like making fire fall from heaven, and makes people worship the image of the first beast which appears to come alive.

Some interpret the appearance of the second beast with horns "like a lamb" as a priest or member of the clergy. The three additional crowns obtained by the beast could have something to do with the Pope since he traditionally has a triple tiara. St. Hildegard von Bingen had a prophecy of a false pope:

> "When the great ruler exterminates the Turks almost entirely, one of the remaining Mohammadans will be converted, become a priest, bishop, and cardinal, and when the new Pope is elected (immediately before Antichrist) this cardinal will kill the Pope before he is crowned, through jealousy, wishing to be Pope himself; then when the other cardinals elect the next Pope, this cardinal will proclaim himself Anti-pope, and two-thirds of the Christians will go with him. He, as well as Antichrist, are descendants of the tribe of Dan."

At the end of Chapter 13 is one of the most well-known prophecies in the Bible, that of the mark and number of the beast. The Antichrist will force everyone to have a mark placed on his right hand or forehead and without the mark he will not be able to buy or sell anything. The mark is associated with the number of the beast, or his name, and is the number 666.

In Hebrew and some other languages numbers are associated with letters (gematria), and so you can add up the numbers corresponding with the letters in a name to come up with a total number for a name. Various names have been linked to 666 in this way. The Roman emperor Nero was one.

It is interesting to note that the numbers one, two, and three when added or multiplied give the number six. Six times six is 36. If you add all the numbers from one to 36 you get the number 666. There are 22 letters in the Hebrew alphabet and 22 chapters in the Apocalypse. Psalm 118 (DRB) has 22 sections, each with eight verses beginning with the same Hebrew letter. So the ancient Jews were very conscious of numbers.

The number seven is associated with perfection. The seventh day was the day of rest in Genesis. The number seven occurs many times in the Apocalypse. The number six is one short of seven and is associated with imperfection. So 666 would be triple imperfection.

Apocalypse: Chapter 14

The Fourteenth Chapter of the Apocalypse opens with the 144,000 that were first mentioned in Chapter Seven. They have the mark of God on their foreheads, as opposed to the people in the previous chapter who had the mark of the beast on their foreheads. This can signify that the people dedicated to God have him foremost in their minds, whereas the people dedicated to the things of this world have material goods foremost in their minds. You cannot serve God and mammon (Matt. 6:24).

Several angels appear in this chapter, the first preaches the gospel throughout the world. This is the angel that St. Vincent Ferrer claimed to be. The second angel says that Babylon is fallen, meaning that the powers of the world have failed. The third angel proclaims that all who accepted the mark of the beast will be punished eternally in fire. A voice is then heard to say that those who die in the Lord are blessed.

Jesus appears as the Son of man and holds a sickle in his hand which he thrusts into the earth in order to gather the harvest. Another angel appears and does the same thing. This signifies the harvest of souls at the end of the world (Matt. 13:49).

Apocalypse: Chapter 15

The Fifteenth Chapter of the Apocalypse mentions seven angels having seven vials containing the seven last plagues, filling up the wrath of God. Three is the number of God (Trinity) and seven is the number of perfection. In this chapter we have three groups of seven.

Ven. Mary of Agreda said that the wrath of God mentioned in this chapter signifies a new punishment, "greater than which neither before nor after is possible during mortal existence ... God will avenge with an especial and dreadful chastisement the injuries committed against his most holy Mother; for the insane daring, with which they have despised her, has roused the indignation of his Omnipotence ... since thereby men have not glorified, acknowledged and adored him in this tabernacle [Mary] and have not made use of this incomparable mercy." (*Mystical City of God*, Volume I, The Conception, Book One, Chapter XVIII)

Apocalypse: Chapter 16

The Sixteenth Chapter of the Apocalypse describes what happens when each of the seven vials is poured out on the earth: 1.) Sores break out on men with the character of the beast, 2.) The sea turns to blood and everything in it dies, 3.) The rivers turn to blood, 4.) The sun burns hot, scorching men, 5.) The kingdom of the beast grows dark, 6.) The Euphrates river dries up to prepare the way for the kings from the East, and 7.) A voice cries out "It is done" and there is a great earthquake, and every island and mountain disappears, and there is a great hail. The Euphrates river actually did dry up recently when a reservoir behind a dam on the river was being filled.

If all the oceans and rivers turned to blood, that would be quite a traumatic event, as would the disappearance of every island and mountain, not just Ireland. Even though many of the descriptions in the Apocalypse are symbolic, these seven events seem to be more literal. So when they happen, you will know that we are very close to the end of the world.

Apocalypse: Chapter 17

The Seventeenth Chapter of the Apocalypse concerns the infamous Whore of Babylon. This woman sits on a scarlet beast that has seven heads and ten horns, just like the previously mentioned beast, only without the crowns. The woman is described as a city, having power over peoples, and nations, and tongues. The seven heads and ten horns are kingdoms.

Various anti-Catholic preachers have identified the Whore of Babylon as the Roman Catholic Church. It may be that the city of Rome is the Whore of Babylon because the visionary Melanie of La Salette said that the Blessed Virgin Mary revealed to her that, "Rome will lose the Faith and become the seat of the Antichrist."

It is said that the corruption of the best is the worst. In the Old Testament, the people of Israel are likened to prostitutes when they cease to follow God and his Commandments. So it could be that a corrupt Catholic Church could also be represented by a prostitute.

The beast is described as being one who was, who is not, and shall come up out of the bottomless pit, and go into destruction. There is a theme in various places in the Apocalypse of an evil once having power, then losing it, and regaining it again. This seems to be the case for Russia, and of the eventual resurgence of evil after the Era of Peace. Finally, however, in the end all evil is vanquished and God reigns supreme.

Apocalypse: Chapter 18

In the Eighteenth Chapter of the Apocalypse the fall of Babylon is described. An angel with great power cries out in a strong voice to the people of the earth that the city of Babylon has fallen, and that they should get out of that city. The kings and merchants weep over the fall of the city, which is said to occur in one hour. Babylon is said to have been righteously punished for the corruption and luxuriant living happening there, sins which reached heaven.

The four sins in the Bible mentioned as crying out to God for justice are: 1.) Murder of the innocent (Gen. 4:10), 2.) Oppression of the poor (Exodus 3:9, Job 34:28, and others), 3.) Withholding wages from the workers (James 5:4), and 4.) The sin of Sodom (sodomy – Gen. 18:21, Jude 1:7). These four sins are essentially recognized as rights today: abortion and euthanasia, usury and oppressive taxation, global minimization of wages, and legalization of homosexual acts or homosexual "marriages."

The long war of homosexuals against Christian America is documented in the book *Making Gay Okay* by Robert Reilly. Homosexual activists have essentially bullied the medical establishment, pastors, politicians, and the Supreme Court into enshrining their desires into law with the cooperation of the complicit media and an apathetic populace. They label their critics as being "homophobic," as if homosexual practices were not repulsive to anyone with common sense. The failure of Christians to explicitly expose abhorrent homosexual practices was perhaps the greatest single factor in making all this possible. St. Paul was correct in saying:

"For the things that are done by them in secret, it is a shame even to speak of." (Eph. 5:12)

The word "delicacies" is mentioned in this chapter of the Apocalypse three times (DRB). The only other place that word is used in the Bible in in Prov. 19:10: "Delicacies are not seemly for a fool: nor for a servant to have rule over princes." This chapter of the Apocalypse is also replete with the mention of the goods of this world, and how the world has become intoxicated with them.

The Christian life is one of warring against the temptations of the world. St. Paul said: "But I see another law in my members, fighting against the law of my mind, and captivating me in the law of sin, that is in my members." (Romans 7:23) St. Peter said: "Dearly beloved, I beseech you as strangers and pilgrims, to refrain yourselves from carnal desires which war against the soul." (1 Peter 2:11) Mortification of the flesh is necessary for advancement in the spiritual life (Romans 8:13).

We need to use the goods of the world to a certain degree. We all need food, clothing, shelter, and usually a source of fuel for heat. But it is foolish to get caught up in the desire for worldly goods for their own sake if we know that they are quickly passing away.

The intellect should be in control of the appetites and not the other way around. The verse from Proverbs quoted above ("nor for a servant to have rule over princes") means that it is not appropriate for bodily desires ("the servant") to rule the mind ("the prince"). One of the effects of Original Sin

The World from Beginning to End and the Era of Peace

was that the perfect rule of the mind over the body was lost.

The story of the servant of the centurion of Capernaum in the Eighth Chapter of Matthew serves the same spiritual lesson. The centurion tells Jesus that when he tells his servant to go, he goes; when he tells him to come, he comes; when he tells him to do this, he does it. The body should be the servant of the mind, and not the other way around.

If we allow the desires of the senses to rule over the mind, we end up merely pursuing pleasure and avoiding pain. The philosopher Lucretius who wrote *On the Nature of Things* developed the pleasure principle to a high degree. He obviously had no belief in an eternity after this life. St. Jerome said that he eventually went mad and committed suicide. A painful death is something to be avoided at all costs by those seeking only pleasure in this life, hence the rise of assisted suicide today. No thought is given to the fact that "Thou shalt not kill" applies to yourself as well as to others.

The city of Babylon can also be thought of as the "Earthly City" in St. Augustine's *City of God*. There are any number of civilizations that have reached a high level of prosperity only to fall into ruin through corruption and vice. Ancient Rome is a prime example. The United States today seems to be following the example of Rome very closely. There is a prophecy of St. Hildegard that says:

> "Before the comet comes, many nations, the good excepted, will be scoured with want and famine. The great nation in the ocean that is inhabited by people

of different tribes and descent by an earthquake, storm and tidal waves will be devastated. It will be divided, and in great part submerged. That nation will also have many misfortunes at sea, and lose its colonies in the east through a tiger and a lion. The comet by its tremendous pressure, will force much out of the ocean and flood many countries, causing much want and many plagues."

Traditionally, the nation mentioned is England. However, the United States is in the middle of two oceans and has many immigrants. It is losing its influence in the Eastern Hemisphere, due largely to the four Asian Tigers, which are the economies of Hong Kong, Singapore, South Korea and Taiwan. The symbol of Jerusalem is a lion.

When speaking about the Third Secret of Fatima in Fulda Germany in 1980, Pope John Paul II said this:

"Given the seriousness of the contents, my predecessors in the Petrine office diplomatically preferred to postpone publication so as not to encourage the world power of Communism to make certain moves. On the other hand, it should be sufficient for all Christians to know this: if there is a message in which it is written that the oceans will flood whole areas of the earth, and that from one moment to the next millions of people will perish, truly the publication of such a message is no longer something to be so much desired."

[grasping a rosary] "Here is the remedy against this

evil. Pray, pray, and ask for nothing more. Leave everything else to the Mother of God. We must prepare ourselves to suffer great trials before long, such as will demand of us a disposition to give up even life, and a total dedication to Christ and for Christ"

"With your and my prayer it is possible to mitigate this tribulation, but it is no longer possible to avert it, because only thus can the Church be effectively renewed. How many times has the renewal of the Church sprung from blood! This time, too, it will not be otherwise. We must be strong and prepared, and trust in Christ and His Mother, and be very, very assiduous in praying the Rosary."

Recently (2014) a biography of Sr. Lucia of Fatima called *A Path under the Gaze of Mary* was published that had a passage from her writings that said something similar to what Pope John Paul II said at Fulda:

"I felt my spirit inundated by a mystery of light that is God and in him I saw and heard: the point of a lance like a flame that is detached, touches the axis of the earth, and it trembles: mountains, cities, towns and villages with their inhabitants are buried. The sea, the rivers, the clouds, exceed their boundaries, inundating and dragging with them, in a vortex, houses and people in a number that cannot be counted. It is the purification of the world from the sin in which it is immersed. Hatred, and ambition, provoke the destructive war. After I felt my racing heart, in my spirit a soft voice said: 'In time, one faith, one baptism, one Church, Holy, Catholic, Apostolic. In eternity, Heaven!' This word 'Heaven' filled my heart with peace and happiness in such a way that, almost without being aware of it, I kept repeating to myself for a long time: Heaven, Heaven."

All three of these prophecies sound similar. Perhaps the "lance like a flame" that Sr. Lucia saw is the comet mentioned by St. Hildegard. It is interesting that both Pope John Paul II and Lucia mention vast numbers of people dying in inundations of the earth in relation to the Third Secret. The officially released text of the Third Secret does not mention inundations, however.

On March 17, 1990 Cardinal Oddi, who had spoken to Pope John XXIII about the Third Secret, told journalist Lucio Brunelli that: "The Blessed Virgin was alerting us against apostasy in the Church." Cardinal Ciappi, who was familiar with the secret, said that: "In the Third Secret it is foretold, among other things, that the great apostasy in the Church will begin at the top [of the Church hierarchy]." Even Pope Paul VI admitted on October 13, 1977 (60th anniversary of the miracle of the Sun): "The tail of the devil is functioning in the disintegration of the Catholic world. The darkness of Satan has entered and spread throughout the Catholic Church even to its summit. Apostasy, the loss of the faith, is spreading throughout the world and into the highest levels within the Church." We seem to be living that prophecy today. Those facts, among others, have led some people to believe that there is more to the Third Secret of Fatima than

The World from Beginning to End and the Era of Peace

what was officially released in 2000.

Apocalypse: Chapter 19

The final destruction of the Whore of Babylon is mentioned in the Nineteenth Chapter of the Apocalypse. It says: "And her smoke ascends for ever and ever." Spiritually, that could be taken to mean that those who were only interested in the things of this world will end up burning in the eternal fires of hell.

In contrast, the next verses describe the marriage supper of the Lamb in heaven. The voices in heaven say: "Let us be glad and rejoice." Jesus is seen as a rider on a white horse who conquers the army arrayed against him. The beast and the false prophet are "cast alive into the pool of fire, burning with brimstone."

St. John falls down at the feet of the angel to adore him, but the angel tells him not to, since he is a fellow servant of God. In the Old Testament, Lot adores angels that appear to him (Gen. 19:1) and they do not protest. It is thought that after Jesus took on human flesh, it was no longer appropriate for men to adore angels, but God alone.

Once again, this chapter presents, in symbolic language, a scene of events that will occur near the end of the world. The beast is clearly the Antichrist, and his being cast into hell will not occur until the end of time. The next chapter presents events that will happen before then, not after.

Apocalypse: Chapter 20

The famous "thousand-year reign" is described in the
Twentieth Chapter of the Apocalypse. There is practically a
cottage industry among evangelicals devoted to this concept.
It is tied up with the idea of the Rapture in which all faithful
Christians will be taken up to heaven in a single event (1
Thess. 4:17).

Belief in a literal thousand-year reign of Jesus Christ on earth
is called Millenarianism or Chiliasm. It has been condemned
by various theologians of the Catholic Church. It was also
condemned by a decree of the Holy Office on July 21, 1944
(Denzinger #2296).

The Bible promises that Christ will return (Acts 1:11 and
Apoc. 1:7). The Apostles' Creed says that Christ will come
to judge the living and the dead. His Second Coming will
not be the start of the thousand-year reign, but the beginning
of the Final Judgment.

It is likely that the Era of Peace promised by Our Lady of
Fatima will be the fulfillment of this prophecy. It may be
that Jesus will reveal himself to certain individuals at this
time, as he did between his Resurrection and his Ascension.

Our Lady of La Salette indicated that the Era of Peace would
last for 25 years of good harvests, or at least people would
become forgetful that sins are the cause of all the world's
problems after that. So how can you reconcile those 25 years
with the thousand-year reign?

Life is full of good and bad events. Much of the time seems

to be taken up by just usual, or ordinary events. If the 25 years of the Era of Peace was similar to the time in the Garden of Eden, as some have said, then it could be thought that the goodness of an ordinary 1,000 years would be packed into 25 special years.

Our Lady of La Salette said that just before the Era of Peace, all the enemies of God would be put to death and the earth would become like a desert. This probably refers to the Three Days of Darkness.

The Three Days of Darkness is a prophecy that has been mentioned by many individuals, especially Marie-Julie Jahenny of France (1850-1941). She said that various periods of darkness would happen before the three days, and that a period of two days of darkness would occur 37 days before the three days.

The great battle mentioned in this chapter of the Apocalypse seems to correspond with the "Battle of Armageddon." The place is mentioned in Chapter 16 (Apoc. 16:16). It is commonly thought that Tel Megiddo, site of an ancient city in northern Israel's Jezreel valley, is where the battle will occur. The white throne judgment mentioned here clearly refers to the Final Judgment.

Apocalypse: Chapter 21

In the Twenty-First Chapter of the Apocalypse, the new heaven, the new earth, and the new Jerusalem are revealed. In them there is no death, mourning, crying, or sorrow. A list of those thrown into the pool of burning fire is given: the fearful, the unbelieving, the abominable, murderers, whoremongers, sorcerers, idolaters, and all liars.

A description of the new Jerusalem is given with 12 gates and 12 foundations. Each gate is likened to a pearl and each foundation is made of a precious stone. The street of the city is gold and transparent like glass. The glory of God is the temple, which continually lights the city, so no sun, moon or stars are necessary.

The dimensions of the city are given as 12,000 furlongs in length and width. A furlong is 660 feet, so that would be 1,500 miles square, or about the size of Australia. That is a really big city! It has a wall that is 144 cubits high, which would be at least 216 feet.

Ven. Mary of Agreda in *Mystical City of God*, Volume I, The Conception, Book One, Chapters XVII-XIX has an excellent meditation on this chapter of the Apocalypse. She likens the new creation to Jesus and Mary and the old creation to Adam and Eve. Verse 21:3 applies to Mary and Jesus: "Behold the tabernacle of God with men [Mary], and he [Jesus] will dwell with them."

Apocalypse: Chapter 22

The Twenty-Second Chapter of the Apocalypse describes the river of the water of life, and the tree of life. The angel tells John that the things he has seen must be done shortly. That and certain words of Jesus gave some of the early Christians the idea that the end of the world would come soon. It seems that every generation has anticipated that

Jesus would return in their lifetime.

Since the lifetime of a man is relatively short compared to all of history, and especially compared to eternity, it can be said that Jesus will come shortly to each man in his particular judgment immediately after death. The world will end at some point and we seem to be getting close, but many events prophesied in the Apocalypse have yet to happen.

Jesus speaks to John here and tells him that he is the Alpha and the Omega, the beginning and the end. He also said that he was the beginning in John 8:25. This is a revelation of the eternity of God; that he is outside of time. Jesus declares that every man will be judged according to his works. A list of those who will not be allowed into heaven is given: dogs (those that behave like dogs – those only thinking of earthly things), and sorcerers, and unchaste, and murderers, and servers of idols, and every one that loves and makes a lie.

The last words of Jesus say that if anyone adds to the prophecies of the Apocalypse, the plagues described therein will be added to him, and that if anyone takes away from the prophecies, his name will be taken out of the book of life. This should be a warning to anyone who wants to change the words of the Bible. Jesus finally says that he is coming quickly. Again, the "quickly" must be taken in the context of eternity.

5.5 Eternity

The end of time marks the beginning of eternity. The Nicene Creed says that Jesus will: "come again in glory to judge the living and the dead, and his kingdom will have no end." So the Final Judgment occurs at the end of time and eternity follows.

Any number of saints and other persons have had visions of heaven, hell, and purgatory. St. Paul said: "I know a man in Christ above fourteen years ago (whether in the body, I know not, or out of the body, I know not; God knows), such a one caught up to the third heaven." (2 Cor. 12:2) He was likely speaking about himself. St. Paul also said here that he: "heard secret words, which it is not granted to man to utter." Many persons who have had visions of heaven say that words are inadequate to describe how wonderful it really is.

Near-death experiences are relatively common. It is said that anyone who has had a vision of heaven no longer fears death. Why would you, when you know that something so wonderful is waiting? It is also said that they cannot stand to watch infomercials, since they realize what a waste of time that is.

Eternity implies endless time, or no perceivable time. Most people have had the experience that pleasant events seem to pass rapidly, as if our sense of time had been suspended. On the other hand, unpleasant events seem to drag on and on.

Since heaven will be the most pleasant experience possible, it will seem as if time did not exist. However, time in hell will seem very long indeed. A woman had a vision of a friend who had died and gone to hell. It had been only a week since she died, but the woman in hell said that it seemed like several years had passed. She revealed that in hell there was no love but only hate and spite.

Sister Josefa Menendez (d. 1923) was taken to hell in spirit several times. She saw many souls there whose greatest regret was their inability to love. She saw that the majority of damned souls accused themselves of sins of impurity, including a child of fifteen who cursed her parents for not teaching her to fear God or that there was a hell. The souls of former religious were especially tormented. However, she heard a demon complain that many souls had escaped his grasp because someone on earth must have been suffering and making reparation for them.

Some people question the concept of an eternal hell. If God is so merciful, how could he allow that? Could just one mortal sin (a serious sin, like murder or any sexual sin, committed willfully with full knowledge) send you to hell for eternity? Although God is certainly merciful, he is also just. Hell is where justice is meted out.

Some sins are so horrible that they deserve infinite punishment. Think of Adolf Hitler. Even a deliberate offense against an infinite God could be said to deserve infinite punishment. However, a person is not able to endure infinite punishment because we are finite beings. Since some people deserve infinite punishment, but cannot endure an infinite degree of punishment, God allows them to be punished infinitely long instead. That is why hell is eternal.

Conversely, God wishes to reward the good infinitely and is able to do so since he is infinite. Again, since we are finite beings, we cannot receive an infinite degree of reward. So

God will just reward the good for an infinitely long period of time. That is why heaven is also eternal.

Obviously, your time on earth is limited. Scientific advancements may be able to increase the time, but you will eventually die. If heaven is so wonderful and lasts for an eternity, and hell is so awful and is also eternal, then you would think it would be worth any effort to attain heaven and avoid hell. Even if you doubted the existence of hell, it would be a good bet to behave as if it existed, just in case. That would seem to be a particularly good bet, especially since many societies in the history of the world have had some belief in a place of punishment in eternity for those who behave badly in this life. Besides, if everyone acted like there were no eternal hell and did exactly what they pleased, life on earth would become a hell. People with no internal restraints need to have external restraints, now and perhaps in eternity. The fear of punishment can be a powerful internal restraint, no matter how you look at it.

Many people today seem to have the opinion that every decent person goes directly to heaven immediately upon their death. The concept of purgatory has largely been forgotten. However, only the very holiest of saints managed to avoid all or nearly all sins. The Bible indicates that even a just man sins seven times a day (Prov. 24:16 and Luke 17:4). Those would be small, or venial, sins and not committed deliberately but only unintentionally.

The Bible says: "It is therefore a holy and wholesome thought to pray for the dead, that they may be loosed from sins." (2 Mac. 12:46) A soul in heaven does not need prayers, and prayers are useless for a soul in hell. What St. Paul said in 1 Cor. 3:13-15 seems to indicate that bad works will need to be burnt off:

> "Every man's work shall be manifest; for the day of the Lord shall declare it, because it shall be revealed in fire; and the fire shall try every man's work, of what sort it is. If any man's work abide, which he has built thereupon, he shall receive a reward. If any man's work burn, he shall suffer loss; but he himself shall be saved, yet so as by fire."

The book *An Unpublished Manuscript on Purgatory* is a series of revelations that a nun had from a fellow nun who was in purgatory. She had these revelations for 16 years, from 1874 to 1890. The nun in purgatory said many things including: 1.) There is a special place in purgatory for those religious who have caused trouble to their superiors. (Jacinta of Fatima said that they gravely displease Our Lord.) 2.) Purgatory is in the center of the globe and there are various levels. 3.) God does not wish anyone to desire ecstasies. 4.) God uses suffering to purify souls in purgatory and on earth; he wishes special souls to be partners in his crucifixion. 5.) The Holy Eucharist should be the main focus of your life. 6.) The Way of the Cross is most beneficial for souls, next to the Sacrifice of the Mass. 7.) Everything should be done to satisfy God alone. 8.) St. Michael takes many souls to heaven on his feast day, but the greatest number on Christmas, although only on All Souls' Day do all souls in purgatory benefit by the prayers of the Church. 9.) Purgatory for many Protestants is long and rigorous. 10.) The secret societies and their master, the devil, are stirring up trouble.

11.) Give correction as you would receive it. 12.) Speak to Jesus as your most sincere and devoted friend.

Any material fortune that you amass on earth will do you no good after you die. As the saying goes, "You can't take it with you." However, spiritual fortunes do follow you into eternity; punishment for bad deeds, rewards for good deeds. Jesus said to store up treasures in heaven by doing good on earth (Matt. 6:19-20).

Since heaven consists in the direct vision of God, hell is the lack of that vision of God. Anyone who dies not in the state of grace, but in the state of serious sin – a conscious rejection of God – will be deprived of that vision. Another requirement mentioned by Jesus Christ is to have been baptized: "Jesus answered: Amen, amen I say to thee, unless a man be born again of water and the Holy Ghost, he cannot enter into the kingdom of God." (John 3:5)

There is a general consensus among theologians that this verse speaks of water baptism, and that one may also be baptized by a desire, or by being a martyr (baptism by blood). Any one of those methods removes Original Sin. The requirement of baptism appears to be absolute, however, judging by the words of Our Lord.

Since everyone is born with Original Sin (Jesus, Mary, and John the Baptist excepted), and since it seems that infants cannot desire baptism or be martyrs (the Holy Innocents excepted), the Catholic Church has always taught that she knows of no other way for infants to be baptized, other than by water baptism. That is not to say that we know God provides for no other way, it is only to say that no other way has been publicly revealed. For the same reason, the Church has also always taught that children should be baptized within a short time (a week or two) after birth.

Since heaven and hell are the only two states that we know exist in eternity, you will either end up in one or the other. There may also be a state of natural happiness for unbaptized infants or good pagans which has been called limbo. There are various levels of heaven and hell which are merited by our works. Dante had visions of them.

Jesus indicated that there are various levels in heaven when speaking about John the Baptist: "Amen I say to you, there has not risen among them that are born of women a greater than John the Baptist: yet he that is the lesser in the kingdom of heaven is greater than he." (Matt. 11:11) It is thought by some that St. John the Baptist is actually third in heaven, after Mary and Joseph. Anyway, if there are lesser in heaven, there must also be greater. The same applies to hell.

Even if we cannot get perfect justice in this world, there will be perfect justice in the next. Everyone will get exactly the reward that is deserved. Those who die with greater sins will get greater punishments. Those who die with greater love will get greater rewards.

If we think about what God has done for us – our creation, redemption, sanctification, and countless blessings – then our motivation for being with God in eternity will not be just for the sake of rewards. We will love God because he is our highest good, and will love others for God's sake. People in this life will go to all kinds of extremes for fleeting fame or fortune, or just for curiosity. George Mallory attempted to climb Mt. Everest "Because it's there." Apsley Cherry-Garrard wrote *The Worst Journey in the World* about a trip that he made with Dr. Edward Wilson to recover penguin eggs in the Antarctic winter, thinking that they would prove the later discredited theory of recapitulation (the idea that an embryo recapitulates its evolution). Perhaps if more Christians showed that kind of enthusiasm for their faith, Christianity would be more attractive.

If our love reaches the level of the saints of heaven, it will become a fire burning within us. Those outside of heaven will experience a different kind of burning. Jacinta of Fatima said to Lucia: "If only I could put into everybody the fire that is burning within me that makes me love Jesus and Mary so much!" St. Gemma Galgani (d. 1903) had such a burning love for Jesus that burn marks appeared on her skin, along with the stigmata. St. Teresa of Jesus (Avila) had an ecstasy where an angel appeared and pierced her heart with a spear of fire (transverberation). Padre Pio had a similar experience. The Bible says: "For our God is a consuming fire." (Heb. 12:29) Jesus said: "I am come to cast fire on the earth; and what will I, but that it be kindled?" (Luke 12:49)

CONCLUSION

Many errors have been propagated throughout the world in modern times in the name of "science." We have been taught that: 1.) Billions of years ago, the universe came about through an explosion, 2.) Galaxies, stars, and planets formed spontaneously from the results of the explosion, 3.) Life on earth came from non-living matter by natural means, 4.) All life evolved from that first living organism, and 5.) The earth is moving rapidly around the sun in some far corner of the universe. None of those propositions can be proven and they are all contrary to the Word of God.

The Bible teaches us that: 1.) God created everything from nothing in six days, only thousands of years ago, 2.) The earth was created first, before the sun, moon, and stars, 3.) All plants and animals were created in their "kinds" and that God was finished creating after the six days, 4.) The original world was destroyed by a flood, and 5.) The earth does not move. None of those teachings can be disproven by science.

What does it really matter if we believe in those things or not? It matters that we believe that the Word of God is trustworthy. The Bible says that: "They that fear the Lord, will not be incredulous to his word: and they that love him, will keep his way." (Ecclesiasticus 2:18) Pope Leo XIII in *Prodvidentissimus Deus*, On the Study of Holy Scripture (#18, 1893) said: "... if they lose their reverence for the Holy Scripture on one or more points, are easily led to give up believing in it altogether ... so if it [science] be perversely imparted to the youthful intelligence, it may prove most fatal in destroying the principles of true philosophy and in the corruption of morality."

So, we see that although God created the world "very good," history is full of disorders. The closer we get to the end of the world, the worse the disorders become. Jesus said: "For if in the green wood they do these things, what shall be done in the dry?" (Luke 23:31) We have been promised an era of peace shortly before the end, however. It is likely that many people living today will experience it.

It does not do much good to worry about the end of the world if your own life is not in order. Our own death could come at any time. And what will we have to say at our particular judgment, where our own sins are revealed, let alone at the general, Final Judgment where everyone's sins are revealed (Luke 12:2-3)? If we expect to live for eternity in heaven with God, his angels, and his saints, then our lives must have been lived in harmony with God's laws.

I hope that by reading this book you will come to the understanding that modern theories have not disproven the truth of the Bible or the teachings of the Catholic Church, but that they are trustworthy. Forewarned by prophecies of the future, you will be able to maintain your composure in the midst of traumatic events, knowing that nothing happens without God's knowledge or permission and that everything in your life has been arranged for your spiritual welfare.

I look forward to seeing you at the Final Judgment in the Valley of Josaphat!

BIBLIOGRAPHY

Agreda, Ven. Mary of, *The Mystical City of God, A Popular Abridgement*, Tan Books and Publishers, 1978.

Agreda, Ven. Mary of, *Mystical City of God*, Refuge of Sinners Publishing, Inc., 2010.

Behe, Michael J., *Darwin's Black Box*, Touchstone, 1996.

Behe, Michael J., *The Edge of Evolution*, Free Press, 2007.

Behe, Michael J., Dembski, William A., and Stephen C. Meyer, *Science and Evidence for Design in the Universe*, Ignatius Press, 2000.

Bennett, Art & Laraine, *The Temperament God Gave You*, Sophia Institute Press, 2005.

Birch, Desmond A., *Trial, Tribulation & Triumph*, Queenship Publishing, 1996.

Bollyn, Christopher Lee, *Solving 9-11*, 2012.

Burpo, Todd, *Heaven is for Real*, Thomas Nelson, 2010.

Carre, Marie, *AA-1025 The Memoirs of an Anti-Apostle*, Tan Books and Publishers, 1991.

Catechism of the Catholic Church, 2nd edition, Libreria Editrice Vaticana, 1997.

The Catechism of the Council of Trent, Tan Books and Publishers, 1982.

Charles, R. H., *The Book of Enoch*, Artisan Publishers, 2009.

Connor, Edward, *Prophecy for Today*, Tan Books and Publishers, 1984.

Cooper, Bill, *After the Flood*, New Wine Press, 1995.

Corbin, B. J., *The Explorers of Ararat*, Great Commission Illustrated Books, 1999.

Cornuke, Robert and Halbrook, David, *In Search of the Mountain of God*, Broadman & Holman Publishers, 2000.

Cruz, Joan Carroll, *Mysteries Marvels Miracles in the Lives of the Saints*, Tan Books and Publishers, 1997.

Culleton, Rev. R. Gerald, *The Reign of Antichrist*, Tan Books and Publishers, 1974.

Cuozzo, Jack, *Buried Alive*, Master Books Inc., 2003.

De Liguori, St. Alphonsus, *Uniformity with God's Will*, Tan Books, 2013.

De Montfort, St. Louis, *True Devotion to Mary*, Tan Books and Publishers, 1985.

Denzinger, Henry, *The Sources of Catholic Dogma,* 30th edition, Loreto Publications, 1955.

Derose, Noel, *If the World Only Knew* – Fernand Crombette:

The World from Beginning to End and the Era of Peace His Life & Works, CESHE, 1995.

Dörmann, Johannes, *Pope John Paul II's Theological Journey to the Prayer Meeting of Religions in Assisi, Part I*, Angelus Press, 1994.

Downey, Kirstin, *Isabella – The Warrior Queen*, Doubleday, 2014.

Duke, Charlie & Dotty, *Moonwalker*, Thomas Nelson Inc., 1990.

Dupont, Yves, *Catholic Prophecy*, Tan Books and Publishers, 1973.

Emmerich, Bl. Anne Catherine, *The Dolorous Passion of Our Lord Jesus Christ*, Barnes & Noble Publishing, 2005.

Emmerich, Bl. Anne Catherine, *The Life of Jesus Christ*, Tan Books and Publishers, 2004.

Emmerich, Bl. Anne Catherine, *The Life of the Blessed Virgin Mary*, Tan Books and Publishers, 1970.

Eusebius, *The History of the Church*, Penguin Classics, 1989.

Ferrara, Christopher A., *The New Rosary*, The Remnant Press, 2005.

Ferrara, Christopher A., *The Secret Still Hidden*, Good Counsel Publications, 2008.

Frale, Barbara, *The Templars*, Arcade Publishing, 2011.

The Saint Gemma Galgani Collection, Catholic Way Publishing, 2013.

Gitt, Werner, *In the beginning was information*, Master Books, 2005.

Gonzalez, Guillermo and Richards, Jay W., *The Privileged Planet*, Regnery Publishing, Inc., 2004.

Gouin, Fr. Paul, *Sister Mary of the Cross – Shepherdess of La Salette*, 1981.

Graham, Rt. Rev. Henry G., *Where We Got the Bible*, Tan Books and Publishers, 1987.

The Great Encyclical Letters of Pope Leo XIII, Tan Books and Publishers, 1995.

Guimaraes, Atila Sinke, *In the Murky Waters of Vatican II*, Tan Books and Publishers, 1999.

Haigh, Paula, *Canonized Heresies: Father John Zahm of Notre Dame*, 2004

Haigh, Paula, *Father Stanley L. Jaki: Evolutionist*, personal letter, 2000.

A Handbook on Guadalupe, The Academy of the Immaculate, 1997.

Hart, Robert T., *Those Who Serve God Should Not Follow the Fashions,* Third Edition, Little Flowers Family Apostolates, 2004.

Hebert, Albert J., *The Three Days' Darkness*, 1986.

Helfinstine, Robert F. and Roth, Jerry D., *Texas Tracks and Artifacts*, R&J Publishing, 2007.

Herrin, Judith, *Byzantium*, Princeton University Press, 2008.

Hock, Rev. Conrad, *The 4 Temperaments*, The Pallottine Fathers & Brothers, Inc., 2002.

Horvat, Marian Therese, *Our Lady of Good Success*, Tradition in Action, Inc., 2006.

Jarboe, Michael, *The Illinois Jarboe Family*, 2012.

Johnson, Ken, *Ancient Post-Flood History*, 2010.

Johnson, Phillip E., *Defeating Darwinism by Opening Minds*, InterVarsity Press, 1997.

Johnson, Wallace, *The Death of Evolution* (formerly *Evolution?*), Tan Books and Publishers, 1982.

Johnston, Francis, *Fatima: The Great Sign*, Tan Books and Publishers, 1980.

Jones, E. Michael, *The Jewish Revolutionary Spirit*, Fidelity Press, 2015.

Keane, Gerard J., *Creation Rediscovered*, Tan Books and Publishers, 1999.

Labarge, Margaret Wade, *Saint Louis*, Little, Brown and Company, 1968.

Letter From Beyond, America Needs Fatima, July 16, 2012.

Mahoney, Timothy P., *Patterns of Evidence – Exodus*, Thinking Man Media, 2015.

Martin, Louise, *Immodest Dress – The Mind of the Church*, Catholic Treasures, Monrovia, CA.

The Message of Fatima, AMI Press, 1968.

Mondrone, Domenico, *Mama! Why Did You Kill Us?*, Tan Books and Publishers, 1970.

Nelson, Vance, *Dire Dragons*, Untold Secrets of Planet Earth Publishing Co., 2011.

O'Gara, Most Rev. Cuthbert M., *The Surrender to Secularism*, Cardinal Mindszenty Foundation, 1999.

Pernoud, Regine, *Joan of Arc: By Herself and Her Witnesses*, Scarborough House, 1990.

Petersen, Dennis R., *Unlocking the Mysteries of Creation*, Creation Resource Publications, 2002.

Phillips, Rev. G. E., *Loreto and the Holy House*, Loreto Publications, 2005.

Posch, Helmut, *The True Conception of the World*, The Kolbe Center for the Study of Creation, 2016.

The Principle, producers Rick Delano and Robert Sungenis, movie, Stellar Motion Pictures, 2015.

Ratzinger, Joseph, *The Ratzinger Report*, Ignatius Press, 1985.

The World from Beginning to End and the Era of Peace

Reilly, Robert R., *Making Gay Okay*, Ignatius Press, 2014.

Ripperger, Fr. Chad, *The Metaphysics of Evolution*, Books on Demand GmbH, 2012.

Schmoger, Carl E., *The Life and Revelations of Anne Catherine Emmerich*, Tan Books and Publishers, 1976.

Scott, Donald E., *The Electric Sky*, Mikamar Publishing, 2006.

Seiss, Joseph A., *The Gospel in the Stars*, Cosimo Classics, 2005.

Sellier, Charles E. and Balsiger, David W., *The Incredible Discovery of Noah's Ark*, Dell Publishing, 1995.

Smith, Wolfgang, *Teilhardism and the New Religion*, Tan Books and Publishers, 1988.

Smith, Wolfgang, *The Wisdom of Ancient Cosmology*, The Foundation for Traditional Studies, 2004.

Sungenis, Robert A. and Bennett, Robert J., *Galileo Was Wrong ... and so was Einstein*, CAI Publishing, 2006.

Sungenis, Robert A., *Galileo Was Wrong: The Church Was Right*, CAI Publishing, 2007.

Sungenis, Robert A., *The Geocentric Universe: According to the Visions of St. Hildegard of Bingen*, CAI Publishing, 2014.

Swift, Dennis, *Secrets of the Ica Stones and Nazca Lines*, 2006.

Sypeck, Jeff, *Becoming Charlemagne*, Harper Perennial, 2007.

An Unpublished Manuscript on Purgatory, 20th printing, The Reparation Society of the Immaculate Heart of Mary, Inc., 2006.

Vennari, John, *The Permanent Instruction of the Alta Vendita*, Tan Books and Publishers, 1999.

Walsh, William Thomas, *Isabella of Spain – The Last Crusader*, Tan Books and Publishers, 1987.

What You Aren't Being Told About Astronomy, Volume I, II, & III, Spike Psarris, DVDs, www.creationastronomy.com.

Woodmorappe, John, *Noah's Ark – A Feasibility Study*, Institute for Creation Research, 1996.

Wynne, John, A *Catholic Assessment of Evolution Theory*, 2011.

Wynne, John, *The Catholic Teaching on Scriptural Inerrancy*, 2014.

INDEX

In 1864, Blessed Fr. Louis-Édouard Cestac had a vision of demons swarming all over the earth, as foretold at La Salette. This was the same year as the founding of Thomas Huxley's subversive X Club, and the year that Pope Pius IX issued the *Syllabus of Errors* in an attempt to combat many evil ideas that were circulating at that time. After seeing so many evils, Fr Cestac was given a prayer by the Blessed Virgin Mary which is as follows:

> Majestic Queen of Heaven
> and Mistress of the Angels,
> thou didst receive from God
> the power and commission
> to crush the head of Satan;
> wherefore we humbly beseech thee,
> send forth the legions of Heaven,
> that, under thy command,
> they may seek out all evil spirits,
> engage them everywhere in battle,
> curb their insolence,
> and hurl them back into the pit of Hell.
> "Who is like unto God?"
> O good and tender Mother,
> thou shalt ever be our hope
> and the object of our love.
> O Mother of God,
> send forth the holy Angels to defend us
> and drive far from us the cruel foe.
> Holy Angels and Archangels,
> defend us and keep us.
> Amen.

ABOUT THE AUTHOR

Eric Bermingham is a Catholic creationist and has been an aerospace engineer since 1987. He first became interested in creationism after reading the book *The Incredible Discovery of Noah's Ark* in 1995. Becoming convinced of the literal truth of Genesis, in the year 2000 he wrote a small book, *Creation vs. Evolution*, which sums up the arguments for creation and against evolution.

He is an advisory board member of the Kolbe Center for the Study of Creation: www.kolbecenter.org. He has given presentations on creationism and geocentrism to various audiences.

His home is not too far from Ark Encounter in Kentucky and its full-scale replica of Noah's Ark. One day he would like to go to Mt. Ararat to see the original Ark.

Eric promoted the movie *The Principle* when it came out in 2014. It was a documentary featuring interviews of cosmologists and scientists concerning the Copernican Principle – the idea that there is no special place in the universe. He is convinced of our special place in the universe, and he would like to see God and his creation returned to their rightful places in the minds of mankind.

Made in the USA
Columbia, SC
27 December 2022

75051870R00200